COLLECTING
PAPER

A Collector's Identification & Value Guide

By Gene Utz

ISBN 0-89689-096-1

BOOKS AMERICANA
INC.

TABLE OF CONTENTS

ACKNOWLEDGEMENTS

To say thank you to all who helped with this book would require another chapter. Numerous dealers, vendors, and auctioneers, as well as trade papers the like of P.A.C., *AntiqueWeek,* and *MidAtlantic* among others went far out of their way to supply expertise, photos, and current prices.

Research librarians, public and university, smiled, then used their electronic wonders to find facts and figures otherwise unobtainable. Individuals, people with names such as Louise Mallen, Bob DeLorenzo, Eileen McLaughlin, dug deep into their memories and collections to help. As did museums and special collections - where would anyone be without them and their directors and curators: Robert Pelton, David Jasen, Conrad Schoeffling, Robert Chandler.

To these and dozens of others, a hundred thousand thanks.

Credits:

New York Alive
Cape Cod Antiques
Long Island Heritage
North Shore Newspaper Group
New England Antiques Journal
The Appraisers Standard
Main Antique Digest
AntiqueWeek
MidAtlantic Antiques Magazine
Old Cars Weekly
Mass-Bay Antiques

PAPER TIMETABLE

B.C. 300 - Called papyrus, a form of paper is made from river reeds in Egypt.

2000 - Parchment appears in the Mid-East.

250 - Camel hair brush invented. Used to write on woven cloth. Led to the first book, a manuscript scroll.

A.D. 1/99 - Palm leaves used for written records in India. Bound together with cord to make a book.

105 - Paper invented in China by Ts'ai Lun.

610 - Paper made in Japan of mulberry bark.

700 - Sizing of paper developed.

751 - Paper made in Samarkand factory by Chinese papermakers, probably prisoners of war.

1035 - Waste paper first repulped and recycled for papermaking.

1151 - Paper made in Spain.

1276 - Paper made in France.

1390 - Paper made in England

1450/1455 - The first printing by Western man using movable type - the Gutenberg Bible.

1490 - Englishman, William Caxton, the first English printer, refers to an English paper mill in a book he printed.

1625 - First newspaper advertisement in England, printed on the back page of a London newspaper.

1690 - The first known paper mill on American soil starts production in Germantown, Pennsylvania, by William Rittenhouse.

1799 - Louis Robert, a French clerk, invents a protoype paper making machine

1840 - England introduced its first postage stamp.

1841 - The first paper made from wood pulp, in Halifax, Nova Scotia.

INTRODUCTION

Collecting paper is serious fun.

As a group, the paper collector knows that our past contains mysteries. The collector seeks these enigmas, removes them from their dusty covers to look at them from a contemporary viewpoint.

They are the few among the many who know that nothing lasts - that no fad, trend, or object is immutable. Everything changes. That's what makes the collector's world so fabulous. The paper collector does not abandon the past. He knows that without it, the future holds no meaning.

Such collectors are a classless grouping with income they consider disposable. Their spouses may not agree. They, the collectors of paper memorablilia, are housewives and doctors, taxi drivers and lawyers, any occupation one cares to name. Baseball cards and comic books draw, on average, a younger clientel.

Paper collecting is a tremendous subject, historically and socialogically. It wears many faces, so many that no one person, no one book, could possibly describe them all.

This book, simply titled, should be considered primarily a workbook for paper collectors, beginners or expert, who desire a more initimate knowledge of the other aspects of their collecting mania.

Background, history, the development of paper in its collectible forms, are subordinate to the main concept, to key collectors collecting.

All forms of paper represent history. All paper collectors are historians.

The weekly newspaper that was printed on April 14, 1865, announced a change in the history of the United States: Lincoln Assassinated. Reading that 128 year old headline and the story that followed, gives the collector a glimpse of a country being torn further apart, and of the mindset of those involved.

Paper collectors don't deal with new processes, new technology. They deal instead with remembrances of things past: of the overlong women's legs drawn by calendar artists Petty or Vargas, of the graphic likeness on a piece of sheet music of a songstress who once sang 'Over the Rainbow'.

There is so much paper. Too much for someone to corner and make a market. So much that prices are in the main, affordable. An $8 children's book or a $15 dime novel cannot be too heavily influenced by the fluctuations of the arts market.

To cover the entire field of paper collectibles in one volume is not feasible. This book has tried to balance what the collector wants to know about major segments, against minor collectibles, in sharply defined chapters.

Now, with all paper collectors in mind, it only remains to dedicate this book to Tsai'Lun, a court official and a Chinese of genius, who at the end of the second century A.D., invented paper made from mulberry bark pounded into a felt-like mass. Dedication then is to this first paper collector, Tsai'Lun. And to Ruth. She knows why.

CHAPTER I

Chinese dolls from the early 1900s, made of colored tissues and metallic papers, with thread for beards, and painted faces.

PAPER DOLLS

By the end of the second century A.D., the Chinese had invented paper made from mulberry bark. It was a hand process, labor intensive, slow, and expensive. Trimmed scraps were saved for further use.

Printing was far in the future.

Paper was a product to be used only by those who could afford it - the government as represented by the ruling warlord and his court. Soothsayers first used it to replace the sticks and arrows then used it for fortune telling. Scribes brushed its surface with their inks to record the glories and edicts of their Emperor. And somewhere in a humble home, a papermaker assembled a few trimmed scraps to make a paper doll for his child.

Jumping 1300 years into the future to the 1440s, we find jointed paper figures; a paper version of puppets. They were first used as adult amusements, then as models for women's clothing, and finally as children's toys.

By 1791, a German fashion journal reported an import from England of a paper doll, "rightfully a fashion toy for little girls."

A half century later, in 1854, the first American paper doll, Fanny Grey, was published in Boston by Crosby, Nichols and Company. Anson Randolph followed by publishing The Paper Doll Family; a group of paper dolls in a box. By 1859 *Godey's Lady's Book* published figures of six boys and girls, with costumes to match. Other women's magazines followed and a trend was unknowingly set for today's collectors.

Like most paper collectibles, there are specialists: public personalities, advertising promotions, company brands, or illustrators.

Advertising gave birth to the greater number of paper dolls, reflecting the vogues and fads of a particular time, with some thought as to what was important to a little girl: what she wanted to be as a grown-up. Thus Queen Victoria's busty figure was as prominent a part of a little girl's playtime then, as was Shirley temple dolls in the first half of the 1900s.

Paper dolls came from the local stationary or toy store, from product boxes on the shelves of grocery stores, or were cut from or used as inserts in magazines or newspapers. Betsy McCall, as an example, first appeared in the pages of *McCalls* in May 1951 as a paper doll drawn by Kay Morrison. It is difficult to recall another era where paper dolls made such an imprint on the public as the 1950s.

Most paper dolls are under twelve inches in height; 6 to 10 inches was more the norm. There were other sizes, difficult to find now. There was a 'penny size' (the price) about 1900. Only three inches tall, highly destructable. There was a 1936 doll of Shirley Temple, 34" tall that was received by the buying public with little enthusiasm. The small 6 to 10 inch dolls were the most popular, just right for a child to handle.

As with most paper, those dolls, made by hand and hand colored, dating from before 1850, are the most prized. Hand coloring, usually in watercolors, helped make of these old dolls, a rare prize.

Color lithography was invented as early as 1837 but it wasn't until the 1860s and later that the color process was sufficiently perfected to create a resonably cheap form of advertising which helped major expansions of several manufacturers. Would the Joseph Campbell Soup Co., as it was known then, be as large a figure in its world today without having once hired Grace Gebbie Dayton to work in its advertising department?

Grace created the Campbell Kids characters, big eyed, fat cheeked children, based on her comic strip. Bobby and Dolly. To recall the Campbell Kids, think Campbell Soups.

She drew the Campbell Kids for the best part of twenty years; meanwhile drawing Dolly Dingles for the *Pictorial Review* and Dolly Dimples and Bobby Bounce for *St. Nicholas Magazine*.

Grace Dayton made her niche, but so did Queen Holden with another winner, Baby Nancy.

Drawn by Queen Holden and published by the Whitman Company in 1931, it was only the second book by Holden.

PAPER DOLLS

In the first year, Baby Nancy and Her Nursery, sold three million copies. Reprinted in 1935, it is still thought to be the best paper doll seller of all time.

Then there was Rose O'Neill and her Kewpie Kutouts. At this writing, there is a proposal to open a Kewpie doll museum in the midwest. Not bad for a chubby, fat cheeked doll drawn first on a piece of paper.

JAPANESE DOLLS

Four thousand years ago, Japanese dolls were symbolic ancestors. Not until 105 A.D. did the first records appear of dolls as toys, in Japan of course.

By the end of the Heian period (796-1185) there were records of dolls made of grass, believed to be the precursers of the paper doll. Five hundred years later, during the middle of the Edo period (1615-1868) paper dolls were wildly popular throughout Japan. The Edo period was one of the most culturally colorful in Japanese history, bringing the common people unto the cultural stage alongside the dominant aristocracy.

During this same time frame, Japan's justly famous woodblock prints embossed on patterned paper began to be used in the making of paper dolls. Specialized forms appeared or evolved in the various districts of the country and the making of paper dolls left the humble precincts of the peasants cottage to be produced commercially.

A form of paper doll developed that followed the dictates of feminine style. Japanese fashion decreed that only three items of feminine dressage were important, the kimono, the sash, and the hair styling. Therefore paper dolls, of primary importance in Japan, are made to be viewed from the rear; the face not to be seen.

These then are two dimensional dolls. Technically, many old Japanese three dimensional dolls may be viewed as paper collectibles as many of the older doll bodies were made of rolled paper, with the clothing glued on; difficult to identify, equally difficult to find.

No other nation has convinced itself that dolls have souls. The Japanese word for doll, "Ningyo" translates as 'human form' or 'human shape' and has remained unchanged since antiquity.

From this belief in a dolls soul comes the belief in a paper doll rubbed against an ill persons body to protect him from illness. As an extension of this, a doll of paper, was placed in the bedroom of the sick person. In the morning the doll was sent to sea bearing the illness with it.

For the Japanese doll nothing was impossible.

The paper bodies and clothing of Japanese Kimishimo dolls are mounted on a frame. From the 1920s, the doll derives its name from the winged jacket and the wide trousers. Ottervic collection.

Japanese toys and dolls are used as playthings, as artistic toys for display, and as charms by both children and adults. Ottervic collection.

Dolls such as these and on page 3 are of museum quality and have insurance valuations only. Similar dolls made for the tourist or retail trade may be found occasionally for $50-200.

This doll, similar to the one in the previous photo, and varied according to the region of origin, is made completely of colored papers folded to resemble layers of a kimona, then stiffened with glue. Ottervic collection. Made for trade would have values between $50-200

The Miharu doll of Japan is a traditional paper mache' doll used to decorate the house on festival or harvest days. Ottervic collection. Trade dolls $50-200

Whether of paper dressed for a Japanese Girl's Day Festival, or a book cut-out of Giselle MacKenzie, dressing dolls as playthings knew no era nor national boundaries. Ottervic collection. A Giselle doll with two outfits was auction priced at $25

3

BETSY McCALL

Betsy McCall, born 1925, has never grown old,
and has spent her life having fun. E. McLoughlin.
It was bought 8 years ago for $75

Betsy McCall, as conceived by the editors of *McCall's* was a middle class, six year old brunette, who grew up but was never any older than the child she played with. Born or conceived in 1925, she spent her life having fun at the beach, the circus and at school. She went to flower shows, met children's radio personalities, went to camp, and ate the carrots that she herself had planted.

She acquired a family the easy way, the editors invented them. In this manner she acquired a twin brother and sisters named Kerry and Merry. An active child, she involved herself in all manner of activities, from a trip to Sanibel Island, to joining the Girl Scouts, and soliciting for UNICEF.

So involved has Betsy McCall been in the lives of *McCall's* readers that she has received thousands of letters. Most asked is the question, "How old is Betsy?"

Reply the editors in one of their Betsy McCall pages, "Just as old as the child who asks."

Since *McCall's* licensed Betsy's name to such commercial paper doll publishers as Simon and Shuster, Samuel Gabriel and Son, and Avalon industries, the collector is not limited to back copies of *McCall's* in his search for the paper doll who wouldn't grow up.

BOOK CUTOUTS

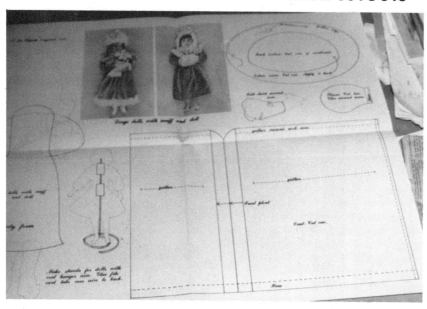

Cut-out diagram for Victorian doll ornaments. L. Mannell. Prices could run as high as $10-30

When Hollywood was the center of the universe, almost every male and female star made at least one appearance as a paper doll, mostly in books as cutouts.

Fictional paper dolls were printed in magazines and newspapers. Books of cutouts appeared not only of real or

PAPER DOLLS

fancied people but of the homes they lived in, the trains they rode or the pets they owned.

Betsy McCall has been mentioned. Before Betsy there was The Lettie Lane Paper Family which was serialized in *The Ladies Home Journal* starting in October, 1908. Created by Sheila Young, the family consisted of a boy and girl paper doll in uncut pages, followed by friends and relatives in a series of activities and period clothing styles.

Collectors need not concentrate on these. There was Dolly Dingle, the Kewpie Kutouts, Topsy, Amelian, Baby Nancy, Little Alice Busy Bee, Barbara and Dolly Dingles brother Dicky. If you include movie stars, the collectors horizon is endless. Shirley Temple alone may have more than eighteen cutout books with her name in the title.

Older books, uncut, are prime collectibles, but few survived the savage handling of young children. Books from the 1950s are easier to locate.

Reprints may present a problem, unless you are one of those who try to find all the reprints.

Of all the paper dolls, Kewpie Kutouts may be the most desired. The mania for Kewpies has lasted better than half a century, as strong today as ever.

Barbar's six inch cut-out height was just right for a young child to handle. E. McLoughlin. The price paid was $35

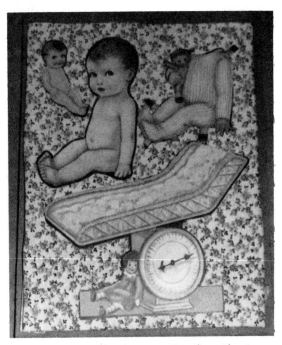

Babies and scales always went together, at least since scales were invented. E. McLoughlin. Bought at doll show for $15

Dolly Dingles baby brother Dickey, from the *Pictorial Review*, February, 1923. E. McLoughlin. Bought for $10.

Baby Nancy was created by Queen Holden and published by Whitman Company in 1931. It sold three million copies in book form the first year. E. McLoughlin. $30

Dolly Dingle still says it all for many paper doll collectors.

Victorian cut-outs as decorations are being reproduced. Two of the many are pictured here.

Paper dolls such as these - or most others - were stereotyped. Little girls playing with these cut-outs were supposed to be teaching themselves a girl's, or women's values such as clothes fashions, hair fashions and home making. Only prices have changed from nickels and dimes to current ranges of $5-45

PAPER DOLLS
Prices:

34" Shirley Temple paper doll. Auction - $15
Dolly Dingle Paper Doll, dealer - $7
Uncut sheet Betsy McCall, 1958 Easter, dealer - $5
Paper Doll book by Saalfied, "The Coronation of Queen Elizabeth, uncut, copr. 1953, dealer - $45
Dolly Dingle Paper Dolls, 1922/1924, dealer each - $35
Paper Doll, National Velvet, 1961, Liz Taylor - $30
Paper Doll, Sandra Dee, 1959, uncut, in box, two dolls, four outfits - $45
Dolly Dimples, Diet or Die, first edition, the Dolly Dimple Story Book - $30
Paper Dolls, Dolly Dingles Friend Peggy by Grace Dayton, 1919/1920 - $8

Clubs and Associations:

International Rose O'Neill Club (Kewpies) care of Jack Crotser, Box E, Nixa, Missouri 65714. Jack Crotser, Phone: 417-725-3291.

Books:

A Picture Book of Paper Dolls and Paper Toys, 79 Parkridge Drive, Pittsford, New York, 14534. Pub 1974 by Barbara Whitton Jendrick.

Antiques of American Childhood, Katherine Morrison, McClinton Clarkson N. Potter, publishers, New York, 1970.

Paper Dolls and Their Artists, Mary Young, 1040 Greenridge Drive, Kettering, Ohio 45429. Published 1975.

Museums and Collections:

Shelburne Museum, Shelburne, Vermont. Not always on display.

Museum of the City of New York.

Children's Museum, New Orleans Recreation Department.

Children's Museum, Detroit Public Schools.

Magazines:

Paper Doll Gazette, Shirley Hedge, RD 2 Princeton, Indiana, 47670.

Paper Collectors Marketplace, P.O. Box 128, Scandinavia, Wisconsin 54977-0128.

Midwest Paper dolls and *Toy Quarterly*, Janie Varsolona, P.O. Box 131, Galesburg, Kansas 66740.

Doll Life, P.O. Box 514, Mt. Morris, Illinois, 61054.
Published by All American Crafts, Inc.

CHAPTER II

A paper toy may take any form, even that of a tigress and her cub if made of papier mache'. Ottervic collection.

PAPER TOYS

Paper dolls were only one manifestation of paper's versatility. The Victorians took an unusual delight in die-cut figures: machine stamped, lithographed, cardboard cut-outs. Their use of paper as everyday toys and party accessories was accelerated by the innovative use of honeycomb paper to create three dimensional figures such as rabbits, bells, eggs, flowers, Christmas decorations, banners, and streamers. Did frugality help? A honeycomb rabbit could be folded flat, to be put away for the following year. Chocolate rabbits simply disappeared.

The success of honeycombed paper led to further experimentation that introduced a child's carriage of cardboard. Paper trains and train accessories followed. During World War Two, Lionel Corporation made cardboard trains.

As early as the 1400s, convection currents from the heat of a stove or a fireplace, was used to make paper figures move. By the 1700s, Germany, always an innovative source of toys, was the fountain head of paper toys made to be cut out and glued to cardboard.

It was the English who bested them by being the first to make cut-out mannikin figures with extensive, changeable wardrobes. To the French of course, it was another mode of exhibiting miladies fashions.

Cut-out dolls with jointed, movable arms and legs, and with slots for movable heads, appeared.

Doll house furniture of cardboard to fit doll houses of the same material appeared in America in the late 19th century. A patent was taken out by an Emily Russell in 1865 for a cardboard doll house with paper dolls. Twenty years later, folding cardboard houses were being made by Converse and McLoughlin Brothers, two of the most important paper toy manufacturers of the time.

In 1934, the Sears, Roebuck catalog offered a five room, fiber board doll house, 28½"L by 15⅝"H. The front door opened, and it was lithographed with flowers around the base and in the window boxes. For 59¢ it included a breakfast porch and a garage.

Picture puzzles, halfway between the original English irregular cut pieces and the later interlocking jigsaw puzzles, appeared in those same catalog pages priced at 39¢. Described as cut-up pictures, colored reproductions of paintings, they were printed on heavy cardboard, then cut into odd shapes.

They adjoined a complete toy village listed at 29¢. Twelve nicely lithographed, substantial cardboard houses already set up and firmly glued was the set's description. A 3½" high church towered over the other eleven houses, all built to porportion.

As the doll house craze was dying out during the late 19th century, advertising paper dolls and advertising puzzles replaced them in popularity. They advertised sewing thread, coffee, bicycles, clothing, food, or sewing machines. Newspapers took up the fad, printing uncounted pages of paper dolls.

PAPER TOYS

To be sure, complete sets and mint condition may be fantasizing, but enough of them exist, still comparatively inexpensive, to make of their collection a possibility.

These cardboard houses, richly detailed, were offered at an antique and collectible show in New York. They were too nice to have remained unsold, especially at their price of $10 each.

HONEYCOMB PAPER

Those sheets of colorful tissue paper, glued and folded flat, to be made to open and appear as the cells of a bee's honeycomb; what could be more recognizable as a decorative object at a holiday affair or a party? Their low prices keep them popular, their handy manner of folding flat to be stored for the next occasion displays their foremost asset - they endure. What other collectible, so fragile in appearance and fact, can do so?

They appeared first in Europe, inventor unknown, as stars, bells, flowers, eggs, or baskets. A home grown genius may have been the one to glue a cardboard figure of a rabbit or Santa to these convoluted bits of tissue paper. When the honecomb was unfolded, the cardboard figure appeared to sit in a basket or stood or sat unaided.

In the 1930s, these folding bits of paper and glue reached their peak of popularity - 5¢ bought a rabbit, 10¢ (a weeks allowance) bought a rabbit sitting in a basket, with a few folding eggs thrown in.

Their popularity started to fade in the 1940s. By the late 1950s, they were a curiosity found mostly in attic trunks.

The honeycombed art held brief sway at Christmas time in the form of bells and stars and angels, but for Easter they had become a thing of the past.

Except in Pakistan. There, honeycomb can sometimes be considered a mania. Taxis and buses have streamers decorating the windows. A hotel room may have so many streamers and banners hanging from the ceiling that entrance visibility is a form of guessing where you last saw the bed. A year round form of national paper-mania.

While endurance seems integral to these collectible honeycomb objects, low, affordable prices appear to be built in with the love that created them.

A rich variety of forms may be found of honeycomb paper. Turkeys, Santas, holiday and welcome banners, or wedding bells, among hundreds of others. Courtesy of L. Mannell.

Sky high are the prices for kites, three and four figure prices are not unknown. This Japanese paper kite pictures two of the seven Lucky Gods. Ottervic collection. New kites sell for $100 and up, older ones, fragile in construction, are scarce; could easily go for $1000 to a purse heavy collector.

PAPER TRAINS

This Dover reprint of "An Old Fashioned Train" stands behind an original scale model locomotive and tender from which the plans were drawn. Robert De Lorenzo.

During the years of World War II, toys had to change or die. Steel was inaccessible for toy production, so was most metals. Toy companies solved part of the problem by adapting paper and cardboard as working materials.

"Lionel Steel Has Gone To War". The most renowned manufacturer of model railroad trains and locomotives used that phrase as a legend on a box containing a freight set. Based on Lionel's regular 0 gauge line, the box contained 250 pieces, slotted and tabbed, some to be folded, of paper and cardboard, difficult for even grownups to assemble.

The 'paper train' was actually manufactured by Samuel Gold, a manufacutrer of premiums and prizes for candy manufacturers. Supposed to run on cardboard track - if ever assembled - it was not a prize Christmas item for long. The fact of its failure in arousing buyer interest has now been reversed, making of its moderate rarity, a paper collector's prize. One was offered at a train show in December 1992 for $45 unassembled.

PAPER TOYS

Other manufacturers joined the trend to cardboard.

A Dover reprint of "An Old Fashioned Train" by A.G. Smith, is a cut-out book in color, of period trains that appears to interest model train enthusiasts as much as susceptible children.

The Skyline Manufacturing Company of Philadelphia, Pennsylvania, in company with The Model Builder of New York City, manufactured cardboard accessories for model train sets, amongst them a cardboard engine house. No slots, no tabs, these accessories, scaled to the size of the train models, were of heavy cardboard printed in color, with wooden strips on strategic edges where glue held them together upon assembly.

A slip enclosed in one set states: "Because of wartime shortages we are unable to obtain metal tubes (squeeze tubes then were made of soft, malleable metals, not plastic). As a consequence we have been compelled to substitute dry glue from the Model Builder's cement normally used in our sets. You will find the dry glue in an envelope."

Metals had gone to war, even from the playroom floor.

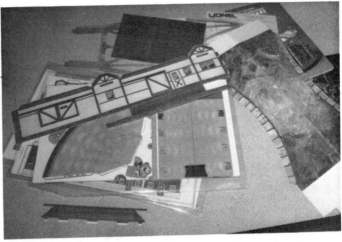

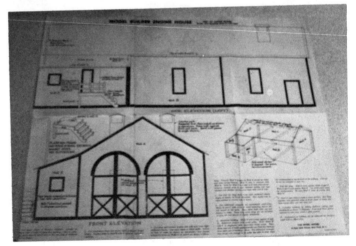

To go with "An Old Fashioned Train" cut-outs, these scale model barns, freight warehouse, and engine house were made in the early 1940s. Die-cut from heavy cardboard, they were put together with the help of wooden strips and powdered glue. Despite their 50 year vintage the prices are only $20-35 with an occasional high of $85. Robert D. Lorenzo.

DIE-CUT TOYS

Die-cut and die casting are related mostly as a means of mass production. Die cast would be the manufacture of permanent molds from molten zinc or white metal alloy. From them flowed a fount of inexpensive toys appropriate for the world's 'five and ten's' and its variety stores.

Die-cutting was the machine handles knife or cutting die used to stamp out figures of desired shape, sometimes of cardboard, with sharp, clean edges. Preformed, sharp edged dies with a cavity shaped to accept the material, is the Brittanica's description.

Cardboard cut-outs so formed, then had pre-cut colorfully lithographed, paper figures glued to the same shaped cardboard.

Germany was the leading producer of toys during the 1800s, die-cut cardboard figures amongst them. By the 1870s, Germany had become a toy exporter, sending its production to neighboring France and Great Britain, and further afield to the American market. During the late 1800s and the early 1900s, Nurenburg could boast of 300 toy factories.

When John McLoughlin opened his small shop in New York City in 1828, he could only have fantasized that when he and Edmund McLoughlin formed a partnership in 1837, their enormous output of books and paper dolls would eventually exceed that of all other publishers combined.

Certainly no one could guess then that more than a century later collectors would spend large sums to own these early die-cut figures.

German die-cut figures from the 19th century held an appeal that was difficult to resist. Even today. Prices for these are easy on the wallet ranging mostly $8-20

Probably an advertising premium, from the 1920s, this heavy cardboard doll carriage is only four inches long. In near mint condition, it bears no markings. As one-of-a-kind item a price on something like this is strictly a matter of negotiation. $10-500. E. McLoughlin

Sometime at the beginning of the century, at the same time commercial radio appeared, some advertising person thought of a miniature doll carriage as an advertising give-a-way.

Only four inches overall, with a movable sun screen hood, it was made of heavy cardboard, with a handle and wheels of wood. There were no marks, no indication of who made or distributed the item. Perhaps it came with a paper insert since lost.

Of superb craftsmanship, its reddish tan is the color of fine leather. Like a veiled woman, it is shrouded in mystery, its origin uncertain.

It is said by the collector to be a promotional piece from the 1920s. Handed down by word of mouth, who is there to step forward and say, "I know that veiled woman, I know that doll carriage."

Someone out there must, for nothing is born or made in a vacuum. Not even a four inch paper doll carriage.

The most popular trains of all time were those that appeared in the Lionel catalogs in time for Christmas. Some of these catalogs were the foundation of a large publishing house. Finding old Lionel catalogs today is as popular as finding the old trains, the second most active collecting field, in terms of money, in the world. Suffolk County Historical Society. 1992 catalog prices for 1949 through 1978 were valued between $4 and $89, with the years 1949 to 1954 the highest: $25-89

Prices:
Victorian die-cuts: authentic, not English reproductions:

Hands holding flowers, Raphael Tuck and Sons - $15
Children with dogs, Raphael Tuck and Sons - $15
Children, Raphael Tuck and Sons - $20
Cats and Dogs, Raphael Tuck and Sons - $20
Men and Ladies, Raphael Tuck and Sons - $15
Men Rowing Boat in Ocean - $15
Tropical Birds BB #80 - $15
Eight Cottages, by L. and B. Germany #31825 - $8
Boys and Girls by Z.U.M. Germany - $6
Angels Holding Christmas Trees by L. and B. #2431 - $30
Wind and Grist Mills, German - $20
Child Drying Dish, uncut - $45
Two Girls With Flowers, mid 1800s - $22

Miscellaneous:

Die-cut Calendar, 'Singers', American singers, eight panels of birds - $45
Cardboard Model Train Railroad Station - $85
Paper Train Cut-out Book - $20
Honeycomb, 1900/1910, two tables centerpieces, Hartford paper-mania show - $35
Honeycomb, 1920, Rabbit in basket with six eggs, from Port Washington show - $18
Honeycomb, single standing rabbit - $12
Paper dolls, Sandra Dee, 1959, uncut in box, two dolls, 34 outfits - $45
National Velvet, 1961, complete but outfits cut - $30
Advertising toy, Doctor Miles Puzzles, four pieces, c.1900 - $8
Kiss Me Gum Cut-outs, American Chicle Company, Louisville, 1900/1910 - $12
Lion Coffee, paper toy, Dorothy and her card - $25
Lion Coffee, paper toy, Lion Coffee line Trolley Car - $25
Lion Coffee, paper toy, Lion Coffee Automobile - $25
Lion Coffee, paper toy, Lion Coffee Tug Boat - $25

Associations and Clubs:

United Federation of Doll Clubs, P.O. Box 14145, Parksville, Missouri 64152, Phone: 816-741-1002, Jan Quisenberry, President.

Toy Train Collectors Society c/o Bob Byledbal, 4868 Holly Place, Hamburg, New York 14075, Phone: 716-649-6479

Antique Toy Collectors of America c/o Robt R. Grew Carter, Ledyards, and Milburn, 2 Wall Street, 15th floor, New York, NY 10005, Phone: 212-238-8803, Robert R. Grew, Asst. Corresponding Secretary.

Magazines:

Toy Collector Magazine, P.O. Box 4244, Missouli, Montana 59806, Phone: 406-549-3175, Gordon Rice, Publisher

Toy Shop, Kraus publications, 700 East State Street, Iola, Wisconsin 54990, Phone: 715-445-2214, Jim Mohr, Manager

Dolls, Collector Communications Corp., 233 Spring Street, New York, NY 10013, Phone: 212-620-8000, Krystna Poray Goddu, Editor

National Doll World, Woman's Circle Publications 306 East Parr Road, Berne, Indiana 46711, Phone: 219-589-8741, Rebekah Montgomery, Editor

Antique Toy World, P.O. Box 34509, Chicago, Illinois

Paper Collector's Marketplace, P.O. Box 128, Scandanavia, Wisconsin 54977-0128, Doug Watson, Publisher/Editor

Books:

Chromos: Guide To Paper Collecting, Francine Kirsch, 1981.
Antique Book Fair and Paper Show Directory Margerie Parrott Adams, 1987.

Auctions:

Richard Opfer Auctioneering Inc.
1919 Greenspring Drive, Timonium, Maryland 21093, Phone: 301-252-5035

Philips Auctioneering, 406 East 79th Street, New York, NY 10021, Phone: 212-570-4830

Theriault's, P.O. Box 151, Annapolis, Maryland 21404, Phone: 301-269-0680

Country Store Antiques Auctions, P.O. Box 51, Bath, Ohio

Paper Show Promoters:

Bob Gallagher, 72-39 66th Place, Glendale, New York 11385, Phone: 718-497-6675

Nostalgia Con, George Downes, P.O. Box 421, Nutley, New Jersey 07110, Phone: 201-661-3358

Bernice Bornstein Shows, P.O. Box 421, Marblehead, Massachusetts 01945, Phone: 508-744-2731

Collections:

Children's Museum, Salem, Massachusetts

Shelburne Museum, Shelburne, Vermont

Museum of the City of New York

CHAPTER III

BOARD GAMES

Spiderman games satisfy an urge for 'fantasy' for pre and early teenagers.

Consider the late 1800s and early 1900s as the Victorian age; an age of strict morality. Gaming tables were a popular furniture item, large enough for a family to gather around, small enough for everyone to see the game's progress. It was an age of games, the most popular of which were board games; their lithography colorful, their graphics irresistible. They were mostly played with dice or spinners. Whomever piled up the most money, presents, or property, was the winner.

In an age of strict moral turpitude, the object of most games was greed.

More realistically, games were races, a race between players to reach a lithographed goal first. Obstacles barred the way, penalties were garnered by unreasonable luck or awkward skill. Scattered across the board were lucky spots, free throws, and free passes.

The boards varied from the 64 square checkerboard style to the 19 vertical and 19 horizontal line on a board dignifying the more than 2,000 year old game of Go.

While many collectors are interested in the remarkable variations of the games, to many, the interest lies in the art work, the lithography, or the graphics of the boards or their box covers. The best, the most colorful, were those of the 19th century. The lithography is a product of their times, and changes, as social and economic variables impinged.

Of all the manufacturers, McLoughlin Bros., Inc., New York, were the best when the turn of the century color and art work are to be considered.

Board games followed the science and technology of their times. Railroad transportation was the high point of technology of that day in the early 1900s. Board games mimicked their popularity. When baseball became a national mania, manufacturers followed the trend and baseball games and flowed into the marketplace.

Ives, the venerable W. and S.B. Ives Co. of Massachusetts, that was eventually swallowed by the Lionel Corporation, was the producer of the first American board game, Mansion of Happiness. That makes it the ancestor of all American board games. In turn, Mansion of Happiness was descended from a game of the 16th century called Goose.

The odds against finding the spiral track of a game of Goose from the 16th century are astronomical. The chances of finding one of the first mid 19th century hand colored, cardboard squares of Ives first board game are slim. Chances get progressively better as we go through the eras of the McLoughlin Bros. to the Milton Bradley Co. (who absorbed McLoughlin).

The usual rules apply, legwork to find the games, condition before you buy, and rarity after you get lucky.

The collectibility of these games will never die. New games appear regularly, the holiday being a hot spot. They still follow contemporary fads and science and they still have the built-in possibility of one day in the near future of being a sort after collectible.

Fantasy heroes with miraculous powers also seem to have staying powers in popularity ratings. They also have high prices. Superman was $350.

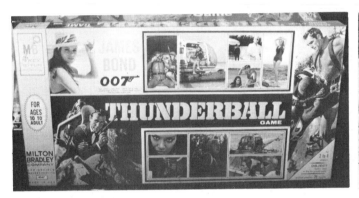

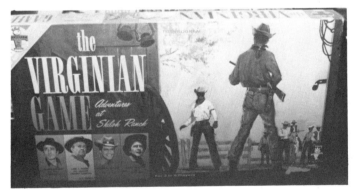

The man with a gun remains the mainstay of many board and family games - providing he's on the side of the law.

PLAYING CARDS

Venerable Charley Chaplin makes a most appropriate playing card joker with an $18 price.

By the Tang dynasty of ancient China (618-907 A.D.) playing cards were a form used for fortune telling. Since paper had been invented at least 400 years before the beginnings of the Tang dynasty, it requires no great jump of the imagination to believe such cards, made of mulberry bark paper, if not superceding the earlier painted sticks and arrows of the fortune teller, were at least companionable adjuncts.

How the idea of playing cards invaded Europe is not known. One thought is an Indian nomad caste, the gypsies, brought cards with them. Another thoughtful group lay it to the Moorish invaders of Spain who arrived earlier then the gypsies.

These earlier versions of playing cards were used in categories almost identical with those of today - educational, divination of fortune telling, amusement, or gambling. They may be art inspired in their design. Normally they are stylized today, mass produced decks of cards with the number of cards necessary for particular games; 52 cards for the so called poker deck, 48 for the pinochle deck.

These two decks lend themselves to an endless varity of games. To transcend the ordinary we must go back in time for the hand painted, hand colored decks of the earlier centuries, or for the modern touch, look to todays Tarot cards.

The earliest such cards were the tarocchi di Mantega, by the artist of that name c.1470. A 50 card deck divided into five groups, the Muses, the planets, the arts, science, and the virtues. A 78 card deck was introduced which was expanded to 97 cards in the 15th century. This then shrunk in size until it was a deck of 32 cards in France or 40 in Spain.

With the invention of lithography in the early 1800s and with todays photograving process, wood block and hand colored cards passed into history and into the purvue of todays collectors.

Television personalities are often used for their name recognition value as were the Addams Family. Milton Bradley Company used them as the keystone of a boxed 1965 card game. The price seemed reasonable at $20

Kits containing playing cards were, and still are, popular with travelers. This otherwise unmarked kit had been made for the Bank of Bloomfield, New Jersey as a give-a-way. No longer given away it had a $125 price tag at a New Jersey show.

JIGSAW PUZZLES

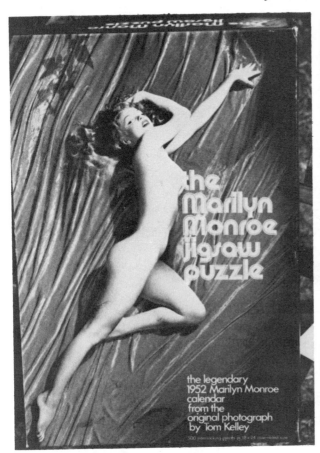

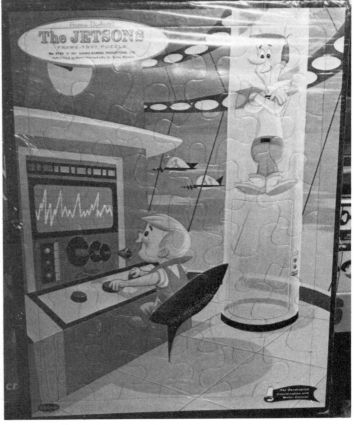

Whether of real people such as Marilyn Monroe, or imaginary folk like the Jetsons, a jigsaw puzzle will have its followers and collectors. They were your choice at a Connecticut show for $70 and $25

Television and radio were prime sources for jigsaw puzzle subjects, as were the movie screen's cartoon characters. Collectors love them all. Prices can see saw wildly depending on the dealer of auction bidding. These items varied from $10-85

JIGSAW PUZZLES

If today's children knew that the jigsaw puzzle was invented as a teaching aid for the study of geography, would they still appreciate receiving one as a present?

Good question, but back in the 18th century, one John Spilsbury, a London printer, mounted black and white maps on sheets of mahogany - some say cedar - cut them into pieces by sawing around a nations perimeter, and sold them as just that - a teaching aid.

They were sold mostly to the aristocracy and the well to do, who were the only folk then who could afford them.

It was Spilsbury's imitators who invented the interlocking pieces, and 25 years later, another map dissector, John Wallis, who made the first puzzle to be used for amusement rather than teaching. Color lithography was introduced to the puzzles early in the 19th century. By the middle of that same period, jigsaw puzzles had emerged fully blown as a child's amusement. Jigsaw puzzles and their manufacturers proliferated. With the invention and development of the die press, the puzzles became inexpensive.

By the beginning of the 20th century, Germany and Austria were predominant in the field, mostly making puzzles for export beyond their boundaries.

America dipped its toes into the jigsaw puzzle pond cautiously, by importing puzzles. By 1850, the first made in America puzzle appeared in the didactic English manner; squarish pieces, interlocking, used to instruct. Our citizens waited another ten years before a lithographed, interlocking puzzle, in a box, titillated their esthetic sensibilities. It was not an overnight success.

It was the invention of cardboard that put jigsaw puzzles on the map as it were.

It is also jigsaw puzzles that make us realize just how long a few of our toy companies have been doing business. Selchow and Riohter (think Scrabble) started using cardboard instead of wood, slicing it into long, straight lines. Milton Bradley and Company of Springfield, Massachusetts, captured a large part of the jigsaw puzzle market in the 1860s with several cheaply produced puzzles of lithographed cardboard. E.P. Dutton sold toy books and puzzle packages around the turn of the century, and Parker Brothers joined the business just about the time jigsaw puzzles invaded the adult market. This last initiated a craze that still lingers today.

Picture postcard puzzles became a parlor game, helping to sustain the astounding sales figure of two million puzzles a week. By the 1930s the craze had leveled off but no one is thinking of writing its obit.

Instead, big money has invaded the game as exclusive puzzles, mounted once again on wood, and hand cut, are designed by specialists for corporate or private customers. For one of these one-of-a-kind pieces $2,000 may be a low figure.

CHESS BOARDS

An integral part of many board games is a chess board or a variation. This twelve by twelve version dates from the mid 1800s, and was show priced at $80

Ranks and files remind us that chess beginnings have always been supposed to be war oriented. So much so that the chess board itself, whether of onyx, jade, stone, wood, metal, or more usually, of cardboard, is divided into eight vertical rows called files, and eight horizontal rows called ranks.

The 32 light colored and 32 dark colored squares accommodate a light and dark set, each of 16 chessmen.

The board has expanded its usefulness by being used to playing the game of checkers.

In the 16th century, a variant of chess, the couriers game, was played on a board eight squares wide by twelve squares long. It is recognizable in a Lucas van Lyden painting, 'The Chess Players'.

The chess pieces may be made of any conceivable material including gold and silver, yet without that mundane, multirow, chess board, even one of simple cardboard, there would be no game of chess as such.

In 1866, Milton Bradley and Company, used the basic chess board of 64 squares as the foundation for their game, The Checkered Game of Life. Each light square was marked with a number representing points gained or lost, and a corresponding word signifying a station in a players life such as wealth, prison, ambition, bravery, politician, 32 stations in all. It was one of more than 200 games from the collection of Arthur and Ellen Linman exhibited at the Miriam and Ira D. Wallach Art Gallery at Columbia University in New York City.

FAMILY GAMES

What's the difference between a board or a family game? Well now. That's not so easy. A useful division would be to classify board games as a game of skill between two players. Family games would then be a game of skill, or luck between any number greater than two, a family, for instance.

Games have never had problems crossing family, tribal or international boundaries. Chess moved from Asia to Europe. Dice games, evolving from knucklebones, were played by Roman soldiers. Is there a country in the world that does not have games played with dice?

Games are played whether by a single player with a deck of cards playing solitare or a family gathered around a Monopoly board watching paper money change hands for imaginary real estate.

In the early 20th century, it was thought the family was losing its function. By WWII that was reversed as a resurgence of interest in a family as a working, playing unit resisted the previous decline. How much 'play' as such contributed to this rise in togetherness is conjectural. It is interesting to note that games played by families filled the shelves of what were then simply known as toy stores. The supermarket concept came shortly after.

GAMES

Games, family games, multiplied. Old games that amused tribes and families for hundreds or thousands of years disappeared. Who of us has heard of Poch, Chinesinspiel, Snakes and Ladders, or Shoot the Box? Or Glueckshaus or Bell and Hammer? Some games survived to become perennials, stock numbers on a dealers shelves, collector's items if in original boxes, Chinese Checkers, c.1880, Dominoes, c.1700, Lotto c.1530, even the first unboxed Monopoly games, c.1930.

The last game was a product of the Great Depression, hand colored and packaged on a kitchen table by its inventor, Charles Darrow, an unemployed engineer. One of those kitchen table originals would be an item offered by a Sotheby or Butterfield auction house for big dollars. A 1935, mass produced edition by Parker Brothers was offered by a dealer at a 1991 toy show for $65. It was a reasonable but not remarkable return for an original investment.

Milton Bradley's 1866 Checkered Game of Life appeared at a collectible paper show, framed, with glass front and rear so both sides of the folding game board could be appreciated. The first folding game board, this one in its gold and black graphics on the rear, had a $25 price tag. *Mid Atlantic Magazine*

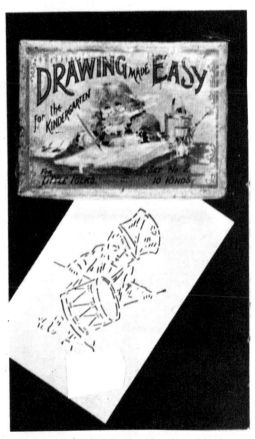

McLoughlin's 1897 drawing kit, adapted for four to six year olds by including stencils as drawing guides sold at auction for $30 plus the 10% premium

A deck of playing cards from England, 1860-1870. They were made for the American market by Reynolds and Sons. This deck came with trump markers and two of the picture suits matted and framed. It also came with a $650 price.

An early, c.1860, French version of a jigsaw puzzle, used eleven pieces of polished wood to create a child's version of a psychologist's test equipment. Found at a Phoenix, Arizona show, it's asking price was $145

This Cantelope and The Lost Diamond games was offered in two different collectible shows two months apart in 1992. The one pictured was framed, in near mint condition and priced at $80. The second, was in only good condition, showed wear, unframed, and was priced at $80.

Both of these board games appeared on a dealers table at a model railroad train show. The Sea Wolf game by Politoy, described as rare, had the rare price of $180. The Space 1999, Moon Base Alpha by Mattel, was only in fair condition and was priced accordingly at $50.

The most popular trains of all time were those that appeared in the Lionel catalogs in time for Christmas. Some of these catalogs were the foundation of a large publishing house. Finding old Lionel catalogs today is as popular as finding the old trains, the second most active collecting field, in terms of money, in the world. Suffolk County Historical Society. The years between 1949 and 1954 have a value range of $25-89

Prices:

McLoughlin's Rhinoceros Puzzle, c.1870 - $30, Auction.
Milton Bradley's Space Patrol. Mint with wrapper - $125, Auction.
Toy Policeman Motion Toy, cardboard - $30, Auction.
Pair of early children's playing cards, matted - $75, Auction.
Playing cards, c.1930, prohibition set, Indian, oversize, Advertising - $15, Auction.
Selchow and Richter box game of Snake Eyes - $80
Hustler Basketball Game in box, by Technofix - $300, Auction
Two piece lot, Snow White and the Seven Dwarfs game, and Sorcerers Apprentice - $85
Marvel's Pop-up Pinball Game, c.1950 - $350
Milton Bradley, Jack Daw game - $40
Playing Cards, double deck, Chessie, in box - $45
Three Ball Tally, Milton Bradley, 1932 - $45
Playing Cards, A. Dougherty, New York, c.1800, incomplete, 40 cards - $35
Jigsaw Puzzle, Easter Morning, Parker Brothers, March 1931 - $10
Playing Cards, double deck, Illinois by MacPherson, in Win Lose or Draw book box - $20

Magazines:

Hobbies Magazine, monthly column about playing cards.

Inside Collector, P.O. Box 98, 657 Meachem Ave., Elmont, NY 11003.

Collector's Showcase, 7130 S. Lewis, Suite 210, Tulsa, Oklahoma, 74136.

Timeless treasures, P.O. Box 341, Lexington, Missouri, 64067. Current price reports, published four times yearly.

Clubs and Associations:

International Backgammon Association, 1300 Citrus Isle, Fort Lauderdale, Florida, 33315. Phone: 305-527-4033. Susan L. Boyd, Sec./Treasurer.

National Scrabble Association, care of Williams and Company, P.O. Box 700, Greenport, NY 11944, Phone: 516-477-0033, John D. Williams.

American association of Backgammon Clubs, P.O. Box 12359, Las Vegas, Nevada, 89121. Phone: 702-792-3609, Linda Kreugel, Exec. Officer.

American Checker Federation, P.O. Drawer 365, Petal, Mississippi 39465. Phone: 601-582-4554, Charles C. Walker, Sec.

American Game Collectors Association, 4628 Barlow Drive, Dept. E., Bartlesville, Oklahoma 74006. Anne D. Williams, Sec.

American Go Association, care of Roy Laird, P.O. Box 397, Old Chelsea Station, New York City, NY 10113-0397, Phone: 718-768-5217, Roy Laird, Editor.

American International Checkers Society, care of Jack Birnman, 11010 Horde Street, Wheaton, Maryland 20902, Phone: 301-949-5920, Jack Birnman, Sec./Treasurer.

Collections:

National Gallery of Art, Washington, D.C., Cincinnati Art Museum, The United Playing Card Company's collection is on permanent loan here.

The Margaret Woodbury Strong Museum, 1 Manhatten Square, Rochester, NY, Children's books, games, puzzles.

Miriam and Ira D. Wallach Art Gallery, Columbia University, NY had 200 games from the Arthur Ellen Linman Collection on display.

Books:

Games of the World, Frederick V. Grunfeld, Holt, Reinhart and Winston, NY, 1975.

The Game of Tarot, Michael A.E. Dummett, Duckworth, 1980.

Playing Cards of the World, Kathleen Wawk, U.S. Games Systems, 1982.

Jigsaw Puzzles, Anne D. Williams, Wallace-Homestead Book Co., Radnor, Pennsylvania, 1990.

The Jig Saw Book, Linda Hannas, The Dial Press, 1981.

CHAPTER IV

TRADE CARDS

Display of trade cards for $100 or less at a paper show gives an idea of the wide variety available.

Playing cards are known to have been used as calling cards but only one card in each deck is an actual trade card and that is the joker. With its graphics and company name it is the ideal of a trade card's use of advertising the publisher while being handed out freely to the buyer, within each purchased deck of playing cards.

There are those who claim trade cards were the genesis for the baseball card. All things are possible. Trade cards originally varied in size from 2" by 3" up to the size of a movie window card or poster. It may be. Or it may not. The cards themselves are mute.

The cards we know have been printed mostly on paper or thin cardboard; many were chromolithographed, some were silk screened.

Closely associated, possibly the true beginnings of baseball cards, starting in the 1880s, were the cigarette cards. In the early 1900s, a coupon was enclosed in each package of cigarettes. This coupon, with 5 or 10¢ in coin, was exchanged for silk screened card bearing the likeness of an early baseball player. The investment was sound. In 1991, $7,000 was the last quoted price for one at a paper show.

With the picture on these trade cards, there was usually a name, either with the picture or on the reverse. The name could be a tradesman's, of a company or a manufacturer. Sometimes a service is mentioned, and with little change they became the first business cards.

The larger trade cards known were so unwieldy that they were probably advertising posters.

On average, the most common size to be found is about 4" by 6". Almost all post 1850 cards will be embellished with vivid colors and usually have a border of decorative lines or leaves.

The earliest cards we know of that still survive are from c.1730. Even Paul Revere was known to have had a fling at designing trade cards.

Lithographers during the 1850s, joined in the business of engraving these bits of advertising with lavish use of color. Among those we know to have worked in this field were Currier and Ives. A single page list of stock cards waiting for a name to be added is known from 1880.

Trade cards as collectibles are not new. Our Victorian forebears were scrapbook collectors. In them (no corner mounts then), were pasted and glued the trade cards collected from daily buying trips to the neighborhood stores. Mom and dad may have brought the cards home but it was the son or daughter who collected them and pasted them in glorious confusion in the household scrapbook.

It was the color that excited them. Lithography was booming. Television and the movies were names of the future. Trade cards were now! They were the boom collectible of the late 1800s.

As an advertisement it was cheap, but accepted. It cost the merchants nothing, or at the most, a few pennies. Most were supplied as low cost advertising by the major suppliers to the neighborhood stores. They were handed out to the customers, or with the merchant's name added, usually on the back, passed out house to house by the neighborhood's willing child volunteers.

TRADE CARDS

As with postcards, the categories are numerous. Unlike postcards, the back of a trade card is the most important side. That's where the name of the business doing the actual work of passing out the cards would appear, as opposed to the company who paid for the printing.

Sometimes the back is blank. As long as the front bears a logo or a name, that doesn't matter. Like postcards, trade cards are collected for the pictures.

Some are quite rare such as clipper ships, Currier and Ives, Coca Cola or other drink cards, multi-color bank cards, or anything before the 1850s.

Again, like postcards, children were popular subjects. So were household tools, food products, animals, or farm equipment.

Bank trade cards, those picturing the cast iron mechanical banks popular then, are a specialist form. Collectors and dealers have been known to pay extraordinary prices for them. As recently as 1991, in Philadelphia, a Punch and Judy card sold for $1,650.

Collectors in general, usually prefer mechanical bank cards that were printed with more than one or two colors. A multi-color Eagle and Eaglet card sold at that same auction for $450.

On the other hand, the price of mechanical bank cards have, in general, remained stable for the past decade with prices averaging well under one hundred dollars.

Because of the Victorian urge to paste everything in scrapbooks, they, the scrapbooks, are the best means of collecting some excellent trade cards. Also the most frustrating. The glues used (fish and animal glues were popular then) makes it difficult to remove the cards without damage.

There is no easy nor totally safe method of doing this if there is handwriting on the back. Bestine, available at art supply stores, has been used with some success. So has ordinary lighter fluid. Neither method is guaranteed.

One of the joys of childhood, was hovering around stores asking shoppers for their trade cards. As late as the 1920s and early 1930s they haunted cigar stores begging cigar store coupons. What do the kids have now, grocery cents off coupons from the newspapers? Where's the fun in that?

Clipper ship advertising cards. They look good. They should, they're reproductions. If original, $5,000 would not be unreasonable. As reproductions they sold for $85.

These 1909 tobacco cards, like the earlier bubble gum cards, were still small, less than 2″ by 3″. Their price wasn't small. These were $100.

BUBBLE GUM CARDS

These tobacco cards, midway between bubble gum cards and the later baseball cards, were advertisements for UZIT cigarettes, billed, in 1909, as, "the new mouth piece cigarette baseball series."

The public school that doesn't have a nearby candy store is a rare one. Those same candy stores, since about 1885, were the crucibles where future collectors of bubble gum cards were forged. They were the source of those wonderful cards issued, before 1930, as bubble gum cards.

There is a claim that, by the turn of the century, at least 500 different sets had been published, of which only 5% were of sport figures.

They led some of these novice collectors to investigate food related cards, bakery and non-bakery items, and the early tobacco cards.

Bubble gum cards were small by definition of user and use. They had to fit the wrapper around the approximately 2″ by 3″ square or oblong package of pink, chewable chicle. The cards pictured an array of animals, trains, ordinary people, and sports figures, up to and including discus throwers.

The term 'bubble gum cards' as generic, to describe all those may be anathema to today's serious collector, but to the knicker clad youngster who competed with his 'gang' by spending off-times pitching these cards against a building's wall, or a crack in a cement sidewalk, that was the only term they knew.

As they grew up, life became more complicated and so did the cards with which they once played. Could they believe then, that those same cards would not only proliferate into the world's largest collectible - baseball cards - but further expand into an industry that spewed more than 600 categories, and thousands of sets, of non-sport cards by the 1980s and 1990s? In addition to the full range of spectator and participant sports as we know them today?

All of these cards have a value, most of them moderate. Age, subject, and scarcity are three predeterminates to research. Of more - or most - interest is condition. Rounded edges, creases, tears, or water stains, will naturally have much to say about the final price. Actually the most to say.

One more caveat. If at all possible, buy full sets of any card issued after 1960. Buy them in mint condition, then store them - and the wrapper - in a plastic sleeve.

The future of these cards were assured, for they eventually led, in the period between 1930 and 1941, to the introduction of baseball cards as we know them today.

BASEBALL CARDS

Baseball cards are presently the world's largest and most active collectible.
In major cities there are advertisements for as many as seven shows a week.

To be a serious collector of baseball cards you must first learn the language of such topics as Topps Bowman, Fleers, Donruss, Score and Upper Deck, individual cards or sets, rated rookie or first cards, traded sets or VG-EX sets. Then there are the names such as Don Mattingly, Roger Clemens, Mark Grace, Wade Boggs, Doc Gorden, and Ted Williams.

And were you there when Babe Ruth hit the first home run in Yankee Stadium? Or when he blew a kiss to Claire, his second wife, as he crossed home plate, the day after he married her?

If you were there then perhaps you can translate the code names of early baseball card sets, T205, or T206.

The T205 set, an ACC designation, was issued as the first Gold Border set in 1911 in packages of cigarettes. Brands such as Sweet Caporals, American Beauty, and Fatima's carried the cards. These were products of the American Tobacco Company, later broken up by the government as a monopoly. The advertisements for the various cigarettes were on the backs of the cards, below the biographical and team standings of the pictured player. This would seem to make these early baseball cards descendents of the earlier trade cards.

All baseball card collectors know what they want for Christmas and that is a T206, 1910 Honus Wagner card. A T205 Gold Border Cy Young would also be acceptable.

When, in 1992, Sotheby's auctioned a Honus Wagner card, one of forty known to exist, they may have been hoping to beat their 1991 record. In 1992, the card claimed by Sotheby's as, "may well be within the top ten in terms of condition," was offered, the final bid of $220,000 was not even close to that realized in 1991.

At that sale of March 22, the team of hockey great, Wayne Gretzky and McNall, combined to bid the 1910 Honus Wagner card to a world record price of $451,000 (ten percent premium included).

After that, you'll settle for the Cy Young card that sold for $41,250.

There is no longer a single baseball card market. Categories now number in the dozens from rookie to bubble gum and early trade cards.

A recent pier show in New York City of over 200 vendors, featured stacks of mostly 1991 and 1992 cards on these same 200 tables, which gives some idea of the hundreds of thousands of each card printed. Early cards are to be found in limited quantities only by good legwork.

Each year a pundit predicts the early demise of this craze. Each year the cards proliferate. Not only are baseball cards just for kids, but they have burst their boundaries separating them, not only from other sports, but also from global events.

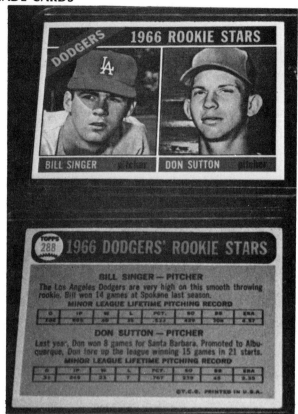

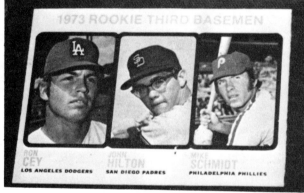

Rookies and stars, single imprints or triple group photographs, are all grist to the serious baseball card collector.

Baseball cards now take in any sport imaginable, including basketball, war, and crime. Are they all sports?

TRADE CARDS

TOM ZACHARY

BIG LEAGUE CHEWING GUM

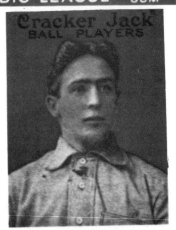

Cracker Jack BALL PLAYERS

TINKER, Chicago - Federals

HENRY "HEINIE" MANUSH

BIG LEAGUE CHEWING GUM

F. CLARKE, Pittsburg

BURLEIGH GRIMES

Chicago

BIG LEAGUE CHEWING GUM

McGRAW, N. Y. NAT'L

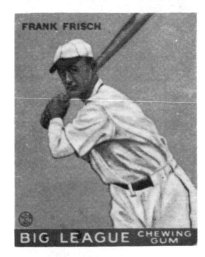

FRANK FRISCH

BIG LEAGUE CHEWING GUM

These were the old timers, names that meant something to the pre-1948 sport fan. That's the years most baseball price guides seem to assume baseball card pricing began. Despite current economic conditions, said a recent Action Packed Trading Cards survey, 57% of those known as heavy collectors, said they would never sell their entire collection. Despite this survey, a collection from a California collector active from 1948 through 1875 appeared at a Dallas, Texas auction in 1992 where a 1961/1962 Fleer complete set in NMT/MT sold for $3,850.

Cracker Jack BALL PLAYERS

WHEAT, Brooklyn - Nationals

CHARLES (CHUCK) KLEIN
PHILADELPHIA NATIONALS

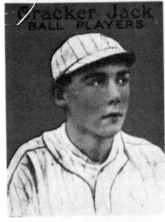

Cracker Jack BALL PLAYERS

ROUSCH, Indianapolis - Federals

33

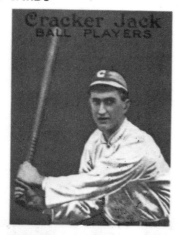

MARANVILLE, BOSTON - NATIONALS

LAJOIE, PHILADELPHIA - AMERICANS

CHASE, BUFFALO - FEDERALS

GROH, CINCINNATI NATIONALS

BIG LEAGUE CHEWING GUM

CICOTTE, CHICAGO - AMERICANS

BIG LEAGUE CHEWING GUM

M. BROWN, ST. LOUIS - FEDERALS

BIG LEAGUE CHEWING GUM

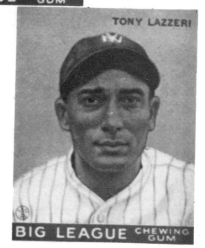

Great names: Big League Chewing Gum and Crackerjack. Larger than life names, the players: Tom Zachary, Tony Lazzeri, McGraw, Burleigh Grimes, and Tinker, of Tinker to Evans to Chance legend. Crackerjack remains as an active name. Players like Frank Frisch made the Baseball Hall of Fame in 1947, Burl Grimes in 1964. Of more interest to the average baseball card collector would be the prices of Lou Gehrig's cards: 1933 Delong, $3000, 1934 Goudey, $3100.

BEYOND BASEBALL CARDS

There is a world of sport cards to choose from like football, soccer, basketball, boxing, wrestling and more. There are cards from the Persian Gulf War. Not enough? There are cards for Civil War buffs; a 100 card set, historically accurate, picturing the human side of war. The set, at $12.50, is a venture by Dave Ryan, a writer from Richmond, Virginia, who has two additional sets planned.

Still not enough? Tuff Stuff is developing a set commemorating the 50th anniversary of Pearl Harbor and trading cards featuring the Peanuts comic strip character, 'Snoopy', an exclusive.

Due in July of 1992 was the 110 card True Crime series incorporating serial killers Ted Bundy and Jeffery Dahmer. *Newsday* (NY) reports that a state assemblyman and a state senator have introduced a bill in Albany that forbids the sale of these cards to minors.

Sport card collectors can hardly wait for the expected rise in prices this ban promises when the new cards come out.

From 1910, trade cards from the English firm of J. Wix and Son. Silk embroidered, botanical in content, they came with a booklet explaining the flower and it's propagation. Priced at $35 each they moved well.

TRADE CARDS

Say Currier and Ives and immediately we think prints. Rarely do we think of that firm publishing trade cards. Here are two from their American View series that were offered at $350 each.

Prices:

Trick Pony bank card - $650

15 Stevens one color cards - $900

O.J. Simpson rookie card - $125

Home Run Baker, 1914, Cracker Jack - $850

Tris Speaker, 1914, Cracker Jack - $1800

Cracker Jack cards, 1914, 49 pieces, including nine Hall of Fame - $2250

Babe Ruth, 1933, Goudey, Ex-Mint - $2500

Dizzy Dean, 1934, National Chicle Gum Company, Batter Up series - $1100

Joe DiMaggio, 1937, Wheaties cereal box collection - $1300

Bob Feller, 1938, Goudey, Heads Up series - $900

Bill Dickey, 1934, Diamond Star series - $800

Duke Snider, 1952, Topps - $700

Topps, 1964, 587 full set, Mint - $4000

Duke Snider, 1954, Bowman - $125

Willie Mays, 1954, Bowman - $250

Connie Mack, 1900, Fan Craze - $600

Topps, 1956, 340 pieces, complete set - $5000

Singer Sewing Machines, 1926/1927, five cards, Song Bird series, VG-EX - $7 ea.

Lion Coffee Cards, Woolson, fifteen cards, advertisements and premium offers on back - $50

Victorian scrapbook, VG, 315 trade cards plus die-cuts and valentine - $185

Hires Root Beer card, 5" by 7", late 1800s, chromolithographed, GD - $10

Lobster Boy card, for side show attraction description on front, facsimile autograph on back, signed Grady Stiles - $15

Cigarette cards, 40, Turkish Trophies, Fable series, Fair-VG - $15

Cigarette card, Between the Acts and Bravo, 2" by 4", fancy back advertisement, lithograph by Heppenhamer, New York - $25

Cigarette card, same company, Kate Gerard, actress, VF - $30

Cigarette card, same company, Modjeska as Camille, VF - $30

Trade Card, 'The Archimedean Lawn Mower, specifications and prices, F - $15

Trade Card, Smoke Topsy Tobacco - $15

Trade Card, Mrs. Winslow's Syrup, calendar of 1886 on back - $10

Trade Card, Superior Land Roller and Seeder - $10

Trade Card, Hampden Watches - $10

White Mountain Mechanical, trade card, die-cut in shape of ice cream freezer - $45

Jenny Lind Concert, facsimile of 1820 ticket issued by P.T. Barnum - $20

Trade Card Album, 216 cards, Wills and Odgen's Cigarettes, neat mint - $80

TRADE CARDS
Collections:

Sports Hall of Shame, P.O. Box 31867, Palm Beach Gardens, Florida 33420, Collectible memorabilia from bloopers and wacky blunders.

Metropolitan Museum of Art, New York, NY 10028, Public information phone: 212-269-7710, ext. 3441, The Burdick Collection.

Associations:

Past in Review, P.O. Box 3864, Las Vegas, NV 89036-0864, Phone: 702-452-2292, Page Rea, President

Magazines:

Baseball Research Journal, Society for American Baseball Research, Inc., P.O. Box 93183, Cleveland, OH 44101, Jim Kaplan Editor

Basketball Hall of Fame Newsletter, Basketball Hall of Fame, 1150 West Columbus Ave., Box 179, Springfield, MA 01101-0179, Phone: 413-781-6500, Jerry Healy, Editor

Sports Collector's Digest John Stommon, P.O. Box E, Milan, Michigan 48160, Phone: 715-445-2214

CHAPTER V

SPORTS MEMORABILIA

Baseball cards have become so much in demand as a collectible, they call for book length copy as a subject. A simpler manner of looking at them is to place them under the all-encompassing umbrella of sports memorabilia. Here paper is offered and collected in the form of programs, scorecards, passes, arena tickets, posters and advertising (by Organizations or players). Name recognition is vital.

During the 1980s, baseball cards were king with accompanying paper and other memorabilia riding their coattails as prices soared. Even the recession failed to dampen collector's ardor as sports memorabilia flourished as a hobby and an industry through 1991 and 1992.

Proof? Look back at what the shows and the auctions offered and sold. Collectors were bidding on and buying, anything from old player signed checks, to golf scorecards, wrestling programs, original art, contracts, autographed photographs, sports magazine, team stock certificates, sports related comic books, calendars, boxing licenses, and original lithographs by Muhammad Ali.

These items and other sports memorabilia, have zoomed in popularity and are now, as of 1992, a one billion dollar annual industry. Baseball accounts for about ninety percent of this activity. It should. It contains the broadest array of collectibles, those that bring the best auction prices.

By augmenting their staffs with experts, the larger auction houses such as Sotheby's, Christie's, Butterfield's, Oliver's, and LeLand's, have all helped to boost memorabilia prices to new records.

The high prices realized at some of these auctions, have drawn discretionary monies to the markets by professionals seeking better investment opportunities. They are competing with investment money from Japan, France, and Italy.

It is not required to know where the 3,000 specialty shops are that deal in memorabilia. It's not even necessary to leave home to become a participator. Mail and telephone auctions abound, mail order companies flourish, and a catalog request to an auction house can make of you an absentee or a telephone bidder.

Remember, prices can go down as well as up, that not every item is valuable.

Five thousand, 1985, Topps, assorted mint stars, rookies, and commons were offered for $60, postpaid, in a collectible magazine advertisement. How many Hall of Famer's were you expecting in that assortment - at that price?

Silks and felts were used as well as paper for cigarette cards of the 1870s through the early 1900s. Four by six inch silks with players and team names from college sports were yours then for the coupon from a cigarette package and 5¢ in coin. The felts were only made for one year by a cigarette company. Felts may be found at shows for $15-45. Silks, normally reasonably priced may go as high as $7000 retail for exceptional pieces. More usual are silks such as these from a Westhampton, New York show at $75

38

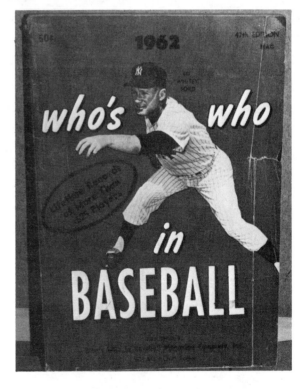

Sports figures' names and faces appeared on postage stamps and the advertising pages. Among the many, Ruth, Gehrig and Mays. Any of the advertisers missed could be found among the statistics of magazines and books on the sport.

SPORTS MEMORABILIA

Paying sport figures for autographs at sports memorabilia shows is not the way to begin collecting unless you are solely interested in current athletes regardless of their problematic future values. They are too available and in all probability will never be worth what you paid to obtain that signature. Forget the hours you stood in line waiting. Remember instead, condition and scarcity are primary.

Realistically, true fans don't seem to mind, but, the more autographs the players sign, the bigger the payoff for the sports star. For the collector, such autographs are the equivalent of junk bonds.

The frenzy for sports memorabilia began slowly in 1969. Until then, sports collectors did so quietly, without a see-what-I-got attitude. Baseball cards were for kids. Other items were cyclic such as press pins, programs, signed bats and balls. In the mid seventies, there were less than 100 dealers throughout the country. Today there are 100 shows in any one week and possibly 35,000 registered dealers involved in the industry and more unknowns working quietly from their homes.

By the 1980s, the larger auction houses, perceiving the large dollars to be made, started specialized auctions. Babe Ruth's brass locker key, with his name and the number three, brought $7,150 at Philadelphia in 1987. Guernsey's, in April of 1990, sold a 1955 Brooklyn Dodger World Championship original photograph for $3,500, and a Bustin Babe, Larrupin Lou's photograph, autographed by Lou Gehrig, and Babe Ruth, for $9,500.

At this same auction, two Cracker Jack baseball card sets of 1914 and 1915 sold for $100,000 without the 10% premium. Baseball gets the big money as other sports tag along. A 1935 complete National Chicle set, the first major football set ever produced, only brought in $8,500.

For the memorabilia collector, sports are forever. More so since the chicle kings put cards in their bubble gum packs as a come-on.

Advertisers picked only the winners hoping their glamor would increase sales. Some advertisers names became as well known as the players they used.

ADVERTISING BY MAJOR PLAYERS

If a baseball player had a good season, the balance of his year was made better as companies selling anything from sneakers to shaving cream, to deodorants and soap, literally pounded on his door with advertising contracts in their hot little hands. What player could resist. Not many.

Honus Wagner did with the world record T206 baseball cards which were issued in 1909 and 1910 by the tobacco companies. Wagner was an early tobacco smoking opponent. He objected to his name being associated with cigarettes advertised on the backs of the cards.

Players other than Wagner, in the early years, normally endorsed only tobacco and sports equipment. Lucky Strike was a heavy 1920s advertiser who used name players from the major leagues.

Two brothers, Dizzy and Daffy dean, lent their names to Beechnut chewing tobacco and Union Leader pipe tobacco during the 1930s. Those advertisements came out as die-cut, four foot high cut-outs, much like a movie lobby cut-out.

Chesterfield cigarettes entered the game late in the 1940s. The names they signed are still household names to collectors and sports fans today - Joe DiMaggio, Ted Williams and Stan Musial.

Babe Ruth would sign anything, so why not an advertisement? The 'Babe' was so willing to sign his name for his fans that when he was unavailable, he authorized 'ghost signers'. In 1923, Babe Ruth was only a four year veteran of Colonel Jacob Ruppert's Yankees baseball team. The Yankee Stadium was only one year old, but before and after every game, Yankee fans lines up hoping for an autograph from Ruth. It remains the most coveted, but not the most difficult to find.

He signed for many company advertisements, including Quaker Puffed Wheat and Rice, and a drinkless Kaywoodie pipe.

Among the big names that formed advertising partnerships, were Coca Cola with Phil Rizutto, Lucky Strike with Lloyd Waner and Ted Williams with Moxie (a soft drink).

Gillette Razors signed and used Duke Sniders likeness in their advertising c.1955. A year earlier, in 1954, they had signed Willie Mays to a similar advertising contract.

Some advertising agencies had a degree of precognition in signing future diamond stars. The Pennsylvania Leather Company was using Jackie Robinson's name for advertising purposes in 1954. Don't bother looking in the record books, that was Robinson's rookie year.

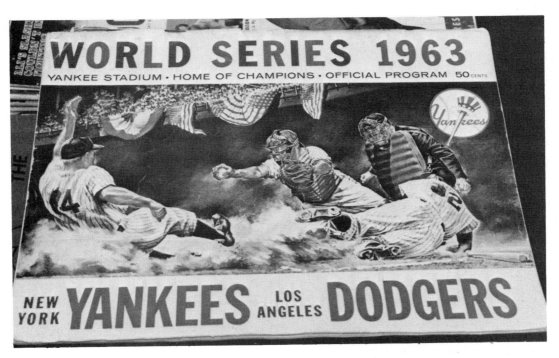

This 1963 World's Series program between the New York Yankees and the Los Angeles Dodgers came with a $275 price tag at a recent auction.

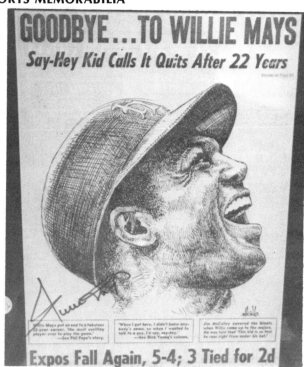

For only $45 at a 1992 show, a collector could have owned this autographed copy of a farewell to one of baseball's greats - WIllie Mays. *MidAtlantic*

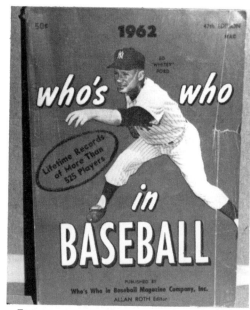

For any year, someone needs to know baseball 'stats'. Publishers hustle to satisfy this need. In 1962, for fifty cents, you could have the lifetime records of 525 players. Thirty years later, the same issue would have cost $35.

SPORTS MEMORABILIA
Prices:

Sen Sen Gum advertising scorecard - $65

Small colored pamphlet, 'Men of America', Bobby Jones on cover, inside - 'Big Bill' Tilden, Johnnie Weissmuller, Rogers Hornsby - $45

Notre Dame vs. Purdue, Oct. 22, 1955, football program. Back cover advertisement Lucky Strike - 65

1936 Wheaties advertisement, full page color, with Lou Gehrig, Foxx, Cochran - $15

1959 Harlem Globe Trotters program - $20

18" by 24" Willie Mays Coca Cola poster - $10

15" by 30" St. Louis Cardinals, Budweiser Calendar, 1980 - $18

Ten baseball player, 1940s, Sunday comic section, color advertisements - $25

Wheaties, 1935/1936, Carl Hubbel, New York Giants, 'Field Those Hot Ones', by John Lewis, Washington Senators, 3rd base - $30

Wheaties, Charles Wasicek, All American 1935, guard, Colgate - $30

Army vs. Notre Dame stubless football ticket, Soldiers Field, Chicago, 11/29/1930 - $35

1936 Sugar Bowl program, second annual classic, LSU vs. TCU, near mint - $100

Evening Sun, Fair Play Eagles scorecard, Christy Mathewson on cover, 10/2/1913 - $25

New York Yankees vs. Milwaukee Browns, World Series program at New York, 1957 - $100

Yankees vs. Milwaukee World Series program at Milwaukee, 1958, EX - $175

Princeton vs. Harvard football program at Princeton, 11/11/1950, EX - $25

Floyd Patterson vs. Roy Harris, World Heavyweight Championship program, Wrigley Field, Chicago, August 18, 1958, EX - $150

'Pistol' Pete Maravich signed 1976 Hoops NBA program, New Orleans Jazz, Mint - $200

John Wooden signed 1971/1972 UCLA program, mint - $50

STADIUM TICKETS

1969 World Series at Shea Stadium, full ticket, unused, in 4" by 8" display block, a momento of the Amazing Mets miracle of '69 - $325

1926 World Series Yankees game seven ticket stub - $200

Dizzy and Paul Dean, ticket for exhibition game sponsored by Jax Beer at Farr Park in Longview, Saturday October 19 - $25

1926 World Series Green ticket stub, game two - $100

1931, St. Louis baseball club games season pass, book of ten complimentary tickets issued to Fred Zacknetz. For the account of the House of Delegates, signed in two places across the back of the tickets Frank DeHass Robinson, President - $25

1930 Giants sterling silver season pass, near mint - $1300

1931 New York Giants sterling silver season pass, near mint - $1300

18 American League season passes from 1934/1963, near mint - $325

1926, Yankee World Series ticket stub, VG - $150

1915, World Champs, Boston, American League baseball club championship game pass, with season ticket coupon book, with all coupons removed - $100

1916, season ticket book, Boston, American League baseball club with twenty coupons and engraved invitation for opening game of the season. This was Babe Ruth's rookie season. - $100

There are more World Series programs available than there are tickets and passes, naturally. The World Series programs dating from 1939-1968, at recent 1991 and 1992 auctions, regardless of the teams involved, set a high of $425 (only because it was a lot of two programs) to a low of $60, for the 1968 program of Detroit vs. St. Louis at Detroit. It was the programs from 1926 through 1938 that realized more solid prices, as below:

1926, Cardinals versus Yankees at St. Louis, with Ruth's autograph - $1300
1928, Yankees vs. Cardinals at New York - $1100
1931, St. Louis vs. Philadelphia at St. Louis - $400
1932, Yankees vs. Cubs at New York - $850
1933, Giants vs. Senators at New York - $650
1934, Tigers vs. Cardinals at St. Louis - $100
1935, Tigers vs. Cardinals - $600
1936, Giants vs. Yankees at New York - $400

The year 1973 was the last year the two opposing World Series teams put out separate programs. Blame it on the playoffs. Producing a program, only to be eliminated from the playoffs made it too costly. So 1973 saw the first of the four team programs, with all the nominated players. But not the final roster.

Books:

The Sports Insider Address Book, by Sportsource, Contemporary Books, Chicago, 1990

Associations:

Sports Museums and Hall of Fame, 101 West Sutton Place, Wilmington, DE 19810, Al Cartwright, Executive Director

Souvenir Card Collectors Society, P.O. Box 4155, Tulsa, OK 74159-0155, Phone: 918-747-6724, Dana M. Marr, Secretary

North American Society For Sport History, Pennsylvania State University, 121 White Building, University Park, Pennsylvania 16802, Phone: 814-865-2416, Ronald A. Smith, Secretary/Treasurer

Mail and Phone Auctions:

Country Store Antique Auctions, P.O. Box 51, Bath, Ohio 44210

Philip Weiss Auctions, P.O. Box 278, East Rockaway, NY 11518-0278, Phone: 516-594-0731

ABC Shows, 343 West Market Street, York, Pennsylvania 17401, Phone: 717-845-7577

Sports Auctions of New York, P.O. Box 347, Floral Park, NY 11002, Mark Schafler - Les Wolff

B and E Distributers, P.O. Box 2889, LaGrande, Oregon 97850, Phone: 503-963-6764

Yesterday's Heroes, P.O. Box 371, Wayland, Massachusetts 01778, Phone: 508-568-1086

Mike Safran, 204 East Edisto Ave., Columbia, South Carolina 29205, Phone: 803-771-6495

Dr. J and Sons, 20820 Telegraph Road, Romulus, Michigan 48174, Phone: 313-479-4111.

Museums:

National Art Museum of Sport, 108 North Pennsylvania Street, 12th Floor, Indianapolis, Indiana 46204, Phone: 317-687-1715, Reilly Rhodes, Executive director

Magazines:

Paper Pile Quarterly, P.O. Box 337, San Anselmo, CA 94960, Phone: 415-454-5552

Non-Sport Marketplace, P.O. Box 128 PCM, Plover, Wisconsin 54467, Phone: 715-341-5452, Sue and Jim Nicewander

Diamond Sports Memorabilia, 6160 Fairmount Avenue, Suite C, San Diego, CA 92120, Phone: 1-800-669-4585 or 619-280-3336

CHAPTER VI

NEWSPAPERS

Events larger or small, of trivial or major concern, fill the pages which originated as broadsides, graduated to 'Penny Posts', and have become a standard offering at collectible shows - our daily newspapers. The low prices put on these offerings may sometimes astound the beginning collector who doesn't realize that rarity takes precedence over million copy daily production.

Then why collect them? Because they constitute a historical market unlike any other, a glimpse of the daily lives of ordinary, and extraordinary people. A paper trail of history as it occured, romanticized by its distance from the past, written by the people who lived it.

The historical newspaper market continues to be active, with its collectible segments bringing steady, though unspectacular prices at auction.

An issue of the *Washington Republican* (Mississippi Territory) dated February 9, 1814, was reported sold in February of 1992 for $500. For collectible newspapers that was an unusually high price. It's headline, "Andrew Jackson Defeats The Creeks: Glorious Victory!!" excited the collecting instincts of those intrigued by military events or the plight of Native American. The statement by the auctioneer, Bob Raynor, that the issue was the only known copy helped raise the bidding.

At the other side of the high bid, low bid action, a copy of *Frank Lesters Weekly* from 1865, sold at a paper collectors show for two dollars, despite a complete front page report on Lincoln's Assassination. Even non-collectors would be interested in owning a copy at that low price.

Recent events are just as collectible, an issue of the *New York Daily News*, headline "Mets Win It." It decorates the back wall of a pharmacy store where the owners mental highlights of history revolve around his beloved Mets baseball team. It's price? To him it's priceless.

Which illustrates the wide divergence in why some newspapers are collectible. A quick glance through a mail auction catalog reveals what collectors look for in a collectible newspaper and its association with an emotional event. Things such as the Pearl Harbor Attack, the John F. Kennedy assassination, or its aftermath, and the shooting of the alleged killer Lee Oswald by Jack Ruby are among the many topics. The movie memorabilia emotional equivalent would be the suicide/murder/natural causes death of Jean Harlow or the shooting of John Lennon.

 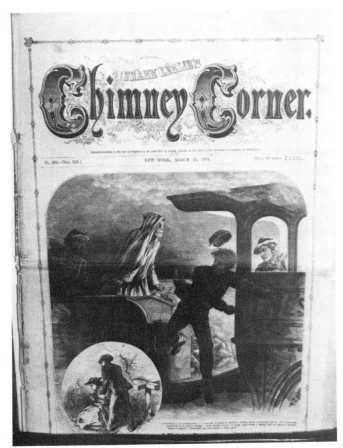

Mastheads change, news retains a sameness, a deja vu. Hurricanes, politics, daily life, and fantasy will always find space somewhere in a newspaper.

NEWSPAPERS

There is no strength in exaggeration. Even the truth is weakened by being expressed too strongly.—*Oliver Goldsmith.*

The Boston Post

THE GREAT *Breakfast Table Paper* OF NEW ENGLAND

TUESDAY, AUGUST 17, 1948

SIGNS CREDIT CONTROL BILL

Truman Flays Knuckling Down to 'Special Privilege' by Congress--- G.O.P. Hits Back

BABE RUTH, BASEBALL'S GREATEST PLAYER, DIES

Idol of Millions Passes Away in His Sleep at New York Hospital at 8:01 P. M. Hub Time---

Illustrators helped make *Harpers* great, but it's the names and events that make headlines. It you are sports minded you may not mind a reproduction of a winners page if it's your kind of sport.

NEWSPAPERS

If it happened and history overlooked it, more likely a newspaper did not. Joe G. and his spouse returned from two weeks in Canada where Joe caught a fourteen pound pike just beyond the Arctic Circle. Come on Joe, how much did that pike weigh?

Someone locally collected that news tidbit. If it wasn't Joe, then it was the local piscatorial expert.

Collectors enjoy the headline proof that Mussolini and his mistress died at the hands of partisons and were hung by the heels in the town square. Another headline read that in April of 1894, several hundred unemployed people, calling themselves Coxey's Army, swarmed into Washington, D.C. asking Congress for help.

They were events that are of interest to someone.

Regional headlines and mastheads excite regional collectors. On January 1, 1868, George A. Trenholm signed a $500 bond for his son, Williamson, guaranteeing payment. Interesting as a source of speculation about integrity as George Trenholm, at that time, was Secretary of the Treasury for the Confederate States - and the Confederacy was bankrupt.

As much speculation was involved on July 4, 1826, as when John F. Kennedy was assassinated 137 years later. On that July 4th, two of our founding fathers and former presidents, Thomas Jefferson and John Adams, died within hours of each other. The speculations could have ranged from coincidence to conspiracy to malevolent spirits; all meat for collectors. It was duly reported by the *National Gazette* and *Literary Register* of Philadelphia on July 11, 1826. The price, in 1992, of a copy of that issue was high as newspapers of that era sell, being $100.

Territorials, weekly or monthly or irregular newspapers from continental areas not yet admitted to the Union as States have their own covey of admirers.

The Salt Lake Daily Herald (Utah) dated February 8, 1871, hard news probably being scarce, took a look at its subscribers reading habits. In that same year the *Yreka Weekly Union* (Yreka, California) ran an advertisement, "Sea Moss Farine, the cheapest, healthiest, most delicious food in the world." Meanwhile the *Mariposa Weekly Gazette* (California) ran a front page story headlined, "Why the Minister Kicked the Deacon."

Headlines from the past, glimpses of ordinary folk and what amused them, and headlines from the past that awed them. They are as follows: the Hatfield-McCoy Feud, Rasputin: the Russian Holy Devil, Joe Louis K.O's Max Baer, Mrs. O'Leary's Cow, The Professor Morse Telegraph, the John Brown Trials, Jesse Jame's First Train Robbery, General George Custer. The current ladie's fashions as reported in Le Moniteur De La Mode, (Paris) December 8, 1906 is yours for only $17.

It was Johann Gutenberg and his invention of movable type and the improvement in the quality of ink, in the 15th century, that made newspapers possible. In 1562, in Venice, Italy, a handwritten news sheet called the Notizie Scritte, sold for a gazetta, a small coin. From such small beginnings probably came our word 'gazette'.

It was not until 1690 that the first crudely printed newspaper of four pages, *Publick Occurrences* Both Foreign and Domestic, was published in what was to become the United States. Being critical of public policy, it lasted one issue. By 1704, a second paper, *The News-Letter*, duly licensed, was printed in Boston. This one lasted until the Revolution.

By 1735, an early keystone of freedom of the press had been established by law when John Peter Zenger was acquitted of libel on the grounds that what he had printed was offensive to the Governor of New York, but the report was true, therefore not libelous.

Historical names such as Alexander Hamilton, Ben Franklin, James Madison, John Jay and Thomas Jefferson are associated with those early newspapers.

It was not until 1830/1860 that newspapers, operating under the 1791 Bill of Rights ratification, became true newspapers in the full sense of publishing 'news'.

'News' may be one of the reasons why an old newspaper is worth $15 or $150 or $500. It's not much to look at or to hold. It may be torn or stained or foxed. But the printer whose stained fingers set the type, the buyer who paid his 1 or 2 or 3¢ for those printed pages; they existed. They lived those headlines of a century or more in the past. As collectors of hundred years from now will surely read ours as rarities. For newspapers are dying. First it was radio, then television, and now electronics, and the people who wish to place an electronic version of the 'news' in every home.

Still, newspapers, and collectors of them, endure. Many of the newspapers founded in those early days are available to present day collectors. Few are yet truly rare and their headlines rare only in context.

Newspapers satisfy our need to know. From local gossip to world shaping events, newspapers satisfy this urge. They illustrate our peculiarities, pecadillos, our persuits and persuasions at a price collectors can afford and appreciate.

Or, Thomas's Boston Journal.

A Weekly, Political, and Commercial PAPER :--Open to ALL Parties, but *Influenced* by None.

'DO THOU Great LIBERTY INSPIRE *our* Souls,--And make *our* Lives in THY Possession happy,--Or, *our* Deaths *glorious* in THY JUST Defence.

15. *The Massachusetts Spy or Thomas's Boston Journal.* Four full pages, 18 by 11 inches, December 23, 1773. The ornate masthead of this newspaper is engraved by Paul Revere, and the paper is printed by Isaiah Thomas. This issue of the *Massachusetts Spy*, printed only one week following the Boston Tea Party on December 16, 1773, concerns itself, in great measure, to news of this historic event. From Boston comes a report of the East India Company tea commissioners who "remain immured at Castle William. Their obstinancy has rendered them infinitely more obnoxious to their country men than even the Stamp Masters were. Their zeal in the cause against the liberties of America must be

154 WELLS AVE., NEWTON, MASS. 02159

The *Massachusetts Spy* or *Thomas's Boston Journal*. Newspapers were thin in content and appearance when this one was printed on December 23, 1773; only one week after the Boston Tea Party. Of particular interest is the masthead, engraved by a Boston citizen: Paul Revere. In 1976 this copy sold for $375. K. Rendell

The biggest laugh of the Dewey - Truman brouha, was the glitch that had Dewey winning the Presidency.

Major catastrophies call for big headlines. The San Francisco earthquake of 1906 qualified on both counts.

A real underground newspaper. This photograph, smuggled out of China during WWII, shows a newspaper being put out under difficulties - in a cave. One of six photographs that sold for $175.

From the mid 1800s until the early 20th century, *Harper's* may have been the best known name in newspapers. *Harper's Young People* and *Harper's Weekly*, were two of the *Harper's* papers that enjoyed popularity. Their covers and the inside engravings were two of the reasons for the paper's success.

NEWSPAPERS
Prices:

American Friend, Marietta, Georgia, December 8, 1820, two pages - $25

American Mercury, 1797, four pages, peace between France and England - $32

Army and Navy Journal, April 10, 1869, signed in type, G.A. Custer, report on Cheyennes - $17.50

Atlanta Constitution, October 5th to October 15, 1920. 1920s World's Series - $75

Black Hills Daily Pioneer, Deadwood, Dakota Territory, June 8, 1882, Frank James (Jesse's brother) - $110

Boston Daily Advertiser, August 4, 1815, Napoleon's abdication, imprisonment - $38

Boston Patriot, October 24, 1810, four pages, G - $18

Boston Weekly Messenger, (52) October 12, 1816 to October 9, 1817, Were in fire - $39

Canal Record, 1908, progress building Panama Canal - $14

Chicago Daily Tribune, November 3, 1948, Dewey Defeats Truman, Mint - $1275

Chicago Ledger, (7) 1921-1922, color action covers - $28

Chinese Communist newspapers (200+) 1949/1950 - $90

Cleveland Leader, September 20, 1881, Death of President Garfield - $25

Cleveland Leader, September 25, 1881, Funeral of President Garfield - $12

Cleveland News, February 25, 1931, Scarface Al (Capone) before Court - $16

Columbian Sentinel, March 31, 1821, Treaty With Spain settling America's claim to Florida - $15

Daily Age, January 23, 1865, Philadelphia pro-South newspaper - $18

Daily Evening Bulletin, San Francisco, March 22, 1856, Gold rush paper - $35

Daily News, New York, September 9, 1974, Nixon quits - $16

Daily Traveler, Evening, Boston, March 20, 1850 - $9

Daily Picayune, New Orleans, August 13, 1840, two reward advertisements for runaway slaves - $22

Detroit Press, August 20, 1881, Jesse James and Pat Garrett - $32.50

Dover Enquirer, 1841, War with Mexico - $4

Evening Fireside, Philadelphia, November 30, 1805 Log of American doctor held prisoner in Tripoli - $20

Evening News, Harrisburg, Pennsylvania, June 6, 1944, D-Day issue - $44

Evening Report, Lebanon, Pennsylvania, May 8, 1915, Lusitania death list reaches 1,400 - $77

Greenburg Daily Tribune, Pennsylvania, May 8, 1937, Zeppelin Death Toll Mounts, Lakehurst, Hindenburg - $24

Harper's Weekly, April 30, 1910, Mark Twain 1835, 1910 - $29

Harper's Weekly, February 26, 1898, Disaster to battleship Maine - $30

Holdin Record, April 9, 1868, Raleigh, North Carolina - $45

Honolulu Advertiser, December 8, 1941, double banner headline, Saboteurs Land Here, Raiders Return - $135

Illustrated London News, Coronation issue, plus Christian Science Monitor Coronation issue, Mint - $38

Illustrated News, New York, April 2, 1853 - $12

Irish Farmer's Intelligencer and Weekly, Dublin, Ireland, March 13, 1819, farmer and horse front page - $22

Ka Haku Hawaii, April 8, 1942, in Hawaiian language - $20

Lancaster Intelligencer, Pennsylvania, April 27, 1865, Booth killed - $50

Leslie's Weekly, November 5, 1859, Harper's Ferry Conspiracy - $25

London Chronicle, April 25, 1758, colony recruiting in France for Canada - $24

London Gazette, 1752, Mohawks say French are gone from Canada - $15

Los Angeles Times, November 23, 1963, Kennedy Assassination in Dallas - $18

Lynn News, September 15, 1848, nomination of Z. Taylor/M. Fillmore ticket - $17

Lynn News, October 8, 1852, Whig nomination of Winfield Scott for President and William Alexander Graham as V.P. - $17

Manufacturers and Farmer's Journal, Providence, Rhode Island, December 14, 1829, Andrew Jackson's State of the Union - $14

Marietta Times (2) October 22/23, 1924, Hunt Pretty Boy Floyd in Ohio - $55

Marietta Times, September 21, 1934, Lindberg Kidnapping Case solved by Hauptman Arrest - $10

Memphis Press-Scimitar, August 17, 1977, death of Elvis Presley - $29

National Anti-Slavery Standard, New York City, August 3, 1861, slave capture at Harper's Ferry, Fine - $30

National Era, Vol. 1, #1, January 7, 1847, four pages, Washington, D.C., Fair - $38

Natchez Weekly Courier, April 29, 1863, address to people of the confederate States by Jefferson Davis - $50

Newport Daily News, October 24, 1929, Stock Prices Crash Again On Exchange - $48

Niles Weekly Register, (34) Vol. 1, September 7, 1811/February 29, 1812, Napoleon's invasion of Spain - $145

Niles Weekly Register, July 4, 1814, war news - $14

Nippon Times, Tokyo, December 23, 1945 England, war items, Fair to Good - $10

NEWSPAPERS

New Orleans Weekly Delta, 1846, official dispatches General Zachary Taylor - $19

New York American, June 1919, first publication in America of the Paris peace treaty - $12

New York Herald, July 14, 1876, General Custer - $45

New York Times, April 28, 1865, reports of killing of John Wilkes Booth - $145

New York Times, June 20, 1930, Byrd and Men Acclaimed by City - $10

New York Tribune, September 3, 1864, eight pages, capture of Atlanta - $23.50

New York Tribune, April 21, 1865, search for Booth - $90

New York Weekly Times, October 6, 1878, Horrors of Lynch Law - $11

Observer, London, September 6, 1684, 307 plus year old single sheet coffee house newspaper - $24

Ohio State Journal, November 19, 1928, Interview of Amelia Earhart - $15

Palestine Daily Herald, Texas, February 14, 1929, Valentine's Day Massacre - $165

Pennsylvania Gazette, printed by Benjamin Franklin and D. Hall, 1760, four pages, French and Indian War - $350
A. Graham as vice-president - $17

Penny Magazine, London, 1832, March 31 to December 29 - $20

Philanthropist, Cincinnati, November 5, 1839, pro slavery riot - $22.50

Public Ledger, Philadelphia, May 22, 1927, Lindberg lands in Paris - $27

Public Ledger, 1862, four pages, Battle of Antietam, Lincoln Proclamation to free slaves - $29

Richmond Enquirer, Virginia, August 4, 1826, front page column on slaves, letters signed by Andrew Jackson and Thomas Jefferson - $23

Salt Lake Daily Tribune, May 10, 1874, Cochise's Indians Raid Into Mexico - $13

Saturday Globe, November 11, 1899, America's first color printed newspaper, story on Sitting Bull - $25

Spectator, London, September 7, 1711, two page coffee house paper, edited by Addison and Steele - $37

Sphere, May 15, 1915, 15 pages of sinking of the Lusitania by German submarine - $35

Sporting News (75) 1970/1972, color covers, sports personalities - $225

The Independent, New York, November 3, 1859, trial of John Brown - $28

The Daily Cleveland Herald, Ohio, July 11, 1863, surrender of Vicksburg - $32

The *Providence Gazette* and *Country Journal,* April 13, 1776 - $228

The Saratogian, New York, May 7, 1945, Germany surrenders - asked $75/sold $35

The Social Justice, May 1, 1939, Pope calls General Franco savior of civilization - $6

Toledo Blade, December 7, 1941, Japan Attacks Hawaii and Manila - $20

Volkischer Beobachter, Berlin, 1940, Official Nazi party voice of Hitler - $235

Weekly Union, Washington, D.C., August 29, 1846, Mexican War, brief notice Lincoln as Congressman - $28

World, The, New York, April 10, 1865, the surrender of Lee - $375

Associations and Clubs:

Newspaper Collectors Society of America, care of Rick Brown, P.O. Box 19134, Lansing, Michigan, 48901, Rick Brown, Editor-in-Chief, Phone: 517-372-8381.

Ephemera Society of America, P.O. Box 37, Schoharie, New York, 12157, William Frost Nobley, President, Phone: 518-295-7978.

International Newspaper Collectors Club, P.O. Box 5090, Phoenix, Arizona, 85010, Charles J. Smith, Secretary, Phone: 602-273-7288.

National Association of Paper and Advertising Collectors, P.O. Box 500, Mount Joy, Pennsylvania, 17552, Doris Ann Johnson, Editor, Phone: 717-653-9797

Past in Review, P.O. Box 3864, Las Vegas, Nevada, 89036-0864, Page Rea, Editor, Phone: 702-452-2292.

Books:

Collecting American Newspapers by Jim Lyons, publisher J. Lyons, Los Altos, California, 1989. Sail to be the only book published on the subject.

The Compact History of the American Newspaper, revised edition, Hawthorne Books, 1969.

The Press and America: An Interpretive History of the Mass Media, fourth edition, Prentice-Hall, 1978.

Magazines:

Ephemera News, quarterly, P.O. Box 37, Schoharie, New York, 12157, William Frost Nobley, President.

Collectible Newspapers, bimonthly, care of Rick Brown, P.O. Box 19134, Lansing, Michigan, 48901.

The Paper and Advertising Collector, P.O. Box 500, Mount Joy, Pennsylvania, 17552.

Mail Auction (s):

Vintage Cover Story, P.O. Box 975, Burlington, North Carolina, 27215. Bob Raynor, Phone: 919-584-6990.

CHAPTER VII
SHEET MUSIC

Sheet music never dies. It reappears in a music collector's magazine titled - what else? - Sheet Music.

In February of 1992, "Unforgettable," a song written more than 40 years before, was chosen Song of the Year at the 34th Annual Grammy Awards held in New York City. Written by Irving Gordon, it had brought Nat King Cole a gold record in 1964 despite the decline of ballads when rock took over in the 1960s.

Was it a comment on today's music or just an unusual occurrence that a song should be remembered after 40 years?

Consider "After the Ball" still played, still remembered, was written and published by Charles K. Harris in 1892. That's 100 years ago. It was also the first popular song to sell several million copies.

Sheet music sales were the yardstick of success for song writers and publishers, more so for 'Tin Pan Alley' (coined about 1903 either by journalist Monroe Rosenfeld or song writer turned publisher, Harry Von Tilzer) Sheet music was also the means by which songs, and the names of song writers, lyricists, publishers, musicians, and singers, descended to become one of today's collectibles.

By July of 1913, Billboard Magazine was beginning to publish the first charts of the weeks biggest sheet music sales. No one then had thought of a Golden Music Sheet, as they have done since with gold and platinum records. But between 1900 and 1910, nearly 100 songs each beat the one million sales figure for sheet music.

The records show that 'A Bird in a Gilded Cage' (Arthur J. Lamb 1900) sold two million copies. 'Let Me Call You Sweetheart' (Beth Slater-Whitson-Leo Friedman) and 'Down By The Old Mill Stream' (Tell Taylor) both 1910, each sold five to six million copies. How are those titles - and sales - for being unforgettable?

Or these. 'When It's Apple Blossom Time In Normandy' (Mellor, Gifford, and Trevor), 'On The Trail Of The Lonesome Pine' (Ballard MacDonald - Harry Carroll). They were among the titles on Billboard's first chart, among the top ten of the early 1900s. They are still sung, or hummed, or tongued out on a harmonica today and still to be found on old sheet music as they were first published.

Irving Gordon, composer of 'Unforgettable', said in his acceptance speech at the Grammy Awards, "It's nice to have a song come out that doesn't scream, yell, or have a nervous breakdown while it talks about tenderness."

That could be one of the reasons old sheet music is still popular. It soothes and it satisfies an atavistic longing for times long gone.

SHEET MUSIC

And the graphics! Don't forget the graphics. The photographs of the singing stars of the stage, the movies, and radio. Photographs of Sophie Tucker, Fannie Brice, or Eddie Cantor. Memories. Still alive within folded sheets of paper called sheet music.

The origins of sheet music as we know it today is not shrouded in myths or legends. It came directly from the broadsides of the 1700s; a poets verse, local in interest, that may have been keyed to a tune first heard in London.

Only ten years after the arrival of the Mayflower, the first broadside, priced at a penny, appeared in New England.

One hundred years later there were categories of sheet music. They consisted of ballads, sentimental, marital, humor, and patriotic. It was early song sheets published by Carr of Philadelphia in 1798 that spread our first national anthem, 'Hail Columbia', from shore to ship, then windborne and around the world.

Another song title, still familiar to us was published about 1812 by John Paff of New York was 'Hail To The Chief' always performed to honor our Presidents. It was in this same year that 'The Star Spangled Banner' was published as a poem in a Baltimore newspaper, *The Patriot*.

Sheet music traces history, whether of a country or an age, of sentiment or satire. From sheet music we learn of 'Daddy' Rice, a historic figure in American popular music who is credited with popularizing the term, Jim Crow.

By the 1850s sheet music had proliferated so that bound copies of sheet music were around. A small proportion of these sheets featured colorful lithographed covers, some hand colored, as were the newly popular Currier and Ives prints.

The backs of these early music sheets were not ignored. Many bore advertisements of other song titles, music stores or publishers. Bound in leather or cloth, few have survived until today.

As the 19th century drew to a close, the categories of sheet music published in America swelled enormously. Minstrel, ragtime, blues, jazz, ballads, nonsense ('Camptown Races'), marches, and dance all found a place, a publisher, and a buyer.

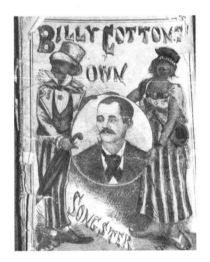  

Song books were popular in the mid to late 1800s. Approximately 4'' by 6'', they were handy to fit into a pocket, had attractively colored covers, and the words for the more popular songs of the day. At a 1992 auction they sold for $12 each.

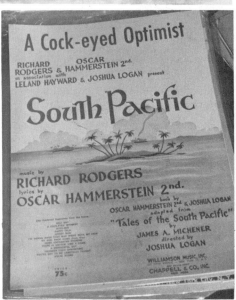

Big names of the day, such as Ziegfeld, Berlin, Hammerstein, Jolson, and Gershwin, decorated the covers of sheet music. The song titles were just as well known. Sheet music sales were in the millions. Al Jolson photo courtesy David Jasen, C.W. Post/L.I.U. The average price for these song sheets is about $15, except the Al Jolson sheet. That will cost between $50-60.

By the early 1900s, 'Tin Pan Alley' was almost a generic term. Sheet music sales escalated under the wave of commercial application of the new breed of publishers.

The music publishing center of the country had by then established itself in New York City - first in the Union Square area. From there, publishers such as M. Whitmark & Sons, Willis Woodward, Hawley Haviland, Dresser, and Leo Feist & Co., proceeded to commercialize the sheet music publishing business. They hired song writers as staff composers, often paying them only whiskey money. They became the hub for song pluggers, that is, those who by charm or chutzpah, persuaded performers to use their publishers songs. Payola entered the country's conscience and language as pluggers used any form of persuasion to seduce a singer to use their song.

Placing a singing plugger, usually a boy with a good voice, in the audience, became a standard ploy on the vaudeville circuit.

All this enthusiastic conniving seemed to rub off on the sheet music endowing it with a splendor further enhanced by enticing graphics and names that are a part of our musical heritage. Need we introduce Weber and Fields, Victor Herbert, Lillian Russell, Gilbert and Sullivan, John Philip Sousa, Johann Strauss, Louis Armstrong, Florence Zeigfield, George M. Cohan? These are recognizable whether or not people enjoy, read, or collected music. The name recognition of those mentioned may be greater than the crop of radio, movie, or television names of the last fifty years.

SHEET MUSIC

Music as interpreted by the notes, bars, and cleffs on a piece of sheet music changed with the altering face of America.

Just before WWI, New Orleans' famed Storyville was closed down by an order from Washington D.C. Even before it's closing, jazz had been immigrating north. With Storyville's demise, the flow of jazz players to Chicago became a flood.

Scott Joplin's time had arrived and classical piano rag was heard from honkytonks to, eventually, the first ragtime festival ever held in Seddia in East St. Louis in 1974.

The syncopation used in song and piano music made ragtime so popular in 'Tin Pan Alley' that it led the ballad in sales.

New old names started to appear on sheet music as composers, lyricists, or publishers. Al Jolson, Eddie Cantor, Irving Berlin, Fanny Brice, Sophie Tucker, and Vernon and Irene Castle were among many.

The songs they made popular racked up astounding sheet music sales. Berlin's Alexander's Ragtime Band sold a million copies in a few months time, together with two to three hundred thousand piano rolls. There is no exact figure. The Darktown Strutters Ball (Shelton Brooks, 1917) sales were of one and one half million pieces of sheet music.

The syncopated music of ragtime, led as much by Sigmund Romberg and Vernon and Irene Castle as by Berlin's music, glided easily into social and ballroom dancing. It's easy to learn and easy to perform. It was two/four and four/four rhythm that made dancing an occasion for people of all ages to join in the fun.

A further demand for after theatre dancing was the genesis for the nightclub. As a side issue of the effects of the songs flooding the country in sheet music sales, the habits of the American woman were changed. Her hair bobbed, her figure slimmed, and her dresses were made simple.

The ballad reappeared, sponsored by Berlin's 'When I Lost You', inspired by a personal loss. Songs crossed and recrossed the country on the vaudeville circuits. The sheet music sales for these songs went on for years.

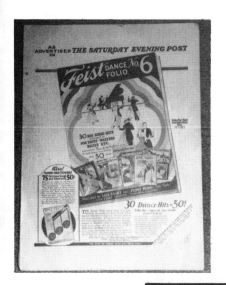

The back page of a piece of sheet music was not ignored. It featured advertisements. These normally were of songs, singers or musicals associated with the publisher.

Vaudeville was the partner of the Broadway musical and the dreamworld of the country. Al Jolson boosted 'Rock-a-bye Your Baby With a Dixie Melody' (Sam Lewis and Joe Young, 1918) in the show, Sinbad, into the million sales range. So did Dolly Hacket in the passing show of 1916, with 'Pretty Baby' (Van Alstyne, Tony Jackson, Gus Kahn).

The 1930s saw vaudeville on its way out taking ragtime with it. But not the Broadway musical theatre. That had a run starting in 1915 that lasted until 1970. During those 55 years sheet music and stories about sheet music proliferated.

SHEET MUSIC

George Gershwin and Irving Caesar wrote Swanee in 1919. Publishers, the full length of 'Tin Pan Alley' turned it down. It had a one week run at Major Bowes new Capitol Theatre where it didn't actually bomb but was close.

At a party, Al Jolson, then touring in Sinbad, heard Gershwin play the song on the piano. Recognizing it as his kind of song, a deal was struck marrying Gershwin's permission and Jolson's singing. Reintroduced to a Sunday evening Winter Garden concert, the song drew cheers. With still more cheers when Jolson added it to the score of Sinbad.

Harms, the publisher of Swanee, scrapped the original Capitol cover on the sheet music, replacing it with a cut of Jolson. That was 1919, the year that Swanee not only sold a million copies of sheet music but also sold over two million records.

On today's market, the Al Jolson cover has a valuation of 50 to 60 dollars. The Capitol cover with only a few weeks lobby sales to its credit has a built in rarity. That cover has been priced at $2,000.

Even with prices such as those, sheet music can be addictive. In 1986, when Ludwig L. went to an auction to buy a few sheet music scores, he didn't know he was going to buy their entire inventory of over 200,000 pieces. His letter to *Sheet Music Magazine* translated to one word - help!

Sheet music can accumulate over the years.

On John Philip Sousa's death, the University of Illinois received as a bequest, his personal collection of music - all nine tons of it.

Collectors collect sheet music as a tonal method of absorbing history. Where else could you learn that Francis Scott Key may not have been the author of the 'Star Spangled Banner' and that 'America the Beautiful' competed with the 'Star Spangled Banner' for thirty six years to be our national anthem and also that the 'Star Spangled Banner' only won out in 1931 when it officially became our anthem by an act of Congress.

Sheet music then is a more than two hundred year parade of what our country was and hopes to be. It is a remembrance of a Hoagy Carmichael, a Gene Krupa, The Mills Brothers, Fats Waller, Frankie Laine, or Mildred Bailey. It is a remembrance of music as living history, a history often taken for granted.

PSALM BOOKS

Psalm books came to this country with the first load of tourists, who then decided to stay and do real estate business with the natives. The first book, Harry Ainsworth's Psalter, came over on the Mayflower. By 1640, *The Bay Psalm Book* was published in Cambridge, Massachusetts. It was the first book of music to be published in this country. A decade later, a new way of distributing popular songs had been conceived; the broadside.

Not psalm books, but close in appearance. These song books from the 1820s were pocket size, with board covers, and brought $110 for the lot at a New York auction.

BROADSIDES

A broadside could be described as one large page printed on one side only. When some early advertising genius folded the broadside in half, it became a broadsheet, which when opened, became one large sheet of advertising. Or the two pages of a song sheet.

They were sold in New England for a penny. More than a century later, broadsheets were still being hawked on the streets, and printed sheet music was being produced by early music publishers. Among them were Boston's Draper and Falsom, and Philadelphia's Benjamin Carr.

An almost modern broadside, a direct descendent of the original in form and usage, was in use in the 1940s as a newspaper advertising insert. Todays versions solicit housewives with coupons.

Broadsides have a long history in this country, appearing in New England before we were a nation. They continue today in altered form. This one, a broadside of a musical score was used as an insert in the *New York Journal American* of October 3, 1948.

MUSIC ROLLS

The first music rolls were made of wood. They had brass or steel pins protruding from their surface which struck the key mechanism generating music. A weakness was that the roll had to be played to its ending in order to change rolls. A hand crank was the motive power.

The roller organ that used these wooden music rolls was the forerunner of the player piano. The key was the music roll, a paper roll adaptation of the barrel organ's wooden roll.

The player piano roll consisted of a roll of paper 11¼" wide, wound on a cardboard tube. It had flanges and a hook arrangement to fit it onto the player piano. The roll was, still is, hand cut, using up to 100 hours to translate the music onto the paper to make a master roll, either from sheet music or on a specially constructed marking piano. This allows a future production of a roll that will play for three minutes to be produced in eight hours.

Because of a lack of concern for the limitations of the human hand, composers were attracted to its possibilities. 'Stravinsky's Etude For Pianola', in 1917, and Hindesmith's 'Toccata', for the mechanical piano in 1926, being two of the better known music roll compositions composed only for the player piano.

Since not everyone had the time, the ability, or the inclination to read music, the player piano, with it's library of music rolls, was wildly successful, just before and after the turn of the century.

Music roll manufacturing companies proliferated. Of all those who sought to get in on this flourishing business, only one remains and that is the QRS Music Rolls, 1026 Niagra Street, Buffalo, NY 14213. Not only can they give you the name of a local dealer, they have recently started the QRS Old Roll Auction, whereby hundreds of rolls are offered each month in a mail auction where they also offer some sheet music.

This 1887 Chautauqua organ, with its brass studded wooden music roll, was an ancestor of both the piano and the paper music roll used on player pianos. The wooden roll had to be played to its end before it could be changed. It sold for $1,600 in mid 1992 with a bonus of 20 wooden music rolls.

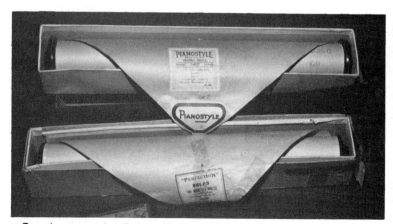

Boxed paper music rolls from QRS, the only company still making these rolls of music. 34, mint in box, player, piano rolls failed to meet their reserve at $85 at a recent auction and were passed. A New York dealer has them priced at $20-35

Prices:

'Buttons and Bows' (Jay Livingston-Ray Evans) Bob Hope and Jan Russell on cover - $4

'For You, For Me, For Everyone' (Ira Gershwin/George Gershwin) Betty Grable and Dick Haymes on cover - $5

'How Deep Is The Ocean' (Irving Berlin) - $2

'I Ain't Afraid of the Policeman' (Carlton G. Garretson) - $15

'The Heroes in Blue' Ed Gardenier-Edwin S. Brill) - $15

'Three Coins in the Fountain' (Sammy Kahn-Jule Styne) - $2

'Swanee I' Caesar/George Gershwin) Al Jolson on cover - $60

Broadside, 20" by 22". "Being a Proclomation by His Excellency, John Davis, Governor of Massachusetts, For a Day of Fasting, etc." - $42

Framed Jumbo March Song, copr. 1862, written to introduce Jumbo the Elephant to the Barnum Circus - $125-$150

The names, faces, graphics, and language on sheet music covers all speak of another day, another time. Only the one universal language remains constant - music.

Magazines:

Sheet Music Magazine, 352 Evelyn St., P.O. Box 933, Paramus, New Jersey 07653-0933

Frets Magazine, P.O. Box 615, Saratoga, CA 95090

Books:

Keys To A Musical Past, Harvey N. Roehl, Vestal Press 1968.

Jazz Masters of the Twenties by Richard Hadlock, The Macmillan Company

They All Played Ragtime by Rudi Blesh, Harriet Janis and Alfred A. Knopf

Mail Auctions:

Joel Markovitch Sheet Music Center, P.O. Box 367, Port Washington, NY 11050

QRS Old Roll Auction, 1026 Niagra St., Buffalo, NY 14213, Phone: 1-800-527-7626

Collections:

C.W. Post Campus, Long Island University, Special Collections, Northern Boulevard, Brookville, NY 11548, Phone: 516-299-2382

The Louisiana State Museum, 751 Chartress St., P.O. Box 2448, New Orleans, Louisiana 70176, Phone: 504-568-6968

The Musical Museum, South Main St., Deansboro, NY 13328

Associations:

The Automatic Musical Instruments Collectors Association, P.O. Box 172, Columbia, SC 29202-0172

The Musical Box Society International, P.O. Box 205, Rt. 3, Morgantown, IN 46160

National Sheet Music Society, 1597 Fair Park Ave., Los Angeles, CA 90041

CHAPTER VIII

MOVIE MEMORABILIA

Music, vocal and instrumental, became intimately connected with plays, radio, television, and movies. Of all, the most interest centers about movie memorabilia. So much so that performers have become the 'guru's' of world wide causes. They have become mayors, state governors, and one made it all the way to become President of this U.S. of A.

Call it what you will, ballyhoo, Hollywood magic, hoopla, or trivia. Anything a performer owns or touches may conceivably end up in a celebrity auction as treasures for the collector of movie memorabilia.

Promotional items provide the base for these collections. The signed photographs alone constitute a minor industry. Two million 'still' photographs are the guesstimate for 1920/1930. Posters run a close second. The quantity that may be found in a movie house about to vacate its premises may boggle the imagination. Large collections have been formed in this manner. Among them, the collection owned by the Long Island University in 1992. Duplicates from this collection were being traded off to dealers and collectors for other wanted items.

The law of supply and demand intrudes when still photographs are mentioned. So many were made with their size so handy for display that although they are basic to a collection their value is low in relation to posters. Many may be bought from specialist dealers for under $5.

Autographed stills, have a higher value, provided the autographs are original, not signed by studio help or a secretary.

The posters and stills are the foundation of a comprehensive collection. Almost anything movie related, such as a hat, a cane, a magazine, even a customized car like Chitty, Chitty Bang, Bang is collectible.

The unique automobile was made for the movie of that name. Unlike some of its sister cars, the one actively used on the set and driven by actor Dick Van Dyke, eventually starred in a Greenwich, Connecticut auction of sporting cars in June of 1991.

Going back a few years to 1970, some 12,000 props and costumes belonging to Metro-Goldwyn-Mayer went on the auction block. Included was a double decker London bus from the movie, 'Waterloo Bridge', 1940, and Clark Gable's trench coat.

Periphrastically, Hollywood gossip columnists are not excluded. A Hedda Hopper hat, alongside a clipping of one of her movie gossip columns would make an ideal collectible for a zealous collector.

Columbia Pictures presents "THE GREAT ADVENTURES OF WILD BILL HICKOK" with Gordon Elliott, Monte Blue, Carole Wayne, Frankie Darro, Reinee Ates, Chief Thunder Cloud, and Mala.

"THE KID FROM TEXAS," A Metro-Goldwyn-Mayer Picture

Movie stills are a never ending collectible source. Often you may find a young Shirley Temple or a Chief Thunder Cloud. A further plus - prices are low, $4 each bought these.

Marilyn Monroe deserves an entire page to herself. This life sized cut-out would be a crowd stopper in any movie lobby.

LOBBY CARDS

Lobby cards were the appetizers that lured the customer to the entree on the screen in the darkened theater. Mounted cut-outs of the major players, or scenes from the movie being shown, helped wet the movie goers appetite.

A life-sized cut-out of Marilyn Monroe was all that was necessary to bring the teenager and his father past the ticket taker to a plush theater seat. Plot? Story line? Who cared? Look at that cut-out. What a woman! Two please.

It was not necessarily sex that lured the customer. An oversized cut-out of King Kong holding Fay Wray in a hairy hand as the gorilla grimaced at the mosquito-like buzzing of airplanes around his head would lure the customer equally well. "Look at the size of him. On top of the Empire State building. Two please."

Perhaps cut-outs should not be mentioned in the same breath as lobby cards. They do fit well alongside the 11" by 14" promotional cards that were normally placed behind glass on a lobby wall. Some collectors put lobby cards with posters. They may be right. Some collectors include cut-outs. They may be right.

To the bidder at an auction - what he wants is what he bids on. Like the lobby card for the movie that never dies, 'Casablanca', 1943, which sold for $3,250, and a lobby card for 'War of the Worlds', 1953, that sold for $425.

Whatever sends you. The lights are dimming. Two please.

Posters, posters, bring on the posters. Color, great names, and the promise of action come with them. No one ever thought of these movie personalities as paper puppets. These $350 movie posters are reminders of their former fame.

Movie posters - all posters - have skyrocketed in price, escalating out of the price range of many collectors.

Posters - not the movie kind - have been around since the Egyptians posted papyrus reward notices for the return of escaped slaves.

Poster art celebrated its heyday in the 1890s, long before Hollywood became the Holy Grail of American teenagers. The subject matter was ordinary, containing women, some nude, all lace and big hats. You could almost smell the perfume. Except for the clothing styles they haven't changed much.

Posters owe their existence to the technical improvement in color lithography and to a French designer, Jules Cheret (1836-1933). He drew an image, framed in color, on a stone with a special grease pencil. The stone was wet, rolled with ink, and the image transferred onto paper when it was pressed against the stone.

At precise intervals the stone was destroyed limiting the number of that particular poster. It made these first, now antique posters, a rarity. Their modern counterparts use a photo offset process. Cheret lived long enough to see posters glorify the great and near great of moviedom.

Posters are advertising in its more colorful sense. They are an art form that communicates. The art work was often created by well known artists and was of high quality. For the Marilyn Monroe collector, the name recognition of one of her movies or its co-stars are the determining factor. May West, Jean Harlow, Humphry Bogart are posters worth seeking. A James Cagney poster, with or without a grapefruit in hand would be a prize.

The same companies who produced circus posters, printed posters for the movie studios. Morgan Lithograph Company, Ohio, and Tooker Lithograph Company, New York come to mind.

What determines the value of a movie poster? The same considerations as any other collectible - rarity and condition. Posters may be graded A, B, or C by a dealer, indicating their condition. Letter 'A' would represent a poster without creases, water stains, or tears, in other words, in mint condition. Rarity would include the number available, the movies title, and the name of the stars.

Poster size is also something to be considered. A 'one sheet' measures 27" by 41", and a 'three sheet' would measure 40" by 80". Lobby cards would be 11" by 14" and window card posters, almost a separate collectible, are mostly 14" by 22".

Posters quite often came in two designs for the same subject: A and B posters. They are not to be confused with a dealers A.B.C. lettering for condition. These A and B posters with their two designs were made to satisfy the reactions of various regions of this country, The Southern bible belt would react strongly to a poster made specifically for the inhabitants of New York City. So two versions of the same poster issued for the same movie were often made and distributed.

Any size makes a hit at an auction. As recently as December, 1991, a Hollywood Poster Art auction in Fort Lee, New Jersey, ran up some impressive totals.

A three sheet paper for 'Stormy Weather', 1943, starring Lena Horne, sold for $6,250, while a duotone one sheet for 'Forty Second Street', 1933, sold for $5,500. Marilyn Monroe's 'Seven Year Itch' in a one sheet size brought in $800, and Tyrone Power, starring in 'Lloyds of London', 1936, sold for the same amount.

Not all posters stay in this price range. As a 1991 Christmas gift for an unnamed collector, Christie's of New York, sold a 1933 King Kong poster for $52,000.

A poster dealer summed up the entire subject nicely when asked what she wanted for Christmas. "Another great poster," she said. And where would you put it? "If," she said, "you are a true collector you would never ask that question. A true collector will find the space."

Guns, swords, love, and laughter, mix and match, add some stars, and a story line, that's the making of a movie as these posters prove.

WINDOW CARDS

When you and I were young Maggie, pre-teen boys earned free passes to the movies delivering window cards to all the neighborhood store owners. The cards were accepted gladly from the young entrepreneurs for they came with free passes for the store owner also. All he was required to do was place the window card where it would be seen by the most neighborhood people, in the window of the store.

Window cards in general, were 14″ by 20″ long and wide. There were some exceptions in size, a few larger or smaller. Usually printed in two colors, they described the dates for a weeks movie shows at the local palace, with further mention of the stars involved. The name of the movie house was featured across the top.

Again, as in posters, the movies stars names on the window card have a deal to do with its value.

A midget window card for 'The Wizard of Oz', 1939, sold for $3,400 at an auction in 1991. At the same auction, a jumbo window card from Disney's 'Fantasia', sold for $950. The relation to the movie titles, as with stars names, in relation to the prices realized is readily apparent.

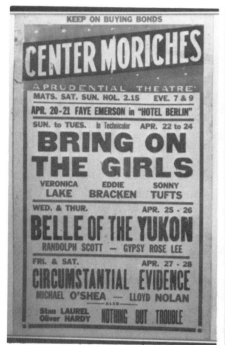

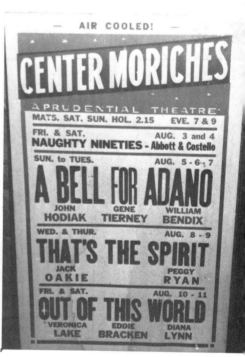

Window cards were reminders to the neighborhood that their local movie house expected and appreciated their patronage, this week and next.

It should be enough that fan clubs for living movie stars multiply upon the land. It releases pent up energies, creates a means of communication with others of like interests.

Admittedly, many are public relation inspired. Those who idolize stars who have passed on to other heavenly theaters, are usually inspired more by emotion. They are also the genesis of many serious collectors.

The list of those whose fan clubs outlived them is not large. Whether or not they were true artists is moot. What they had to give as a legacy to those who still idolized them is not. Actors with the distinction of John Wayne, Marilyn Monroe, Yul Brynner, or Jean Harlow left their admirers with something that can't be bought - a bit of themselves.

No personality cult has more members - not Dean, Wayne, or Lennon. Marilyn Monroe remains a star, an enigma, and a lure for collectors world wide.

Once described by the animation studios, cels are hoarded zealously today; let out to select dealers piecemeal. Anything found with a Walt Disney signature, his won or artist signed has high dollar value.

Al Jolson's blackface routine would be classed as politically incorrect today. His song delivery is timeless. His name recognition excellent for movie memorabilia collectors. A one sheet poster sold for $225 at a 1992 auction.

The French have a passion for Mickey. This book, in French, by a French publisher was a table offering at a 1992 collector show here in the States for $75.

It seems appropriate that early on in the surreal world of Hollywood, pressbooks were often called 'ballybooks', a play on words from 'ballyhoo'.

Pressbooks are not to be confused with press kits. Today, a folder of the movie's stills and a press release of the stars credits and media articles.

The pressbook of yesteryear, could be a folder or a ten, twenty, or more page booklet together with any pertinent, or impertinent, material designed as promotion for a movie. There were bally accessories available such as giveaways and cutouts, posters and banners, gimmicks and gags. The movie moguls of the 1920s and 1930s were concerned with producing high visibility promotions, especially for their 'A' or major releases.

Pressbooks then, were elaborate, so much so that their issues were usually limited to about 500. Nice, right? Built-in rarity, more so considering how many could have been discarded or destroyed.

Like most paper collectibles, pressbooks are time machines taking us back for an intimate look at the times and lives of the movie pioneers.

Pressbooks, the bally, were assigned the task of suggesting to movie managers, ways and means of promoting the movie. Some ideas were far out such as giveaways that included garments or free hair styling advice or renting an elephant to lead down Main Street with advertising posters plastered on its hide.

A synopsis of the movie would be included; well written pieces, imaginative, never dull. Why not? Their authors had name recognition on the screen or on books or magazine covers if not on the pressbook. John O'Hara and F. Scott Fitzgerald among them.

Pressbooks today are but a dim image of what they once were with little of the appeal they generated during the 1920s and 1930s. The closest we can come to what they were, what they represent in those days, is the annual year edition of *Variety*. For the *Variety* magazine began as a 'bally book' for the entire entertainment industry.

Prices:

Posters:
One sheets - 27" by 41":
All the Kings Men, reprint, 1958 - $25
Bill and Coo, Ken Murray, 1948 - $50
The Brave Bulls, 1961, Anthony Quinn - $30

Half sheets - 22" by 28":
The Beachcomber, reprint, 1949, Charles Laughton - $50
Comanche Station, 1960, Randolph Scott - $20

Insert posters: 14" by 36":
At War With The Army, 1951, Martin and Lewis - $30
Little Women, 1949, Liz Taylor - $50

Lobby Cards:
Blondie, eight card set, reprint, 1950 duotone - $30
The Hustler, reprint, 1964, eight cards - $50
Sgt. York, reprint, 1949, eight cards - $75

Window cards:
Sante Fe Trail, 1941, Errol Flynn, Ronald Reagan - $300
Story of Alexander Graham Bell, 1939, mini card - $100

Movie posters:
Lawrence of Arabia, 11" by 14" - $40
Incredible Shrinking Man, 11" by 14" - $125
African Queen 14" by 36" - $650
Shane - 14" by 36" - $400
Marked Woman 22" by 28" - $1,750
One Eyed Jacks 22" by 28" - $175
The Godfather 27" by 41" - $250
Kings row 27" by 41" - $850

MOVIE MEMORABILIA
Miscellaneous:
25" yellow pennant for NBC Radio City - $60
Modern Boy Magazine, December 1934 - $8
Radio City Music Hall Showplace Program September 19th, 1946 - $10
Magic 'Mike' Handout for The Big Broadcast of 1936 - $12.50
Mini Program, Covered Wagon, 1923 - $10
9" by 12" Playbill, Rugged Path, 1945 - $35
Magazine - Photoplay Studios, Ben Hur, 1959 - $8

Pressbooks:
The Actress, 1953, MGM 12 pages - $15
Bridge Too Far, 1977, UA 16 pages - $15
Ceiling Zero, 1935, WB 32 pages - $125

Auctions:

Hollywood Poster Art Auction, 65 Hudson Street, Hackensack, New Jersey 07601. Phone: 201-488-6333. Ron Janis & Joe Burtis

Collections:

The American Film Institute, Washington, D.C. 20566.

Museum of the Performing Arts, New York, NY 10019

Academy of Motion Picture Arts and Sciences, Beverly Hills, CA 90211

Magazines:

Film Collectors World, Rapids City, IL 61278.

Movie Collector's World, P.O. Box 309, Fraser, MI 48026. Neva Bukantis

Disneyana: Price Guide. Timeless Treasures Publishing, P.O. Box 341, Lexington, MO 64067. Phone: 816-584-7441.

Associations:

Poster Society, 138 West 18th St., New York, NY 10011.

Books:

A Concise History of Posters, 1870-1970, John Barncoat, Harry N. Abrams, Publisher, New York, 1972

The New York Times Directory of Films, Arno Press/Random House, 1971

A World of Movies, Richard Lawton, Delacourt Press, New York, 1974

The American Movies Reference Book, Paul Michael, Prentice-Hall, New Jersey, 1969

CHAPTER IX
MAGAZINES

One of the collectible industries that centers on Hollywood is movie magazines. Collectors of these are outdone in their avid search only by collectors of sports memorabilia in their hunt for sports magazines and their covers. Particularly their covers.

A first edition of *Sports Illustrated* is a Holy Icon to the sports collector. If such a magazine cover features a name sports figure, prices rise. If that athlete has signed the cover, prices escalate even more, and the cover is presented matted and framed and as tarted up as the patrons of a Saturday disco.

Everyone saves magazines. They pile up in attics and basements, closets and garages. Is there anyone who hasn't saved *National Geographic*? That's why they can rarely be sold because everyone still has them.

Other magazines vary with prices depending on the year the magazine was printed, its condition, authors, and covers. *Saturday Evening Post* of the 1910s and 1920s, illustrated by Norman Rockwell, have been priced as recently as 1992 at $200 to $300. The 321 covers he painted for S.E.P. just beat out another S.E.P. cover artist, J.C. Leyendecker, by one painting. Leyendecker is known to collectors. To the public, Rockwell is THE name. Leyendecker had started as a magazine illustrator about 1896, doing much of his work for the mass circulation magazines.

At the same paper show where *Saturday Evening Post's* were being offered for three figures, a 1940s *Fortune* Magazine didn't cost a fortune when it sold for only $2.

Magazines follow the same rules as any collectible including rarity and condition, with special emphasis on its cover graphics, illustrators, and authors.

There is no exact definition of 'magazine'. The word derives from the Arabic, meaning 'storehouse'. Periodical may be a better term, but 'magazine' has probably been implanted in the American mind permanently.

The sheer volume of magazine titles in North America alone makes a necessity of pinpointing only one or two categories when one first plunges into this ocean of collectibles. There are an estimated 85,000 magazines published in North America alone.

What one sees on a news stand is the bare peak of a mountain of print. Perhaps there are 100 top flight, mass circulation magazines. Between that 100 and the 'little' literary magazines is a grey mass of specialized periodicals that make up the bulk of what America reads weekly, monthly, or quarterly. They are rarely, if ever, sold from magazine stands.

In America, it was not until the early 1740s that the first magazine was published. That master of being first, or among the first, Ben Franklin, was there when in association with Philadelphia printer Andrew Bradford, published the monthly, *The General Magazine*, dated January 1741. It lasted six issues.

Since that attempt there have been hundreds that didn't last that long and some that seem to last forever. The *Readers Digest* was founded in 1921, *Time* in 1922, and *The New Yorker*, in 1925.

After World War Two, general magazines (those that covered many subjects, many philosophies) foundered in their battle with television. Specialization took up the slack, making it easier for the collector to select his opportunities for collecting. On today's market, despite all those thousands of magazines titles, *Sports Illustrated*, particularly their covers, still leads the pack towards a collector's heart and pocket.

THE
GENERAL MAGAZINE,
AND
Hiſtorical Chronicle,
For all the Britiſh Plantations in America.
[To be Continued Monthly.]

JANUARY, 1741.

ICH DIEN

VOL. I.

PHILADELPHIA:
Printed and Sold by B. FRANKLIN.

America's first monthly magazine, *The General Magazine*, published in Philadelphia in January, 1741, lasted only six issues. One of its two publishers however, scored a first. The first and only publisher whose name is recognizable to the general public 250 years later was Ben Franklin.

Rare Books and Manuscripts Division
The New York Public Library
Astor, Lenox, and Tilden Foundations

COMIC BOOKS

When in 1990, auctioneer Ray Brachfeld introduced his son Joshua, as that evening's auctioneer for the 15,000 copy comic book auction, he prefaced the introduction with an explanation.

"The reason we're late with the lotting and tagging," he said, "is Joshua's fault. He had to read all 15,000 issues first."

All comic book collectors should be so lucky. It lampoons the image of seriousness hovering around collectors. It is common knowledge that comic book values have risen in value abruptly. Nostalgia fuels some of these high value comic book sales, and scarcity blasts others into stratospheric auction records.

Batman was born on December 27, 1939. A copy of *Detective Comics # 27* of that date, in which he first appeared, sold for $55,000 at Sotheby's in December of 1991. The buyer was Harold M. Anderson, owner of a traveling baseball and comic book museum in Florence, Alabama.

If a single copy of that issue costs that much, what hope is there for the average collector with minimal discretionary money to spend. Fear not, collectors, D.C. Comics, like Batman himself, has come to your rescue. If you can't afford multiple thousands for that first edition introducing Batman, D.C. Comics (his publisher), has issued an oversized commemorative edition, printed in 1970, that may substitute. Now a collectible in its own right, when last seen at a 1991 paper show, it was being offered for $15.

Originally, before the early 1930s, all comic books were simply made up from runs of newspaper comic strips. They were irregular in issue, with cardboard covers, and resembled todays comic books only in content.

Men of muscle, steel, or amazing powers. Meet them any day of the year in the pages of the comic books. Spiderman number one had a recent (1992) show price of $4,000.

Famous Funnies was the first to be sold from a news stand but still consisted of recycled comic strips.

If any date can be suggested as a birthdate for modern comic books, it would be 1938 when Action Comics #1, thrust Superman upon an appreciative public. It spawned a plethora of action oriented super heroes, each more unbelievable than the last.

Who could believe that the future of Clark Kent, Robin the Boy Wonder, Captain Marvel, Wonder Woman, The Incredible Hulk, Spiderman, Captain America, or Batman, would include scholarly dissertations and university courses. Weird. As weird as some of those super heroes.

Weirder still are the things that can happen at a comic book auction. Four current copies of Fish Police can, and have, brought a dead silence and a zero bid. Yet in 1988, a then current copy of Miami Mice shot to $100 two months after being printed.

It's moments like that that keep the gleam of hope in a collector's eye.

MAGAZINES

For publishers it's moments like the 'Death of Superman' that keep the presses rolling. Speeding bullets ran second to fans and collectors as they flocked into stores across the nation in November of 1992 to snap up copies of the long awaited Issue Number 75.

It took six issues for arch villian Doomsday to kill off Superman. It took just one day for Issue Number 75 to turn kryptonite into gold - the gold of cash registers ringing.

Fear not you fans of the big red 'S'. Reports circulating in the industry have Superman rising in April as four clones. Another report denies this. Doesn't matter. They can't kill Superman; they would have to kill all that merchandising. Superman is dead. Long live his clone.

SPECIALTY MAGAZINES

It is the specialty magazines, honed and pointed towards specific segments of the professional and sporting worlds that dominate the American market. No one is sure of the count. 10,000 has been mentioned.

Name a field of study, subdivide it into smaller divisions, and there will be a magazine to be found to cover that field, that particular segment.

For someone outside that field, they are not always easy to locate. Gale's Directory of Publications and Broadcast Media index numbers stops at 35,837 entries. Ulrich's International Periodical Directory is right there with Gale's. Between the two, they list a fantastic number of published magazines. It's quite possible to know of some that are not listed in either directory. *Paper Pile Quarterly* and *The Trading Network Journal* are 1992 examples.

Regardless, somewhere within the continental United States and Canada, there is a specific magazine being published just for you and your interest.

The names and the titles are bewildering. The following are some examples: *Desktop Press, Dirt Rider, Kit Car, T'ai Chi, Safty Briefs, Vegetarian Voices, Preservation in Print, Theriogenology*. They roll off the tongue, a babel of individual interests, some so specialized that their circulation figures may never exceed three or four hundred. Most magazines of this caliber will rarely make it as a collectible.

Movie magazines, while specialized, will always be of collectible interest because of their star studded content. Such titles as 'Movie Mirror', 'Movielines', 'Moville Record', 'Disney Channel Magazine', 'Emmy', or 'The Duckburg Times' will make it, eventually, to a dealers table or a collector's bookshelf.

Scientific American is still around. The October 14, 1902 issue featured a cover story on rules for Heavier Than Air Flying Machines. The auction price was $35

Etude Magazine discontinued publication in the 1950s, Until then its focus had been classical music. It filled a niche, still does for collectors; but at low prices, $5-10

Life Magazine at the turn of the century was concerned with Charles Dana Gibson, Biltmore, bridge, and horse shows.

Although *American Agriculturist* was published in New York, its interests were rural, including apple orchards in Ontario, Canada. The photograph shows how not to preserve your paper collectibles. Creases are out. Despite its poor condition it sold for $10

Three specialty magazines from the 1870s and 1880s. *The Electrical Review*, New York, April 21, 1888, ran an article on the future of the photograph, the *Country Gentleman,* July 2, 1874, said Dakota Sioux were not anxious to fight United States Calvary, and the March 1886 issue of *American Druggist* told of the miracle uses of cocaine as a medicine.

The *Electrical Review* sold for $40 at auction, the *Country Gentleman* $35. *American Druggist* was a buy-back by the auctioneer but has since been sold privately.

Literary Digest appealed to a wide range of the reading public. At one time it was recommended reading for public and high school students.

COMIC STRIPS

Comic strips came first, then comic books.
Photo courtesy Jim Fern

Only New Yorkers will remember when, if you had been reasonably good, the Sunday morning choice of a radio program was yours. The only choice was between 'Horn and Hardet Children's Hour' or the 'Little Flower'.

The answer was always easy. Listen to little kids your age singing. Where's the fun in that? "The Mayor. The Mayor," thin voices chanted. The cathedral shaped radio clicked on, an everyone sat back, Mom and Dad included, to hear His Honor, The Little Flower, New York City's Mayor, Fiorella LaGuardia, read the Sunday comic strips over the air.

Was there ever a time like it? Mutt and Jeff, Andy Gump, Moon Mullins, The Katzenjammer Kids, Barney Google and Spark Plug, Krazy Kat, and two even your grandchildren will recognize Gasoline Alley and Blondie today.

Those were the days when comic strips were just that - comics. No deep sociological meanings, political commentary, or moral message. Comic strips were funny.

There is no more provocative form of Americana. Krazy Kat was portrayed as an icon likened in a 1926 essay by Gillet Seldes to Don Quixote. Garfield and Doonesbury are on the best selling book list, while many collectors of original cartoon art consider themselves the equal of Fine Art collectors. All this from one shot - gags and situations that introduced the American comic strip to the 20th century when its predecessor, Richard Outcault's 'Yellow Kid' first appeared on February 16th, 1896, in a yellow shirt in the pages of *The New York World*.

The Sunday colored comics have never been the same.

Magazine covers are the appetizers before the main course. An invitation to the menu of fascinating stories and articles within.

Covers, whether by artists in paints, of pen, or photographic skills, are the open sesame to the world inside. Where the likes of authors we know, or would like to know, hold sway with the written word. Again perhaps, with illustrations by those same cover artists.

Commercial? Of course. Let them sneer who believe true art may be found only in museums. They are partly correct. For collections of works by cover illustrators hold pride of place alongside the masters in art museums across this country.

Something these same home grown critics may not care for: illustrators influenced popular taste much more than those who only painted with museums in mind. The cover illustrator had to work within the limitations set by his publisher. His work was sharper, more defined, for the audience for which it was destined.

Would anyone, critic or otherwise, claim Charles Dana Gibson's, 'Gibson Girl' did not change the look of American women at the turn of the century? Every girl wanted to look like her. As did the women of the 1920s who thought no one ever documented their lifestyles better than John Held Jr's flappers and bell bottomed trousered shieks.

Not only in the fields of fashion. Norman Rockwell's covers showed us an idealized world of homespun characters and old fashioned virtues that we wanted to believe existed once and would again.

Cover art was a world that began with the first high speed color press. A world of news stand sales that ended when subscriptions became more important. It is a world that still exists in a small way through the artistic skills of highly paid photographers and our new cover illustrators. They leave the practicioners of pen and brush to work on record albums, playing cards, specialty magazines, and court rooms where cameras are forbidden.

Covers introduced the reader to temptation to open the magazine to read. *The Esquire* cover for its fortieth anniversary issue was a fold out cover (see page 80). It was the only way they could show the likenesses of all the big name authors they had published between their covers.

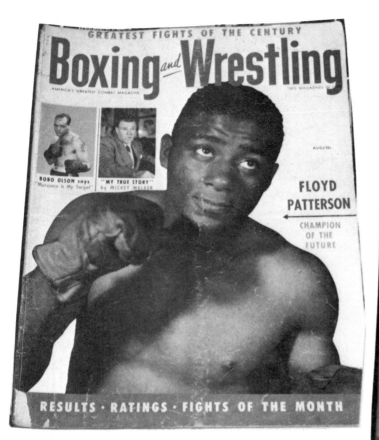

Magazines reach out for specific audiences; their collectible prices varying wildly. While *Star Trek* and *Boxing and Wrestling* could be bought at a show for $5 and *Fortune* magazine for $8, *Esquire*, with its double fold-out 40th Anniversary cover, was priced at that same show at $1 a year - $40 for the issue

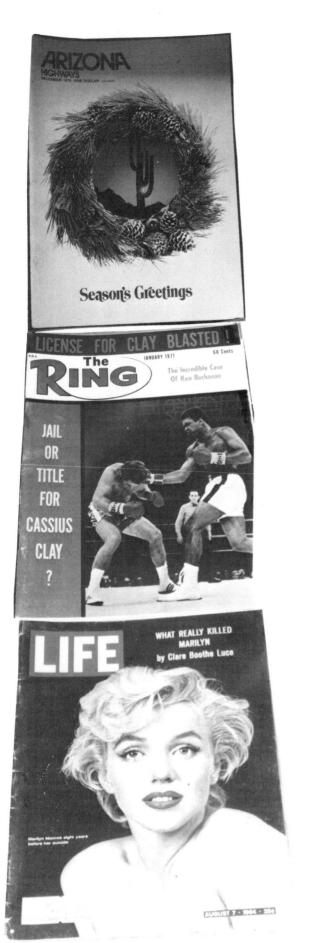

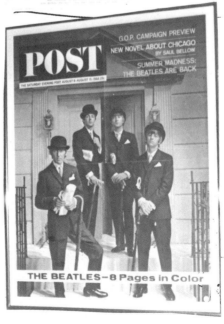

From *Puck* and the *Post* , to *Arizona* or *Life*, and *The Ring* to *Rolling Stone*, magazine covers were all come-ons. Come-on and see what we offer inside. Magazines and their covers have wide variation in price due to the number in circulation or the personalities featured on the cover. *Ring* and *Rolling Stone* were both available at $10 each, *Arizona* only made it to eight. *Puck*, despite its age, could be had for $20. It was Marilyn Monroe and the Beatle covers that set the prices for *Life* at $110, and *The Saturday Evening Post* (framed) at $200.

The first colored comic strip was Hogan's Alley, where Ourcault's Yellow Kid made his yellow shirted debut.

Life magazine may be one of the most avidly collected of all magazines, despite having been issued once a week for 1,878 issues between 1936 through 1972. Covers, inside photographs, and subject matters are the keys to this magazines high ranking with collectors. A copy dated April 26, 1937, with a Lou Gehrig cover, was a $10 offering at a 1992 collector's show.

Ladie's Home Journal, Country Gentleman, Leslie's, American, American Weekly - the listing of magazine titles are not endless - they only appear so. For collectors that's a plus.

  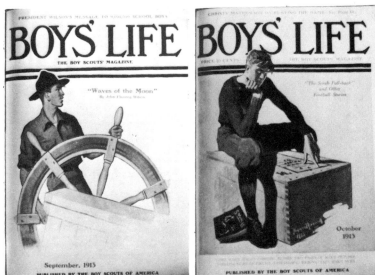 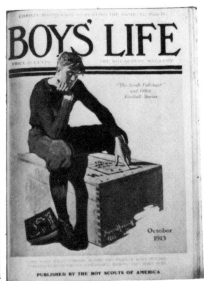

A Presidential profile, and a young, unretired, Johnny Carson, peer from the covers of one of America's most widely distributed magazines - *TV Guide.*

Boys grow up, become men. Their toys and dreams change. They also become more expensive.

Cover Design: Arthur Paul. Reproduced by special permission of *Playboy* Magazine; copyright © 1953 by *Playboy.*
This picture of Marilyn Monroe was on the cover of the first issue of *Playboy* magazine.

THE EMPIRE BUILDERS—By Mary Roberts Rinehar

Once the dream magazine of all aspiring writers, the *Saturday Evening Post* went under as general magazines fell victim to other entertainment fields. Revived, it once again holds promise, but is not the writer's icon it was once.

Literary Digest and *Collier's* both had long, successful careers. Both appear at auctions and shows for collectors now that the magazines can no longer call newsstands home. A *Collier's* cover dated February 28, 1931, sold at $18, while a *Vogue* cover dated January 15, 1922 went for $75. There are more *Collier's* available than *Vogue's*. The price will normally be higher for *Vogue*.

Books and magazines for boys have almost always been winners when the subject matter is limited to a boy's love of excitement, whether in books or in magazines such as *Boy* or *Boy's Life.*

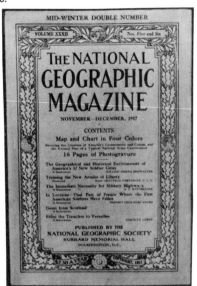

Are you one of the six people in the United States who have never read at least one copy of *National Geographic?* Or saved subscription copies for years and years before discarding them - reluctantly?

There are more *Scientific American* magazines available to the collector than *American Agriculturist's* which accounts for the $10 price for the latter as compared to $6 for the former. *Etude*, a classical music magazine ceased publication in the 1950s; not an unusual occurence in the magazine field. Note the recent folding of most of the American classical music magazines aimed at general audiences. *Etude* may be found for $5-15. High Fidelity, Keynote, and Musical America, newly deceased, are too current to have acquired accurate price listings.

Life magazine has had a long life span; changing format and illustrations to match the times. The highest prices for *Life* are to be found when the cover photograph has name recognition: Mickey Mantle ($120). Otherwise even a Batman cover will bring only $25; others form $3 and up.

PRICES:

ADULT - MEN'S

Ace - August 1958 - $5

Adam - February 1966 - $5

Adam Vol. 1: 1096, Vol. 1 - March 1911 - $10 each

Adam Bedside Reader - 1960 and 1968 - $6 each

Adam Film Quarterly - #2, 3, 1967, #4, 1968 - $7 each

Adam Film World - Vol. 4, #3, Vol. 6 #4 and 5, 1977, Vol. 7, 1979, Vol. 8, #1, 1980, Vol. 8 #8 1982 - $7 each

Adam Special Report - #2 and 3 1969 - $7 each

After Hours - 1963 - $5

Angel, Vol. 1 Denmark - $10

Argosy - September 23, 1933, January, February, March, 1940 - $8 each

Artists and Models - May, July 1927 - $7 each

Artists and Models Annual - Vol. 1 #2 1969 - $7

Bally Hoo - June, September, November - $15 each

Bally Hoo - April 1933 - $7

Best of Playboy - 1954, 160 pages - $12

Briggit - Vol. 1 #4 - $10

Caberet - September, November 1955, January, February, March, May, 1956 - $7 each

Casanova - May 1957 - $10

Cavalcade of Burlesque - September 1950 - $8

Cinemax Monthly - 1876 - $7

Cupcake - Collector's Edition - $10

Dude March 1957 - $5

Eros 1st issue, Spring 1962 - $28

Esquire 25th Anniversary issue, October 1958 - $20

Esquire 40th Anniversary issue, double cover - $20

Esquire January 1942, 12 Varga calendar pages - $42

Laff - Summer 1954 - $10

Millionaire - March 1964 - $10

Mood 1962 - $10

Night and Day - September 1952, Annual 1965, February 1957, Vol. 1 #2 1964 - $10 each

Night People 1974 - $5

Oui Premier Edition, Vol. 1 #1, October 1972 - $10

Outlaw Motorcycle - banned, Vol. 1 #7 1865 - $12

Paris Life - 1953 - $7

Peep Show - 1954 - $10

Pep - March 1933 - $10

Perils of Pauline Vol. 1 #1 - $10

Playmate - September 1959 - $12

Relax - May 1957 - $10

Scandanavia Croquis Models, #70, 72, 73, Denmark - $10 each

Snappy - October 1933 - $10

Wink - November 1968 - $10

OUTDOOR — SCIENCE — MECHANICS

Adironack Life - Winter 1972 - $6

American Rifleman - 54 year run, 1st issue June 1, 1923 through 1977 - $575

Automobilist, The (17) 1926-1929 - $44

Buick - 1955 - $5

Canoeing - B.S.A. 1960 - $6

Conservationist (NY) - October 1972 - $5

Craftsman - Fall 1909 - $35

Field and Stream - August 1904 - $20

Field and Stream - October 1936 - $8

First Cars: Illustrated History of the Motor Car, 1st issue 1970 - $15

Ford Owner and Dealer July 1923 - $20

Holiday - July 1948 - $10

Kodakery - July 1924 - $5

Metal Worker - October 1925, November 1929 - $12.50 each

Model Airplane News December 1933, August 1934 - $10 each

Modern Mechanics and Invention - August 1931 - $30

Modern Mechanics (12) 1935, and (7) 1936 - $9 each

Motor Age - April 28, 1904 - $15

Motor Life - July 1955 - $15

New York Clipper - May 1882, spot issues through April 28, 1883 - $30-$45 each

Pathfinder - (10) 1938-1939, January 9, 1933 April 19, 1935 - $9-$12 each

Popular Mechanics - 1950 - $20

Popular Photography - December 1942 - $4

Popular Science - 1929, August 1934, December 1934, January, June 1937 - $6 each

Rodeo 1958 - $15

Science and Mechanics (6) 1933-1936, with (4) *Popular Mechanics* January, May 1933 - $6 each

Scientific American - February 6, 1875 - $6

Scientific Monthly - (90) copies, 1929-1938 - $75

Scouting 1918, 128 pages - $35

Sports Cars of 1955 - Car Life Annual - $7.50

Sports Illustrated - 1st issue, August 16, 1954, with baseball cards. Two different advertisements, from two different trade journals - $110-$195

Sports Illustrated - April 1955, with baseball cards - $110

Trailways - Spring 1951

COMIC MAGAZINES

Action Comics - #76, 77, 82 - $95 lot

Batman - #5 - $280

Dell Comics (61) 12 cent issues - $70

G.I. Joe - (3) #11, 12, 13 - $20

Happy Hooligan - Opper, bound volume, 1903 - $22

Marvel Comics - #41 - $45

Marvel Comics - (40) 12 cent issues - $40

Mutt and Jeff Cartoons Book Bud Fisher, #3, 1912 - $55

Popeye's Ark - 1936, Saalfied, #1117 - $35

Smiling Jack - 1938 - $55

Spiderman - book and record set - $18

Superman - book and record set - $18

Superman - #8 - $100

Superman #42 and 58 - $80

Tarzan - Big Little Book: *New Adventures of Tarzan,* 1935, Whitman - $40

Walt Disney's Donald Duck *The Fabulous Diamond Fountain* - $12

Walt Disney's Donald Duck and the Boys, 1948 - $10

SPORTS

Autocar - October 12, 1951 - $6.50

Automobile Quarterly - Summer 1966 - $10.50

Baseball Digest - February, March, May, November 1944, Charles Gehringer cover - $8 each

Baseball - December 1937 - $25

Boston Garden Sports News - (3) 1940-1942 - $12

Field and Stream - December 1920, July, December 1923 - $8 each
Outdoors (6) 1931-1945 - $18
Ring - March 1960, February 1960 - $10 each
Sport - October 1950, Jackie Robinson cover - $15
Sport - May 1953, March 1956 - $5 each
Sporting News, The - April 20, 1974 - $15
Yachting - November 1940 - $10

HUMOR

Best of National Lampoon, The - 1972 - $3
Film Fun - 150 photographs - $3.50
Gags - July 1941 - $4
Harlequin (61) 1973-1978 - $25
Judge - October 16, 1926 - $15
Movie Humor - Vol. 2 #9, 1935 - $7
National Lampoon - (58) 1973-1979 - $25
Puck - June 22, 1887, January 2, 1889, July 18, 1888 - $16 each
Puck - March 21, 1888 - $20
Puck - November 16, 1898 - $35
Puck - 1905, Rose O'Niell - $50

ENTERTAINMENT

Film Fun - February, June, August, September 1924 - $12 each
Modern Screen - January, November 1945, September 1953 - $5 each
Modern Screen - September 1953 - $12
Motion Picture - May 1924, April, October, November, 1931 - $35 each
Motion Picture - July 1969 - $5
Motion Picture Herald - March 14, May 9, August 1, October 24, December 19, 1931 - $10 each
Motion Picture News - October 2, October 16, 1915 - $35 each
Motion Picture Story - October 1912 - $35
Movie Fan - September 1953 - $8
Movieland - annual 1955 - $30
Movie Life - December 1938 - $15
Movie Life - November 1949 - $4
Movie Mirror - July 1934 - $4
Movie Mirror - August 1969 - $3.50
Movie Picture - June 1953 - $12
Movie Radio Guide - December 20, 1939 - $7.50
Movie Romances - October 1931 - $30
Movie Story - December 1945 - $5
Movie Story - November 1945, April, November, December 1946, February 1947 - $10 each
Movies - April 1948 - $15
Movie Weekly - February 16, March, 1, March 22, 1924 - $15
Moving Picture Weekly - December 1957 - $20
Photoplay - October 1944, Lana Turner cover - $10
Photoplay - July, August 1945, February, April, May 1946 - $5 each
Photoplay - September 1955 - $8
Radio Digest - April 1930 - $24
Radio Mirror - October 1941 - $6
Radio Mirror - December 1939, Judy Garland cover - $12
Radio News - October 1922 - $15
Radio Stars - December 1936 - $15
Radio and TV News - March 1950 - $25
Screen Album - Summer/Fall 1936 - $10

Screen Guide - June 1938, Jean Harlow cover - $20

Screenland - October 1944, Shirley Temple - $15

Screenland - January, 1954 - $12

Screenland - 1956 through 1960 - $10 each

Screen Romances - October 1936 - $38

Screen Romance - January 1940 - $60

Screen Stories - February 1961, Marilyn Monroe - $25

Screen Stories - 1960 through 1973 - $10 each

Screen Stories - June 1966, Batman cover - $15

Silver Screen - July 1933 - $8

Silver Screen - 1936, Jean Harlow - $14

Show (25) 1962-1963 - $29 lot

Song Hits - September 1940 - $5

Stage - June 1933, August 1937 - $15

TV Annual #2, 1955 - $12

TV Guide - December 25-31, 1948 - $150

TV Guide - April 2-8, 23-29, April 30—May 6, MAy 21-27, June 25—July 1, August 13-19, July 23-30, September 24-30, 1949 - $75

TV Guide - May 20-26, May 22—June 2, 1950 - $50

TV Guide - September 30—October 6, October 15-21, November 25—December 1, 1950 - $75

TV Guide - November 8-14, 1952 - $14

TV Guide - March 17—April 2, 1953 - $15

TV Guide - August 2, 1953 - $35

TV Guide - September 25, 1953, George Reeves and Superman cover - $250

TV Guide - June 8, 1957, Lassie cover - $30

TV Guide - March 26, 1966, Batman cover - $35

TV Illustrated - November 1955 - $8

TV Picture - June, December 1955 - $10

TV Radio Mirror - April 1956, November 1960, July 1961, March 1963, January 1970 - $10 each

Theatre - December 1906, June 1904 - $7 each

Theatre - March 1909, Billie Burke cover - $10

Will Rossitor's Stage Favorites - January 1899, Anna Held cover - $12

GENERAL

Aggie Life - (10) Massachusetts Agricultural College, 1896-1897 - $10

American Cookery - (2) 1922 - $10

American Cookery - March, October 1932, May, June, July, October, November 1939, June, July 1940, February, June, July 1941 - $4 each

American Gardening (28), bound, from October 1893 through December 1894 - $30

American Home (54) 1942-1951 - $25

American Motel - March 1951, February 1953 - $4 each

American Museum Journal - October 1912 - $6

American Restaurant - April, July, August, November 1952 - $4 each

Antiques (7) 1928-1929 - $9

Antiques - October 1926 - $4

Antiques Journal - April 1972 - $4

Antiques Journal - January 1977 - $5.50

Art News Annual - 1944-1945 - $50

Atlantic Monthly - (18) 1954-1958 - $12 lot

Ballou's Pictorial - March 8, 1856 - $9

Ballou's Pictorial - January, June 1863 - $10 each

Bay View - (2) 1899 - $10

Better Homes and Gardens (21) 1926-1938 - $30

Better Homes and Gardens - January 1948 - $5

Better Homes and Gardens - (15) 1946-1954 - $15 lot

Beatles On Broadway 1964 - $18

Beatles Bulletin - May 1965 - $18

Born To Run - Springsteen, 1979 - $5

Boston Cookery School - 1911-1914 - $10

Buffalo Bill - 1904 - $8

Butterick Quarterly Fashion - Autumn 1927 - $35

Cartoons - December 1919 - $8

Century - October 1894 - $10

Child Labor Bulletin - February 1915 - $6

Christian Herald - March 1933 - $5

Collier's Automotive - January 1910 - $10

Connoisseur - (8) 1919 - $9

Cosmopolitan - December 1893, March 1897 - $10 each

Cosmopolitan - (14) 1901-1902 - $30 lot

Cosmopolitan - December 1918 - $12

Cottage Hearth - (10) 1886 - $15

Cultivator and Country Gentleman - (8) 1878 - $30 lot

Dance With the Devil - Rolling Stones, 1975 - $5

Dearborn Independent - October 8, 1927, The Courting of Marry Todd article - $7

Delineatork Fashion - (4) 1892-1896 - $18 lot

Etude - October 1941 - $6

Farmers Wife - (32) 1934-1939 - $65 lot

Fortune - March, May, October, November, December 1931, April 1932, April, October 1933
   February, June 1938 - $10 each

Fortune - (2) August/September 1933, Mint - $25

Fortune - May 1936 - $8.50

Fortune - June 1936 - $10

Fortune - Railroad covers, eight in color, 1931-1939 - $39 lot

Frank Leslie's Boy and Girl's Weekly - (90) February 15, 1879 through February 7, 1882 - $5 each

Frank Leslie's Popular Monthly - January, June 1897 - $10

Frank Leslie's - March 28, 1868 - $10

Godey's Ladies Book - 1837-1844 - $100

Godey's Ladies Book - 1864 - $9.50

Glory Days - Springsteen, 1987 - $6

Good Housekeeping - (16) 1934-1935 - $189

Goose Quill - November 1, 1901 - $20

Harper's Monthly - August 1830, October 1833, July 1834, June, August 1835, March, April, July, August, September 1836
   - $4 each

Harpers Round Table - (6) 1898-1899 - $15 each

Harpers Weekly - November 23, 1861, May 27, 1865 - $30 each

Harpers Weekly - January 18, 1862 - $40

Harpers Weekly - June 3, 1865 - $18

Harpers Weekly - August 19, 1899, black life - $11

Harpers Young People - (5) 1880s - $20

Hobbies July 1933 - $5

Holiday - (19) 1940s-1950s - $6 each

Holiday - July 1948 - $10

Hot Rod - May, July 1955 - $6 each

Hugard's Magic Monthly - March 1950 - $6

Hygeia (19) 1930-1940 - $15 lot

Illustrated London News - (300) 1950-1960 - $2 each

International #1 and 2, adventure - $15 each

Journal of American History - (50) - $40 lot

Junior Red Cross - March, November 1923, April, September, November 1925, January, September 1926, February 1938

Labor Age - December 1921, October 1923 - $4 each
Ladie's Home Journal - Christmas 1892 - $12
Ladie's Home Journal - May 1893 - $22
Ladie's World - November 1896 - $7
Leslie's Monthly - July, December 1885, Woodcuts and Chromolithographs - $49
Liberty - January 18, 1930 through December 6, 1930 - $5 each
Life - (7) 1884-1885, (1) 1891, (10) 1903 - $26 lot
Life - September 30, December 9, December 30, 1897, September 19, 1901, January 22, February 28, July 16, October
    3, 1904, January 28, 1909 with Cole Phillips cover of Divine Service - $15 each
Life - (6) 1912-1925 - $48
Life - April 20, January 9, 1959, August 15, 1960 - $20
Life - May 8, 1950, Jackie Robinson cover and June 12, 1950 with Hopalong Cassidy cover - $25 each
Life - March 13, 1962, Mickey Mantle cover - $120
Life - March 11, 1966, Batman cover - $25
Life - June 4, 1971 - $15
Literary Digest - (2) 1914 - $7
Literary Digest - (9) 1918-1919, Norman Rockwell covers - $100
Literary Digest - November 2, 1935, Charlie Chaplin cover - $10
McClures - April 1899 - $10
Mentor - (4) 1922, (1) 1924, (6) 1925 - $3.50 each
Modern Man - November 1953, Marilyn Monroe cover and story - $25
Nation, The - (6) 1919 - $9
Needlepoint - October 1917 - $10
Newsweek - May 15, 1950, Groucho Marx cover, and March 10, 1947, Albert Einstein cover - $15 each
Our Home and Fireside - May 1881 - $8
Original Beatles Book 1964 - $18
Peterson's (12) 1866 - $40
Peterson's - 1870 - $40
Peterson's - (7) 1860-1874, hand colored fashion plates - $39
Peterson's - 1862, bound, 12 steel engravings, 12 hand colored fashion plates - $69
Photo History - April 1937, Vol. 1 - 4 - $5 each
Pictorial Review - May 1914 - $20
Pictorial Review - April, October, November 1931 - $21
Reader's Digest - (28) 1936-1939 - $1 each
Reader's Digest - (15) 1938-1941 - $23 lot
Red Cross - (3) 1917-1918 - $10
Red Cross - May, July, August 1918, with N.C. Wyeth cover - $28
Ringling Brothers and Barnum and Bailey circus - season 1937 - $18
Rolling Stone's Anthology - 1975 - $5
Rough Rider Weekly - (5) 1905-1906 - $15 lot
Satisfaction Rolling Stones 1965-1967 - $6
Saturday Evening Post - February 20, 1937, Bob Feller cover - $10-$20
Saturday Evening Post - June 3, 1939 - $10
Saturday Evening Post - (17) 1940-1950, Norman Rockwell covers - $90 lot
Saturday Review - (80) 1960-1963 - $15
Sphinx - magic, July 1947 - $6
Springsteen - 1985 - $8
St. Nichols - October 1914 - $7
St. Nichols - December 1913, Will Bradley cover - $15
Sweetheart Stories/Love Story - pulps (2) - $15
Time - March 2, 1931 - $6
Time - January 9, 1933 - $10
Time - September 20, 1943, Bob Hope cover - $8
Time - April 23, 1945, Harry Truman cover - $8
Time - June 1, 1946, Albert Einstein cover - $20
Time - January 12, 1948, Gregory Peck cover - $8

Time - May 16, 1949, Milton Berle cover - $10
Time - August 22, 1949, Liz Taylor cover - $12
Time - May 15, 1950, Coca Cola Cover - $20
Time - December 31, 1951, Groucho Marx cover - $12
Time - (50) 1940s - $75
Tops - Magic, January 1950 - $6
Tourist Court - December 1950 - $4
True - April 1960 - $9
True - (175) 1952-1973 all different - $200
Vanity Fair - March 1915 - $7
Virginia Illustrated - (10) 1929-1932 - $25 lot
Vogue - December 1940, November 1950 - $8 each
Wisconsin Archeologist - January 1919 - $4
Woman's Home Companion - April 1915 - $18
Woman's Home Companion - May 1915 - $15
Woman's Home Companion - (25) December 1933 to 1936 - $175
Woman's World - March 1911 - $10
Young Ladie's Journal - May 1891 - $8
Youth's Companion - January 1891 - $15
Youth's Companion - October 20, 1898 - $25

Museums:

Lied Discovery Children's Museum, 833 Las Vegas Boulevard North, Las Vegas, NV 89101, Phone: 702-382-KIDS

Baltimore Museum of Art, Baltimore, MD 21218

The Cartoon Museum, Orlando, FL 32807

Books:

Comic Art in America, Stephen Becker, Simon and Schuster, 1959

A History of American Magazines, Frank Luther Mott, five volumes, Belknap Press of Harvard University Press, 1930.

The Art of Walt Disney, Christopher Finch, Harry N. Abrams, Inc., 1973

Collections:

Charles Marion Russell Collection, Trigg-Russell Gallery, Great Falls, MT

Frank Schoonover Collection, Brandywine Museum, Chadd's Ford, PA

Edwin Austin Abbey Collection, Yale University Art Gallery

Harvey Dunn Collection, South Dakota Memorial Art Center, Brookings, SD

Arthur I Keller Collection, Museum of American Art, New Britain, CO

Howard Pyle Collection, Delaware Art Museum

CHAPTER X

DISNEYANA

There has been so much written about Walt Disney and Disneyana collectibles, that writing a new chapter about the subject is daunting. The writer finds himself in the same position as the man marrying a woman with eight previous husbands - he knows what to do but how does he make it interesting?

If you are a paper collector specializing in Disneyana, there is no thrill equal to an early black and white Mickey from *Plane Crazy*. This was Walt Disney's first Mickey Mouse production. Created in 1928, it was released after *Steam Boat Willie* and was believed by many newcomers to the Disney cult to be Mickey's first.

The production background of Minnie handing an oversized horseshoe to Mickey as he stands in the open cockpit of a plane, is said to be one of the earliest surviving pieces of orignial art from the Disney Studios.

The average collector may never own one - one sold for $44,000 at a Christie's auction in 1992 - but there are millions of Disneyana items out there, trophies for legwork by the collector - most in an affordable price range. No one, not even the Disney Archives, can list all the various items produced since Disney's first success and the creation of Mickey Mouse in the 1920s.

Yearly sales, here in America, of old and new Disney items, have been estimated at better than $400,000,000. Europe adds more to the total. France alone is Europe's number one buyer of Disneyana. The comic book, "*Le Journal de Mickey*," says one authority, "is read by 10,000,000 French children each week."

While Disneyana has always been an emotionally based area, it was New York's Christie's East, that started the current collector interest, and escalating prices, in 1984. It was then they first auctioned former Disney animator, John Basmajian's private collection of Disneyana. The sale realized three times its pre-auction estimate.

As of this writing, the claim is that more than 350 animated art dealers and galleries are operating around the country. Major and minor auction houses, both on the East and West coasts, and points in between, each hold two or three animation auctions a year.

But is it art? Yes. To the beginner, it's all animation art. The established collector knows that a production cel set against its original background has more value than the 80 or more cels filmed against that same background. He knows the rarity of the original art of the 1930s. He also knows a 'Mickey' will always be worth more.

More important, the dedicated collector knows that not all Disney or other animation art will rise in price. He loves Disneyana as a collectible. Maybe, being human, a small percentage of his mind thinks of a return on his investment. Mostly he just enjoys himself.

Posters, games, stamps, books, annuals, cut-outs, candy wrappers, playing cards, puzzles, sheet music, stationary, stickers and toys are all part of paper Disneyana.

Selected animation cels may make the headlines with there five figure sales, but it is the other, unlimited selections, that keep Disneyana attractive to collectors.

While most everything collectible in Disneyana is highly colorful, movie posters are the one items more likely to be hung on a wall for visual enjoyment.
Courtesy Long Island University.

DISNEYANA

As collectibles, animation art is still affordable. $1,000 or less are the recorded prices for many sales as of this writing. Poster prices continue to climb, the few survivors in pristine condition fueling the escalation.

Posters, aping circus and stage promotions, were the primary means of advertising those first movie cartoons. Hand painted, lithographed, and distributed to theatres, they were supposed to be returned to the studios after the theatre run of its designated film. The studios sent them elsewhere, to another theatre chain for the next showing. Attrition took its toll and few survived in reasonable condition.

One that did, from one of Disney's first, before Mickey, productions, "Alice the Peacemaker," sold at auction in 1992 for $22,000. Other Disney posters sold for less. "Society Dog Show", with Mickey Mouse, 1941, sold for $10,450. "Truant Officer Donald," a 1940 Donald Duck cartoon, sold for $4,620.

Books command good prices, particularly those with superior graphics. A pop-up Mickey Mouse In The Circus, in Spanish, 1934, sold for $260 in a mail auction. Lower on the collectible chain, collectors are buying postage stamps featuring Disney characters from places as far from Hollywood such as Dominica, Grenada, and the Gambia.

Disney has become the mainstay of America's hedonists, with Mickey Mouse being the single most recognized symbol and name in the world.

Some claim Disney enthusiasts having the most fun are the members of the Mouse Club, the oldest of Disneyana organizations, with their annual convention in Anaheim, California.

Others claim that those who attend Disney theme parks are exposed to more Disney collectibles in more apt surroundings.

Does it matter? Some collectors have paid more than $400,000 for a favorite Disney character. Others have paid mere hundreds. There are others who buy what they can at $10, $20, or $30. You know what? They all have fun.

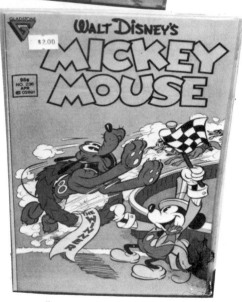

Comic books and their covers are the most readily available collectibles featuring Disney characters.

97

BOOKS

Think Disney, then add books. The normal answer is comics. Mostly that's true. Mickey and friends in a comic book format have flooded the market with the same excess as comics produced by traditional comic book publishers.

Some few have reached that nirvana inspired by collectors who list comic books and their issue numbers in columns of desirability. Amongst them are Donald Duck, black and white, number 16, Dell publishers, in 1938: Donald Duck, four color, numbers nine and twenty nine, also by Dell, published in 1941 and 1942.

Also among the must-haves is the Mickey Mouse book by Bebi and Long, from 1930, and Walt Disney Comics and Stories, numbers 1-35, by Dell in 1940.

Of greater interest than these to collectors could be called an 'almost comic' book. The pop-up books that were published by Blue Ribbon Books, Inc. during the 1930s. Pleasure Books was another publisher who helped develop this book form. A pop-up book is simple. Open the covers and a three dimensional scene pops up relating the pop-up characters to a perceived story line. Unlike comic books, normally printed on cheap paper, these pop-up books were well made. Mickey Mouse has appeared in a pop-up book titled just that, *Mickey Mouse*. So has Pinocchio and Minnie Mouse. Mickey starred in another pop-up titled *Mickey Mouse In King Arthur's Court,* which some collector's privately perceive as the jump off spot for the future Sorcerer's Apprentice.

These pop-up books have become more rare each year. That, however, has never stopped a collector from dreaming.

Another form of Mickey Mouse pop-up book was the *Mickey Mouse Waddle Book*. A telephone auction catalog from Stuart and Maxine Evans of New Jersey, described the book as, "The finest Disney book in existence. Revolutionary story book with characters that actually come out of the pages and walk."

It sold for $1,800, plus a 10% premium.

When the Waddle book was first issued in 1934, the price was $1, then considered high. Right now, some consider the $1,800 realized as low.

ORIGINAL ART

Between 1896 and 1950 were the golden years of comic art. Defining it more closely, we can pinpoint 1928 as the year animation art made two personalities famous world wide - Walt Disney and Mickey Mouse. All because Disney added a sound track to the second Mickey Mouse cartoon, Steamboat Willie.

With this as a beginning, Disney went on to win 30 academy awards, introduced a new method for synchronizing sound with animation, used the three color process, produced the first feature length animated movie, and was literally the father of millions of animated cels.

The original art conceived and developed by the hundreds of talented artists employed by his corporations were once discarded by the studios, thrown out as trash, or given away as table prizes for attending a dinner. Today they are hoarded, released on a limited basis, mostly to individuals or firms dedicated to returning the highest gross monies. Animation is now big business.

It's up to the collector, should Disneyana be judged as a sales item on a shelf, or an investment to be put away like a classic car or a gilt edge bond, to await its accountant predicated increase in value, five, ten, or more years in the future?

To answer that, remember that original animation art was developed as an art form for the millions, for the masses, to whom as Iris or Waterlilies oil on canvas or wisteria panel by Tiffany, are items to enjoy only in museums. Mickey Mouse is to be enjoyed in the home.

Should Mickey or Goofy or a Silly Symphony to be placed in the same class as a self portrait by Brueghel, or an icon by a nameless monk? Right alongside those never-never pieces of traditional art - that's where Mickey belongs. With all his friends.

Sotheby's, the world acclaimed auction house, sees a long term future in original animation art as a collectible. So much so that the house added a special department to handle it. For the kids who grew up with Disney; the buyers of the future.

Original? It's all original art. We have inherited it from the caveman who pecked and daubed it on a cave or canyon wall. We've inherited it right down through the centuries to the day Walt Disney introduced us to his version of an art - original animation art. We're all better for it.

Song sheets may not be original art but what serious collector would turn it down if offered?

Everything about Disneyana is original, from cels (not definitely within the field of paper collectibles) to the concept of Disney characters.

CARTOONS

The original Mickey Mouse Club, formed in 1929, at a Saturday movie theatre promotion, held a five day convention in Anaheim, California in 1992. The members were able to see the first five Mickey Mouse films and the original Silly Symphony with the use of an existing musical composition as background for a matching animated story. From that year (1929) to the 1940s, most of Disney's classics were born.

In 1930, Ub Iwerks drew the original strips of a Mickey Mouse strip for King Features. In that same year, Pluto the Pup, unnamed as yet, appeared for the first time in *Chain Gang*.

The first Sunday color comics featuring Mickey appeared in 1932, as did a Silly Symphony series. Goofy appeared that same year, to be outclassed the following year by the arch villian of everyone's childhood - The Big Bad Wolf - as he tried out his inimitable wiles on the Three Little Pigs.

Failing a roast pig, he tried once again, the following year, in *Little Red Riding Hood*.

The three pigs evaded him long enough to appear, with Donald Duck, in a King Features, Silly Symphony strip; a prelude of things to come in 1937.

In that year, Donald Duck achieved a starring role in *Donald's Ostrich*, and the all time classic of *Snow White and the Seven Dwarfs* debuted.

Was that why Donald Duck appeared in a newspaper comic strip in 1938? He acquired nephews Huey, Dewey, and Louie, a good start for a year that produced another classic: *Ferdinand the Bull*. By 1940, *Pinocchio* and *Fantasia* were introduced, and the name of Disney was implanted for all time in the minds of those then around to see those great, great cartoons.

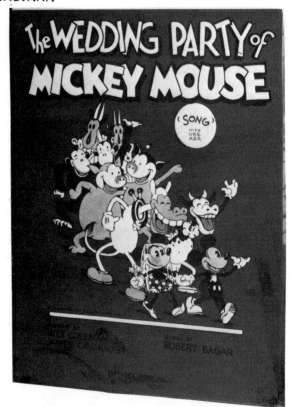

Mickey and Minnie were married? According to this song sheet from 1931, it's true.

From the *Stage* magazine of September 1935 came one of the first Disney stories of Mickey, Pluto, and friends in color.

DISNEY POSTERS

Mickey Mouse fans never completely grew up. There is something wonderful in that.

Whatever the attraction, it gives people pleasure, no matter where they live. Mickey's outgoing allure transcends the barriers of nationalism and language. His appeal, the attraction of all Disney characters is universal. The appeal of childhood.

The posters have that universal magnetism as well. No pastels of meaning, no nuances of shadow or line. The colors are vibrant, alive, primary in their urgency and representation.

The colors, like the characters they portray, reach out, their lines, shimmering quicksilver, play tunes that soar through your mind, taking you to worlds that exist purely in imagination, but with links that define our own lives.

Even the early black and white film had that fantastic feeling of joy. There were no sad Disney films, no joyless Disney posters.

Mickey and all his co-workers had one thing in common - their vitality. Through their posters this vitality was enhanced.

Mickey and his friends live and will always live, if no place else, within our child like hearts. The hearts that like Mickey's will hopefully never grow old and forever remain that of a child's.

DISNEYANA
Prices:

Watercolor Mickey Mouse Nabisco advertising proposal, c.1950, Advertisement for Peter Pan Bread - $400
Book illustration, by Robert G. Stokes, Disney artist for Snow White and *Fantasia* - $575
Mickey's Space Ship. Watercolor illustration c.1950, Little Golden Book - $400
Donald Duck pencil drawing, 1934, *Orphan's Benefit*, Donald's second screen appearance - $700
Donald Duck, Willis Pyle, pencil and watercolor - $65
Pinocchio, Willis Pyle, pencil and watercolor - $110
Donald Duck cel, *Cowboy Donald* on painted background - $330
Donald Duck store displays, 50th birthday, six different - $20
Three Little Pigs, 1933, graphite and colored pencil - $950
Woodland Cafe, 1933, graphite and colored pencil - $775
Silly Symphony, 1936, Country Cousins, graphite and colored pencil - $675
Little Hiawatha, 1936, graphite and colored pencil - $400
Donald Duck Bread, die-cut advertising sign - $175
Cinderella and the Aristocrats, watercolor cel from Disney annual number 215 - $100
Double page watercolor, Disneyland annual, Donald Duck and Nephews, Goofy, Three Little Pigs, Mickey Mouse - $160
Rough drawing, Bambi running with mother - $45
1978, Disneyland annual, page 37, watercolor Pinocchio, Gepetto, and Jimmy - $150
Framed lot of two Bambi sheet music and Walt Disney first day cover - $260
Peter Pan, Capt. Hook, and all characters, watercolor, Disney annual number 40 - $125
Mickey, Minnie, and Mortimer Mouse from the Copper's Catch, publicity drawing - $160
Snow White and the Seven Dwarfs, Disneyland annual number 89, watercolor - $310

Magazine:

Disney Channel Magazine, 3800 West Almeda Avenue, Burbank, CA 91505, Phone: 818-840-6661, Steven Gutman, Publisher

Books:

Walt Disney by Maxine P. Fisher c.1988

The Disney Poster Book, introduction by Maurice Sendak, c.1977

The Disney Studio Story, by Richard Holliss, Brian Sibley, c.1988

The Disney Version: The Life, Times, Art and Commerce of Walt Disney, by Richard Schickel, c.1968

Disneyana: Walt Disney Collectibles, by Cecil Munsey, 1974

Clubs:

The Mouse Club (with more than 800 associated clubs around the country), 2056 Cirone Way, San Jose, CA 95124, Phone: 408-377-2590

Auctions:

Smith House Toy Auctions, P.O. Box 336 CS, Eliot, ME 03903, Phone: 207-439-4614

All American Collectors Show, Glendale, CA, Phones: 213-392-6672 or 818-980-5025

Manion's International Auction House, P.O. Box 12214, Kansas City, KS 66112, Phone: 913-299-6692

Camden House Auctioneers, Inc., 10921 Wilshire Boulevard, Suite 713, Los Angeles, CA 90024, Phone: 213-476-1628

CHAPTER XI

PHOTOGRAPHY

Some photographs and subjects like Marilyn are
timeless

Photography was not invented: it evolved. It began with Aristotle when he first described how light (he never knew of a light wave) behaved when projected through a small hole. In terms of years, the technical achievement of photography is only one hundred and fifty years old.

The early 1850s brought the art to the world's attention when photographic prints were displayed at The Crystal Palace in London.

Through the changing modes and uses of glass plates, paper prints, to glass plates again, then to tintype, a collodion coated metal plate, then back once more, to stay, the use of paper then plastic for film.

As museum accessions, the works of legendary photographers Robert MacPherson, Timothy O'Sullivan, and Matthew Brady in recording both landscapes and battlefields are invaluable. As were the portraitures of Alexander Healy and Louis Carroll.

Their's are museum pieces, out of reach of most advanced or beginning paper collectors. We must look to photographs made from the late 19th century to the present for works that are reasonable but undeniably collectible.

The photographers of the early 1900s were captivated by scenes of immigrants debarking at Ellis Island, of horse drawn trolleys, and of curb-side pushcart markets on city streets. Louis Hines and Alfred Stieglitz are the names to seek.

Timothy O'Sullivan recorded the wonders of our wild West; lugging glass plates and heavy equipment over primitive primitive trails.

Sociology teamed with photography as Jacob Riis chronicled the slums of New York and Louis Hine left his immigrants alone long enough to examine children laboring fourteen hours a day in dismal factories.

Nothing escaped the photographers eye. Dance halls and locomotives, ferris wheels and migrant laborers, court rooms and ballparks were all memorialized in black and white by their skills.

Other newspapers and magazines followed the New York Tribune's lead in publishing photographs along with hard copy. Industrial corporations followed the same lead. Soon photographs of a firm's wares replaced bulky salesman's samples. Major entertainments, World's Fairs recorded everything from exhibits to panoramic views of what they offered to an expectant public.

The entertainment world, the actors and actresses, took to photography as if born with a camera in the cradle. Napoleon Sarony, as much an actor as his subjects, directed their movements, posed and commanded them to bring out his subject's personality.

Without photography there would be no movies, no Wallace Berry to remember in 'The Kid', no Judge Hardy and Son to laugh with, and no shoot-outs in a Western saloon. These were lobby photographs, shown behind glass doors. Your choice at $4 each.

Photographs like these, and those associated with the stage, industry, entertainment, shipping, or transportation, are what most collectors seek today. Time capsules of what was once the ultimate in personality and progress.

Photography realized much of its potential when used with advertisement. Starting in the 1930s, advertising photography gave impetus to the art of public relations.

Photography had grown up. It was moving out upon divergent paths.

PHOTOGRAPHY

History is more personal when touched by a photographers skill. Ships lying too in a British harbor, War veterans growing old, the pride of a locomotive plant, or just good times and good friends, all there for the memories. The ship photo was priced at $800, the war veteran's at $85 and the good friends enjoyed their $95 price.

A stereoscope and the cards to go with one were an evenings entertainment in the parlor of a Victorian household. Average price for run
of the mill cards is about $4. Specific sets can be more expensive. At
a recent estate auction 300 stereo cards, some hand colored, sold for
$2,200.

While stereoscopes, or stereopticans, were first described as early as 1832 and were popular in the 1850s, they reached a peak of popularity in Victorian times. No late 19th century parlor was complete without a stereoscope, and cards to accompany it.

Two not quite identical photographic images would, when viewed through a viewer with two lens, appear as a single, three dimensional, apparently solid image. So popular were these hand held magic viewers that they, and the cards to be viewed, were produced in the millions during the late 19th century and into the 1920s.

Produced in the millions tells the collector much about their values today. Scarcity still determines price.

Stereoscopes using color optics had been applied to three dimensional movies in the 1950s. It was left to an American inventor, Edwin H. Land, to develop the use of stereoscope technology and polarizing filters to eventually produce what we know today as the polaroid camera.

Ambrotypes were a development by a British chemist who found that collodion would hold light sensitive chemicals on a glass plate. Its advantage was that unlike daguerrotypes, more than one print could be made from the original negative.

Silhouettes, after the French Minister of Finance in 1759, Etienne de Silhouette, were sometimes photographs of only two tones, black and white, showing the participents against a light background.

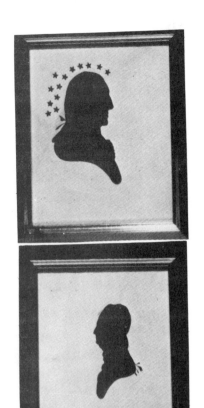

Silhouette artists were noted personalities in their field. Amongst them, A. Edouart, whose works, similar to these, sold at a 1992 estate auction for $240 to $450.

During the 19th century silhouettes reached a peak of popularity. They were divorced from photography at times by being scissored from dark material and mounted on a white background or by having profiles filled in by brushwork.

One of the big names, if not the biggest, in photography was and is Kodak. They knew an eye catching photograph when they saw one, and promptly used this one as a window display poster. The vendor also knew and priced it at $100.

To: Jean,
With Sincere Best Wishes, The USAF Thunderbirds

The United States Air Force Thunderbirds made dramatic photography at any time. This one with autographs of the flight leaders was a $25 show offering.

DAGUERROTYPES

In 1829, one Joseph Niepce entered into partnership with Louis Daguerre. Both had been experimenting, trying to make a camera's image permanent.

After Niepce's death, Daguerre, with Niepce's son, continued the experiments until, in 1839, they had perfected a process, named after Daguerre, 'daguerreotype'. A silver plated, polished, copper plate, exposed to iodine vapors, would create a layer of silver iodide that was photosensitive. Placed in a darkened box with a small, covered hole in one side, a 'camera obscura', the plate would be exposed to light by removing the lens cover.

Developed by exposing the plate to mercury fumes. The finished daguerretype had no grain, resulting in an almost perfect image.

It aided in the rapid development of portraiture as a business. Its major flaw was yet to be worked out. There was no way to make multiple prints from any one exposure. One plate, one print.

That was the peak of photographic development until Talbot's invention of the more convenient coated paper film that could be used to produce negatives and positives in unlimited quantities.

PHOTOGRAPHY

Prices:

Abernathy's Dry Goods and Groceries, Johnston, Iowa - $65

Alaska gold rush, unmounted albumen, Seward Street in Juneau, by LaRoche - $35

Alice in Wonderland, 1900, mounted albumen photo of cast for play in costume - $20

Ansel Adams, (6) Andrew Faninger (2) booklets - $45

Apollo Moon Photograph, Kodak copies of original photos taken on moon, five different - $90

Architectural (32) c.1900, ruins, buildings, European, professional - $29

Artillery Private, Indian Wars, cabinet photograph by Stanton, Fort Wayne, Indiana - $18

Bandsmen, c.1870, tintype, two bandsmen in uniform with band instruments - $32.50

Bandsmen, Parkman, Ohio Buckeye Band, 22 in uniform - $36

Benny, Jack, 1938, autopen signature - $6

Blacks, c.1900, five blacks well dressed - $18

Brass Band, 1918, Franklin Brass Band standing in snow - $18

Buzz Aldrin, eight by ten, NASA color photograph of Apollo II, signed and inscribed by Aldrin next to rocket - $85

Circus (3) 1890s, Campbell Brothers Circus, eating, posing, blacksmith shop - $55

Dina Merrill, 20th century actress, signed - $20

Early Bicyclists, cabinet photograph, two dandies with bikes, Pennsylvania photographer - $18

Early Farm Steam Tractor, eight by ten, mounted albumen photograph - $25

Egyptian Couriers, 1870s, albumen, two Egyptian men in native costume - $40

Execution of Namoa pirates, eight by ten, mounted albumen photograph, 1891 - $85

Float as a blacksmith, by Green in Richland, Iowa - $45

George Washington Bridge, Hudson River, New York, Margaret Bourke-White, c.1930 - $28,600
    Well, you can always ask

Indian Wars, cabinet photograph, officer in dress uniform with sword, Peterboro Cavalry, 1883 - $30

Jack Armstrong on Horse, from Blackstar, and your radio friend J.A. - $35

John Philip Sousa, sepia matte, signature, dated 1910, half length pose - $275

Linberg, Charles, (2) unpublished, unmounted, sepia. Lindberg in jacket by plane, with photographers around Spirit of St. Louis, while man speaks with Lindberg in cockpit; marked on back, 'in Panama' - $150 both

Market Place, York, England, 1870s, albumen print of English Street - $75

Medical, cabinet photograph, c.1890, nurse in uniform holding cup and medicine bottle - $30

Mickey Rooney, signature, with Judy Garland - $10

Midget, cabinet photograph, c.1890, Major Alom, age 25, Image by Eisenmen, New York - $15

Midget, c.1880, cabinet photograph, Miss Jenny Quigly, signed - $32.50

Military Group, 40 men in Uniform with swords by 21 man military band, and 45 star flag, by Schumacher - $100

Mining, (3) silver prints, 1880-1890, French or North African mine scenes - $45 lot

Mondrian, Andre Kertesz - $6600

Motion, (2) 1919, man smoking cigar, moves in and out when photograph is bent - $8 each

Nashville Evening Tennessean, August 16, 1935, Front page photographs of Will Rogers and Wiley post, 'Killed as plane crashes in Alaska fog' - $65

Nazi (6) on back, 'Official Photographer, A.H., Polish Campaigne, 1939 - $75

New York World's Fair, 1939, 360 in envelope Neill Armstrong, eight by ten color, NASA, of Neill in space suit with moon behind him - $150

101 ranch, mounted albumen, of J.H. Kent and his parade Civil War private, cabinet photograph, by Hill, Monroe Michigan - $75

101 Ranch, printed photo card, Tex Cooper with beaded vest, two mailing advertisements, page from show, all 101 ranch - $40 all

Railroad Yard, Warsaw, Indiana, engine, tower, and workers - $15

San Antonio Flood (4) 1900, four views of flood stage - $20

San Antonio, Texas, (3) c.1900, Alamo and street views, albumen - $25 all

Soldier, 1880, cabinet photograph, Lowell, Massachusetts Sergeant in uniform, grey, of 1840, non-commission sword, Mint - $25

Spanish-American War, cabinet photograph, trooper in full field uniform - $12

Steam Engine, largest ever made, Union Pacific, Chicago, Illinois - $20

Stereoviews, Spanish-American War, (3) Mint - $15

Stereoviews (3) cowboys at Sherman Ranch - $15
Stereoview early flat mount albumen, young Indian boy with bow and arrow - $12
Stoker, in front of three boilers and furnace, albumen, photograph, c.1880 - $10
Texas Fishing Club, c.1900, (11) unmounted albumen photographs, club at Arkansas Pass, Sport, Texas - $35
Texas Pioneer, Lincoln S. Conner, 1870 - $50
Texas Rangers, 1910 - $25
Thumbnail Tintype, soldier in frock coat, Indian Wars - $20
The Deadwood Dandies, cowboy photograph, c.1890 - $10
Thrown Steer, albumen photograph, two cowboys, early image - $25
The Sikorsky S-42, Margaret Bourke-White, c.1930 - $14,300
The Redwoods, Bull Creek Flat, Ansel Adams, Northern California, gelatin silver print, 1960 - $7150
Texas Ranch, (6) Ranch scenes - $50 all
Tintype, man in hat with colt - $18
Tintype, David Smails, another of this daughter Ella - $20
Tintype, Civil War soldier wearing great coat, officers sword and pistol. From Zanesville, Ohio - $150
Twins, c.1880s, cabinet photograph, mother, father, Siamese twins - $40
Untitled (Doll in Cobwebs), Frederick Sommer - $6050
UPI Wire Photographs, (4) the assassination of President Kennedy, Mrs. Kennedy's scramble to help after her husband is shot. With two paper lots - $250
Untitled Rayogram (Leaf With Holes), Man Ray, c.1928 - $4675
United States warship sunk in Havana harbor, February 15, 1898 - $10
Vanities, International Yacht Races, Margaret Bourke-White - $9350
Whatchamacallit, c.1925 photograph of home-made snowmobile - $11
WWII Ariel Aviation shots, (450) chloride photographs of various parts of Europe dated 1944-1945 - $300 lot
WWII documentary album of Okinowa by a serviceman - $35

Magazines:

History of Photography, 249 Materials Research Library, Pennsylvania State University 16802, Phone: 814-865-9395, Professor H.K. Henisch, Editor.

Stereo World, The National Stereoscopic Association, P.O. Box 14801, Dept. AC, Columbus, OH 43214

Museums:

Photographic Archives, University of Louisville Libraries, Ekstrom Library, Louisville, KY 40292, Phone: 502-588-6752, David G. Horvath, Curator

Photographic Archives, Special Collections, M.I. King Library North, Lexington, KY 40506, Phone: 606-257-8634, William J. Marshall, Assistant Director

The Daguerrean Society, Inc., 7618 Willow Point Drive, Falls Church, Virginia 22042, Mary Livingston, Secretary

Associations:

American Photography Historical Society 520 West 44th Street, New York, NY 10036, Phone: 212-594-5056, George Gilbert

Stereo Photographers, Collectors, and Enthusiasts Club, P.O. Box 2368, Culver City, California 90231, Phone: 213-837-2368, David Starkman, Technical Director

International Photographic Historical Organization, P.O. Box 16074, San Francisco, CA 94116, Phone: 415-681-4356, David F. Silver, President and Secretary

National Stereoscopic Association, P.O. Box 14801, Columbus, OH 43214, Phone: 614-263-4296, John Weiler, Secretary

BOOKS:

Reality Recorded: Early Documentary Photography, Gail Buckland, New York Graphic Society, 1974.

The History of Photography, Beaumont Newhall, Museum of Modern Art, New York and New York Graphic Society, Greenwich, CT 1964

CHAPTER XII

POSTCARDS

Postcard collectors are a different breed. They may be the only collectors, aside from auction bidders, who require chairs. A postcard vendor at a collectible show is known from a distance. All his customers may be sitting down. Unhurried, serious, each one knowing that somewhere in the hundreds of categorized boxes, and thousands of postcards before them, are the few they need to complete a series, or start a new one. Time has less meaning to a postcard collector.

Deep within him lies the knowledge that there is nothing within the ream upon ream of government regulations that says he himself cannot print his own postcards - providing the sender uses legal postage stamps.

Why should he? Today there are thousands of publishers printing more thousands of chromes and real photograph postcards. Isn't he better off with his chair at a vendor's table, selecting what he likes for a collection, rather than have the headaches of having to dream of new scenes to print?

After all, the first copyright for an American postcard was issued to John P. Charlton of Philadelphia, Pennsylvania in 1861. With only a few of those to be found maybe the collector will be the lucky one. Or perhaps he'll find one of the first government postals issued by the United States on May 13, 1873. Or the first exposition cards of the Industrial Exposition in Chicago or the Industrial Exposition of Providence, Rhode Island of that same year.

Possibly he'll settle for the souvenirs from the Chicago World's Fair of 1893 - full color postcards which were mistaken by many as the first picture postcard.

The first picture postcard was born in 1869, with a Dr. Emanuel Herrmann as parent and the Austrian post office as midwife. As a postcard, it was plain, thin, and buff colored, marked Correspondent-Carte over an emblem of Austrian authority. There is another claim that the first picture postcard was offered for sale in Germany in 1870. It was closely followed by one by an Oldenburg printer named Schwartz, who printed a soldier and a cannon on a government issue postcard.

It was 1898 though, July 1, 1898, that marked the beginnings of American postcard history. On that date publishers and printers were set for production of privately printed cards authorized previously on May 19th.

Postcard collectors can always take the time to look at postcards, even those they have just bought.

POSTCARDS

A postcard dealer knew how to merchandise his cards as these display boards prove.

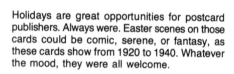

Holidays are great opportunities for postcard publishers. Always were. Easter scenes on those cards could be comic, serene, or fantasy, as these cards show from 1920 to 1940. Whatever the mood, they were all welcome.

The deluge has never stopped. Did Armstrong send a postcard from the moon headed 'one giant step for mankind'? If not, why not? Every conceivable event or location has been honored on a postcard previous to that fateful step.

Can anyone think of a subject, a category that has not been viewed on a postcard? Hand colored, photographed, or embroidered?

The Johnson and Wales Culinary Archives and Museum in Providence, Rhode Island, numbers among their outrageously numerous collections, 16,000 postcards, featuring hotels, motels, restaurants, and diners. There is a postcard collector's club that collects only railroad and transportation cards and another that specializes in covered bridges.

All of these descended from a melange of visiting cards, decorated envelopes, picture headed writing paper, photographic, and advertising cards. The postcard caught the public's fancy - despite objections from the few concerned with the privacy of the written word. The picture postcard stood on the paper pile of the collectibles of its past. From them it evolved.

It has been noted in almost every book on the subject, that when the postcard craze swept Europe in the late 19th and early 20th centuries, diners in Berlin's restaurants and beer halls, bought postcard from perambulating postmen, wrote their brief message thereon, and promptly mailed them in a letter box carried on the postman's back. Was delivery as efficient?

POSTCARDS

It was not only the mass of folk with only a few pennies to spend who doted on these colored bits of thin cardboard. Queen Victoria, it is claimed, was also a postcard collector. Differently from the common fold, it was noted, she had an aide collect and mount them for her.

The craze for sending postcards had come full circle, generating a new craze - collecting them. The postcard fever has, like all collectibles, escalated, faltered and escalated again. But like cartoonists Al Capp's Shmoos, it has never died. Instead it has proliferated into countless categories.

VALENTINES

Valentine postcards are the ultimate personal touch. Not as old as love, they superceded its lustful beginnings as a Roman fertility rite. Civilized to a more romantic holiday form, it took its place on a picture postcard with enthusiasm.

In 1840, England's revised postal system enabled postcard senders to mail valentines at a uniform, low rate. This increased the demand, leading to increased commercial production. This in turn reduced the number of hand colored, home-made valentines which lingers today mostly among pre-school and kindergarten children each February 14th.

Why that particular date? St. Valentines Day is what survives of the Roman festival, Lupercalia, where yound men drew lots for the names of young women and paired off.

A Roman Bishop, Valentinus, was clubbed to death during one Lupercalia celebration. With sainthood obtained, the early Christian Church substituted St. Valentine's name for the pagan celebration. The ceremony became more gentle, less lustful, so much so that flowers and candy replaced the rape and assault as more civilized adjuncts to the Valentine postcard.

The boom in postcard production during the early 1900s, promoted the concept of sending valentines to friends and family as well as lovers. One result of this was the use of children, cupids, and verse on valentines of all types.

Most collectors of American postcard valentines seek those printed between 1900 and 1920. After that period postcards had one of their out-of-favor lapses as valentines in envelopes took precedence.

Valentine postcards are surely not as old as love, but their romance lingers as a remarkable collectible.

Christmas postcards from Germany, c.1920,
featured realism as well as fantasy.

CHRISTMAS POSTCARDS

Right up there with the Valentines are the Victorian Christmas cards in popularity. When in 1898, the government allowed private production of postcards, the Christmas season was not neglected. Popular then and equally popular now among collectors, publishers are using these same Victorian prints in reproductions. Since they are being reproduced as current Christmas cards complete with matching envelopes, the thought of these being passed on as originals is minimal.

The first Christmas card was designed by J.C. Horsley in 1843. Rare it is, but equally rare in its spelling - clearly reading, 'Xmasse 1843'.

It was Germany that introduced a startling array of color on postcards when, as the 20th century dawned, millions of these brilliant cards arrived on the market. Christmas were amongst them.

POSTCARDS

Again, as with Valentines, children were not neglected. Children's artist, Kate Greenway's characters decorated many of these cards.

Victorian Christmas cards for children included such concepts as an idealized anthropology that pictured animals and insects dressed as humans.

Insects for Christmas? The collector can view his collection of these cards and wonder what the artist or the publisher was thinking when between them, they printed this type card.

Manhatten from New York's harbor, a cereal advertisment from Niagra Falls, and a country store all made an appearance on postcards from c.1940.

THANKSGIVING POSTCARDS

Perrenial favorites, thanksgiving cards are abundant, therefore, low in price. These postcards sharing with us our mythological heritage, offer collectors topical cards often enhanced with attached figures.

These attachments were commonly of brass or silver colored turkeys or pilgrims. Some were obviously placed on the card by the publisher, for they belong to the imprinted scene. Others appear to be after thoughts of the retailer or the sender. A few are known with attached feathers adorning a card imprinted turkey. All of these seem to predate 1910.

A model railroad train collector used postcards
with railroad themes as an attractive add-to for
his train collection. Courtesy Robert DeLorenzo.

A single postcard with a fold out section in the
center was a different postcard for a vacationer
to main home. Courtesy L.H. Mallin.

Embroidered postcards, displayed on boxes of
other cards were attractively priced at $5 to $25
by the dealer who offered this grouping.

WEIRD AND WONDERFUL, WACKY AND WILD POSTCARDS OF THE PAST

At one time, from the 1920s back to the Victorian age of the late 19th century, anything could be put on a postcard. Witness the feathers and medallions on Thanksgiving cards. Some cards were slotted so heads or hands could be moved. It was left to the British publisher 'Tuck' to head the listing of the most prolific and wildest.

Forget turkey feathers. Tuck put plumes that rose above the card on his birds. Animals sported furry tails that hung far below the postcard's edge. He sought the heights when he pasted a gramophone record on a postcard and expected the British Postal authorities to deliver it for the ha' penny postal rate. Whether this was the final straw or not, soon after, the British authorities devised new regulations concerning postcards that effectively ended the flow of the imaginative Tuck postcards.

Embroidered products came within the regulations both in Britain and here in the States. While some were the result of skilled Victorian ladies, most were the product of the many publishers of the time.

Think of the postcard as the pattern for a piece of needlepoint. The designs filled and edged with colorful threads in intricate stitching. Today, these conceits cost between $5 and $25 for a card.

More expensive to the collector, would be the hold-to-light postcards. These are die-cut cards with colored glaze work behind the cut-outs. When held up to a light source, the die-cut sections appear illuminated, as the windows of a home would be if the lights were on inside.

Similar to these would be the transparencies, postcards which when held to a light source, would reveal another picture hidden within the sandwiched layers of the card. Of the two, hold-to-light, die-cuts or transparencies, the die-cuts are more valuable, with an average of $50 that can rapidly escalate to $500. Especially if the hold-to-light card pictures a Santa Claus.

At the turn of the century, an Art Nouveau postcard by Alphonse Mucha, signed by the artist (another 'most valuable') was placed in an auction. Mucha, a famed, French poster artist of the times, occasionally turned his talents to postcard design. At a time when the dollar had a real value, the postcard at the auction was sold for $13,600. That auction record for a postcard still stands.

There is a story, sworn to as true, of a young girl in the early 1930s making breakfast pancakes for her carpenter father.

She forgot two things - to use baking powder in the batter and to watch what she was doing. The father claimed that first pancake looked like and had the texture of the roofing shingles he was installing that day.

As a family in-joke he kept the pancake. Eventually, he trimmed it to postcard size, glued on a Thanksgiving paper turkey, a stamp, and address on the reverse, and mailed it to Grandfather. It was delivered.

Grandfather replaced the turkey with a Santa, added a new stamp and address, and mailed it back. The claim is that it went back and forth four times in the next two years. Eventually it disappeared.

The family has a question. Is there a postcard collector out there who owns a pancake postcard that looks like a roofing shingle? They'd love to have it back.

Prices:

Adironack mountains (4) early 1900s, deer hunting - $10
Andy Warhol, signed color, reproduction of his Campbell Soup Cans - $395
Arizona Bill, photograph postcard, scout with 5th Cavalry - $50
Aviation, #23, Ezra Meeker Aviation Meet, Los Angeles, California, 1910 - $10
Aviation, airship, Toledo #1 (lighter than air) - $15
Balboa, Canal Zone (24) 1900s, published by J.J. Maduro, VG - $10
Balloon Races at Indiana Speedway, c.1920, #90 - $15
Barnum and Bailey's Circus (4) two from Warsaw, Poland, 1901, two of Jordon sisters and Marguerite and Hanley, 1908 - $15
Baseball (2) c.1920, National League Baseball Park, Toledo, Ohio - $11.50 both
Brotherhood of Locomotive, Fireman, and Engineers (4) c.1900, fraternal, unused, locomotive, with two men shaking hands - $20 each
Buffalo, New York (9) 1905 - $9
Cabinet photo of Big Tree on display at Columbian Exposition - $10
Century of Progress (5) 1932 - $9
Chang Kai Shek, black and white, signed, bust pose in uniform - $395

POSTCARDS

Charlie Chaplin, publisher B.C. Macter, 1916 - $50
Child's Goat Cart, real photo, young girl in cart, 1934, Boston - $11
Colorado Cowboys, tinted, Denver - $8
CPS Malcolm steamship (9) 1920s, including four other steamships - $38
Deadwood Dick, real photo, in buckskins, holding rifle - $10
Fire Department (9) most recent dated 1916, some horsedrawn equipment - $36
Firestone Tires, 1939 - $5
Fish embroidered card, Fine - $25
Flood, real photo, people in doorway watching flood waters in Main Street - $13
Ford exhibit, Cycle of Progress, 1939 - $5
Ford Motor Company advertising lot (60) - $45
Graf Zeppelin, picture postcard, postmarked, Stuttgart, 1933 - $15
Hog butchering, real photo, used, at Montrose, Iowa, 1914 - $7
Hold-to-light card, Victorian house - $50
Hummel by Emil Fink, Stuttgart (9) one dated 1934, eight colored cards unused - $30
Indian, Native American, real photo - $5
Indy Speedway, 1935, track shows trees in infield - $10
Jack Dempsey, sepia, early boxing pose, signed and inscribed - $85
Lake George, New York (10) 1900s - $20
Leather postcards (17) postmarked - $3 each
Lone Ranger, Gimbals at the New York World's Fair - $10
Marilyn Monroe in Bus Stop, French version - $15
Marines (7) comic 1943 - $10
Mercedes Benz (8) 1956, unused, six color, two black and white - $36
Modern chrome (100) different - $20
Moving wheel, Christmas - $2
New York Highlander Baseball Team, Fair - $50
Old West/mining, armed men, stage coach, horses 1903 - $10
President Calvin Coolidge, real photo, tending his garden, VG - $20
Rochester, New York (14) early 1900s - $20
Schlitz Palm Garden, Milwaukee, interior, early view - $20
Statue of Liberty, Hold-to-light, 1986 - $6.95
Tennis (9) 1910/1920 - $11 all
Tupper Lake, New York (12) early 1900s - $20
Transparency, woman with hidden mirror - $35
Vaudeville, real photo, c.1920, Singers - Piccolo Company - $15
WWI (3) real photo, Prussian soldierson KP, and medical corpsmen 1915 - $20
WWII (12) comic - $10
Yellowstone National Park (100) by Haynes, numbers 10072 through 25150 VG - $35

Associations:

Postal Card Society of America, United Postal Stationary Society, P.O. Box 48, Redlands, CA 92373, JoAnn Thomas, Executive Secretary.

Post Card Collectors Club: International Rail Road and Transportation, P.O. Box 6782, Providence, RI 02940. William S. Diefenbach, President. Phone: 203-637-2801.

Deltiologists of America, P.O. Box 8, Norwood, PA 19074. James L. Lowe, Director. Phone: 215-485-8572.

Organization for Collectors of Covered Bridge Post Cards, care of Kay Lloyd, Seven Squantum Street, Milton, MA 02186. Phone: 617-698-9025.

POSTCARDS

Mail Auctions:

Antique Paper Guild, P.O. Box 5742, Bellevue, Washington 98006. Bob Ward

The First National Post Card Auction, Post Cards International, P.O. Box 2930, New Haven, CT 06515-0030. Phone: 203-865-0814

Ronald D. Millard, Cherryland Auctions, P.O. Box 4086, Tequesta, FL 33469. Phone: 407-743-0010

Museums:

Printers Row Printing Museum, 715 S. Dearborn Street, Chicago, IL 60605, Phone: 312-987-1059

Collections:

Johnson and Wales Culinary Archives and Museum, Providence, RI, Barbara Kuch, Curator, Phone: 401-455-2805

Books:

Post Marks on Post Cards, LaPosta Publications, P.O. Box 135, Lake Oswego, OR 97034

The Picture Post Card and It's Origin, Frank Staff, Frederick A. Praeger, Publishers, NY 1966

The History of the Christmas Card, George Buday, Rockcliff, 1954

A History of Valentines, Ruth Webb Lee, Batsford, 1953

Greetings From Oregon, Gideon Bosker and Jonathan Nickolas, Graphics Art Center Publishing, OR 1987

Magazines:

Barr's PostCard News, 70 South Sixth Street, Lansing, IA 52151. Bill Cote, Editor. Phone: 319-538-4500.

Postcard Art - Postcard Fiction, 143 McGuinness Boulevard, Brooklyn, New York 11222. Martha Rosler, Editor and Publisher. Phone: 718-383-2277

Postcard Classics - Deltiologists of America, P.O. Box 8, Norwood, PA 19074. James Louis Lowe, Editor. Phone: 215-485-8572

Post Card Collector, Joe Jones Publishing, 121 North Main Street, P.O. Box 337, Iola, WI 54945

Post Card History Society, care of John H. McClintock, Editor, P.O. Box 1765, Manassas, VA 22110, Phone: 703-368-2757

Greetings Magazine, 309 Fifth Ave., New York, NY 10016

Picture Post Card Monthly, Reflections of a Bygone Age, 15 Debdale Ln., Keyworth, Nottingham, NG12 5HT, England, Phone: 06077-4079

CHAPTER XIII

MAPS, CALENDARS, PRINTS

There must be as many kinds of maps as there are adjectives to describe them. They speak of time and travel, of distance and exploration, of fair lands and far places, of doorways and windows into a past rich with history.

There is the agricultural map that shows soil qualities and types in underlating, free from patches of varying colors. There is the antique map, drawn before we knew of latitude and longitudes - maps drawn with the capitol of a state or kingdom as ground zero from which all distances were measured.

There are military maps as important in 1777 for General George Washington in his campaigns against the British as they were in the 1940s when the Army Map Service and the Navy Hydrographic Office joined with civilian map makers to fight another war.

The map that makes one dream the most are the antique maps, where blank spaces, unexplored areas, are filled with words to tantalize, "Here be Demons". If the blue of the oceans became too bland, sea monsters appeared that rivaled the dinosaurs in frightfulness. With our current technologies, we spew out enough maps to smother those ancient sea monsters.

In a typical year, Rand McNally sells about four hundred million maps. The company is just one civilian map maker. The United States Government supports 39 federal agencies producing more millions of maps - collectibles of the future. A far cry from the days when maps were the perogative of the government or the well-to-do and were drawn for them by a local or regional artist.

Incredible amounts of information crowd these old maps along with the sea serpents and the gods and goddesses of the winds.

The most appealing of old maps are the hand colored engravings of master printmakers. They were rare even when new.

Information was a viable, secretive commodity as far back as the age of Phoenicians and their sea routes. They invented sea serpents as a protective cover for these same routes to scare off susceptible sea farers of other nations. The Portugese Monarch, Henry the Navigator, made state secrets of his sea routes to the then fabled lands of silk and spices during the 15th century. Maps were secrets protected by the lives of those who used them.

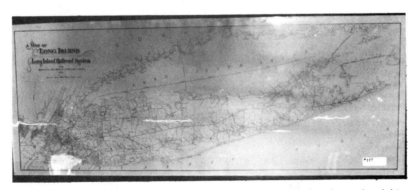

If maps could talk. This one, as difficult to read in this photograph as it was the night it hung in the dimly lit Amagansett (NY) railroad waiting room, is the same map the German saboteurs tried to read that night in the 1940s when a submarine landed them on a Long Island (NY) beach. The bidding at a railroad memorabilia auction for this tid-bit of history ended at $375

Maps are small scale or large scale, richly varied.
They picture the streets, theatres, or piers of a
waterfront metropolis, or the perimeters of a
sporting club.

MAPS

Whether ancient or merely decades old, maps will always have a market, even though they have a tendency to be trendy. As a collectible they have not reached their full potential. Too many are bought because something with a lot of yellow is needed to match a sofa.

Yet all maps have a historical value. All nationalities are intrigued by their sense of history.

They span the centuries from the clay tablets of Mesopatamia, the rectangular grids of the Chinese about 550 B.C., through Eratosthenos of Alexandria who measured the circumference of the earth about the third century B.C., with an accuracy that is still amazing.

The first map drawn, printed, and published in America was by John Foster of Boston. The first printmaker in the Colonies. It was a woodcut, done in 1677, of New England. Benjamin Franklin, among his other skills, was also a map-maker, printing one in 1733 of the Maryland and Pennsylvania borders.

Maps have played an important roll in our society ever since as sources of information about endless topics, a colorful form of a paper computer storing information in thousands of bits and pieces.

Maps are tranquilizers. Try stretching out on the floor to read a map, feel the body relax, the stress drain away as dreams of far shores intrude. Map collectors are fortunate. Their dreams are all about them on the walls and on their book shelves in a form called an atlas.

Maps are also difficult to unroll if not stored properly.

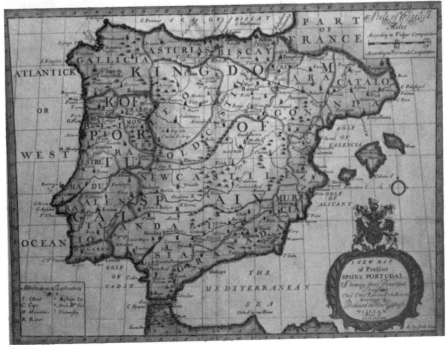

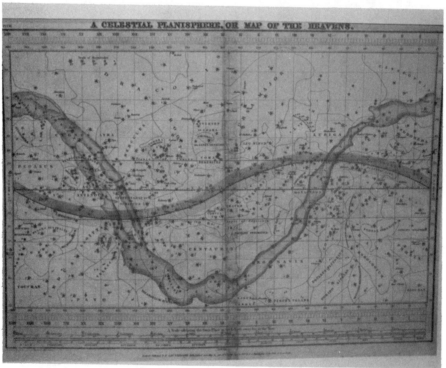

Maps of a continent, a river system, an archipelago, or countries that no longer exist by an old name, may be found in atlases old or new. Or a star map for a future voyager.

ATLASES

Atlas was the Greek mythological giant who held up the world. An atlas currently is any collection of maps between covers - paper or board.

Anything that may be noted on a map may be represented in an atlas such as business, census, county, geological, history, oceans, waterways, utilities, wildlife, the list is endless.

To keep up with change in place names (people often become rabid in the pro and con of their beliefs about name changes) requires changing almost 1,000 place names a year. In 1992 a bill before the New York State legislature was being opposed over changing the name of Wildwood State Park to that of Governor Al Smith State Park. The breakup of the Soviet Union may double or triple the number of name changes for 1993.

Of all the books put up for sale at auction, the atlas generates the most enthusiasm among bidders. Rarely does a dealer let one get away from him to find a home with a casual bidder.

AUDUBON PRINTS

An 1827 edition of John James Audubon's Bird's of America, would be the single most valuable edition that many bird print collectors could hope to find.

An elephant folio, almost three foot tall, four volume set of Birds of America, containing 435 prints, sold at auction in 1977 for $396,000. A single print from an identical folio showed up on a dealers table in a Hartford, Connecticut show in 1991, priced at $4,000. Multiply that by the 435 prints in the four volume set and you arrrive at $1,740,000. That's a telephone number investment.

Why? Why should the price of colored plates supposedly drawn by one man cause such a flurry of money on the market?

John James Audubon, born 1785 in Haiti of a French Admiral and a native Creole, spent fifteen years wandering American wilderness areas in search of birds. He did not draw from life, instead mounted their cold bodies into position, then drew and colored the results. Background was often the work of others.

Unable to find a publisher in the States he took his drawings to England where they caused a sensation. There, in 1826, Audubon arranged for his paintings of birds to be made into book form. It emerged, printed on double elephant folio paper, about 26½" by 39½", with a total of 435 plates. All birds were shown life size which would explain the size of the printed pages. It is thought that no more than 200 sets were printed with a total price for each set of $1,000.

A critical look at these paintings reveals Audubon's use of artistic license in sometimes posing his birds in impossible positions.

A reprint in the double elephant size was made in chromolithograph form from the original copper plates by Julius Bien, in New York. It was evidently a long drawn out process, interrupted by the Civil War, as the years between 1850 and 1868 are quoted as the time used in completing the reissue.

Audubon released a smaller edition, 1841/1844, in seven volumes of which the first edition was hand colored.

In 1845/1848, he produced a three volume set of North American Quadrupeds with John Bachman as a collaborator. In 1849, 1851, and 1854, he again issued a three volume set of North American Quadrupeds, this time without a collaborator, although his two sons, Victor Gifford and John Woodhouse, are known to have done serious work on his last three sets of books.

Few artists retain Audubon's visibility almost two hundred years after their birth. Few artists can claim his fame.

Audubon is not well known for his animal paintings. It was birds and his artful rendition of their colors and habitats that made him famous. Not all his paintings of birds were as natural as these three.

Apples and pears and stone fruits, herbs or
flowers, the salesmen of trees and shrubs and
flowers used hand drawn colored plates as a
merchandising tool. They were most popular in
the 1870s and 1880s here and in Europe.

127

BOTANICALS

One hundred years ago it was not only doctors who made house calls, so did the fish monger, the tinker, the eyeglass man, and the tree peddler. The tree peddler would take out his sales tool, a flip chart of hand drawn color plates, showing water colors of fruit trees, ornaments, and possibly a new flower or two.

The set of plates, popular in the 1870s and 1890s, were not unusual in context, only in their use as a commercial selling tool. It had proud forebears.

In 1768 Captain Cook made his first around the world voyage, taking with him Joseph Banks, scientist and naturalist, and a party of ten naturalists and illustrators. Four survived. The rest died leaving as their legacies, colored drawings of 3,000 plants, one third new to science.

Bound into books, the engravings were individually hand colored, a time consuming task.

No slower, however, than the slow accumulation of medical knowledge, which was helped along its way by these books of plant engravings. Until the 1400s, medical knowledge, which of necessity was largely of the virtues of plants, was passed on by word of mouth or from the few copies available of the early Greek and Roman manuscripts.

The invention of the printing press, and the accurate renderings of plants and herbs by artists such as Leonardi da Vinci and his contemporaries, made possible the wider distribution of illustrated books of plants and flowers.

Called 'herbals' the illustrations between its boards are todays collectible, botanical prints.

CALENDARS

To some folk a calendar is a system for keeping track of the days, the dates of holidays and anniversaries, or phases of the moon. Or the date the mortgage is due.

To collectors, some more sober minded than others, calendars are prints. To casual viewers these prints appear as collections posted mainly on the walls of gas stations or automotive garages.

They may have a point. The most popular calendar of all times seems to be those from the 1940s and 1950s when Petty and Vargas were at their peak as calendar artists. Look closely at one of their ladies. The legs are out of proportion and too long. That was a trick to fool the eye they worked out that was eminently successful. It made the ladies more sensual. Today it makes them more collectible.

Calendars sometimes seem only to picture good looking women. It's not true. Calendars may sometimes illuminate major maternal event: consider this one of the Dionne quintuplets in 1937.

Calendars are a major advertising tool. Low in cost to the advertiser delivering their message 365 days a year, as proved by this 1926 sporting calendar.

A map of New Jersey from 1795 shows the same border outlines we know today. But look at those blank spaces, now filled with crowded suburbs.

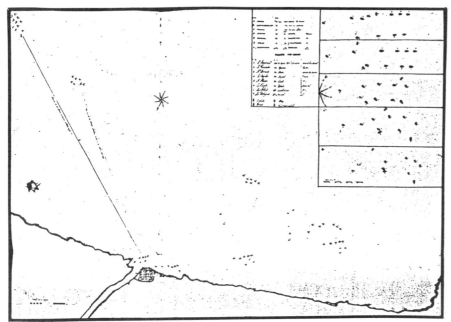

Autographs overlap with maps? Why not? The photograph is of a logbook on board H.M.S. Donegal, commanded by Sir Poulteney Malcolm, May 29, 1805/March 11, 1806. The hand drawn map in the logbook details the names of ships and captains, describing a naval battle between the French and British during the Napoleonic Wars. Priced in 1976 at $1,850. K. Rendell.

There are those who like trains in any form and their number is numerous.

Then there are those whose appetites are more refined, who wouldn't think twice before buying this advertising calendar of 1915 vintage for its twelve and one half dollar asking price. Notice how proudly J. Goodsir was of this Bell Telephone connection.

MAPS

Prices:

John Speed - A Map of Virginia and Maryland, 1676, 12" by 18" - $825
Birds eye map of early Paris Center - $50
18th century map of Susses, colored, (Jansen-Amsterdam) - $100
Early map of Roman Empire, colored - $60
18th century French map of Ottoman Empire - $90
Early map of Northumberland -$125
Early map of Orient (India, China, Japan, etc.) - $1,200
Sand Grouse print, no other information - $25
Pair of decorative botanical prints - $30
Two pictorial maps of Long Island - $140
Print by William Sydney Mount - $30
Pair of monkey prints - $30
Colored lithograph of pears, late 19C - $85
Orange Lilium croentom, hand colored engraving from Hortus Eystellensis, 1613 - $4,500
Map of England and Wales, 1823, hand colored - $70
Audubon elephant litho by Bien, 1860 - $850
Chart of the Whaling Islands of Maderas and the Canary's, 1794 - $235
Vargas calendar, 1948 - $100
Multicolored lithograph after John Gould Cacatua Eos - $85
Map of the Americas, original, 1746 - $650

Books:

Audubon and His Journals, Maria R. Audubon, Dover (reprint) 1986. Originally published by Scribner, New York, 1897

Old American Prints for Collectors, John and Katherine Ebat, Charles Scribner's Sons, 1974, NY

The Story of Maps, Lloyd A. Brown, Little Brown and Co. 1949.

The Book of Calendars: Facts on File 1982, Frank Parise, Editor

John James Audubon, John Burroughs, *Overlook (reprint) 1987. First published 1902.*

Clubs and Associations:

Print Club, 1614 Latimer Street, Philadelphia, PA 19103, phone 215-735-6090.

American Historical Print Collector's Society, P.O. Box 1532, Fairfield, CT 06430, Phone: 914-795-5266, Sec. William F. Stickle

Print Council of America, care of The Baltimore Museum of Art, Art Museum Drive, Baltimore, MD 21218, Phone: 301-396-6345

COLLECTIONS:

Audubon prints: New York Historical Society of New York City.

Maps: Library of Congress, Alexandria, Virginia, 22304.

New York Public Library, New York, New York, 10018

U.S. Military Academy, West Point, New York

Auburn University, Auburn, Alabama, 36830, Phone: 205-826-4500.

Arizona Historical Society, East Second Street, Tucson, Arizona, 85710, Phone: 602-882-5774

University of Colorado, Guggenheim Building, Boulder, Colorado, 80302, Phone: 303-492-7578

Botanicals: Hunt Institute for Botanical Documentation, Pittsburg, PA 15213

Magazines:

Guild of Natural Sciences Illustrators, GNSI Newsletter, Washington, D.C. 20044

The Print Trader, M. Rainone, Middle Village, NY 11379

Paper and Advertising Collector, P.O. Box 500, Mount Joy, PA 17552, Phone: 717-653-4300

CHAPTER XIV

ADVERTISING

When a prostitute in ancient Rome inscribed in reverse on the bottom of her sandals, 'Follow Me', so the imprint would show in the dust or mud, a mindset was born: advertising pays, and some few of its practitioners haven't changed.

Is there anything known in this world that hasn't been used as an advertising ploy? From a crackerjack prize to a hundred foot neon sign destroying the grandeur of a peaceful river?

So many industries, companies - large or small - have used colorful, accurate, or exaggerated advertising. Movies, the circus, the arts, sporting events, television sponsors - they all use the hard sell. Soft drinks, hard liquor, tobacco, sewing companies all joined the wall and roadside poster deluge, the newspaper broadsheet, the magazine display, the cut-out, mail, package, give-a-way, or trade mark frenzy.

Does anyone know the figures? Does it seem that more money is spent on advertising each year than on the national budget? It's conceivable. But look at the bright side. Look at all those great advertising pieces to put away to be the next decades collectibles.

Scenes of yesterday, from old circus acts, minstrel shows, and rodeos, all have their enthusiasts. What will the future collectibles be? TV guides, Yugo car advertising, the original four batteries from that pink, perpetually moving rabbit?

Don't bother guessing. The changing paraphernalia of today's everyday life are what will be collected. As we now collect the ordinary mementos of the last decades, the last century.

Advertising has always been with us and barring our sun going nova, always will. Sometimes as gimmicks, sometimes as words that haunt us. The free calendar at Christmas from the local pharmacist is as important as the Gucci labeled shopping bag.

Before television, advertisers used trade cards, post cards, even playing cards to deliver their message of 'you need this', and 'buy me'. They depend on lavish color lithography or bright packaging before the word 'packing' was invented. Jingles, amusing rhymes that tended to remain in our minds. The Burma Shave jingles on roadside signs, often called 'the Commercial Mother Goose' was an advertising bonanza. They made everyone happy: the sponsor, the agency, and the motorist on a long trip.

People don't buy a product, they buy an image,
Perpetual youth, health, or innocence.

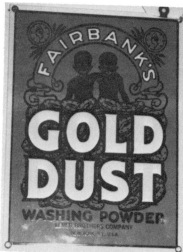

It matters not how old a brand name product is, at least one out of four of these products is imprinted on the readers mind. That's all an advertiser asks, to be imprinted.

ADVERTISING

Like sawdust covered ice cut from a pond, they too are gone. But not forever. Somewhere a collector treasures them, as other collectors horde the labels from a Chase, Isherwood and Company, Buckeye tobacco package, the paper labeled lid from a box of Cadbury chocolates, an Uncle Sam 'I Want You' poster, or a 1963 World Series Yankee year book. Advertising is not only forever, it's almost endless.

Some advertising collectibles are easy to find, like calendars or hand fans, so many were made we should be tripping over them. Others are rare. Even cereal packages from the late 1930s. Figure it. Who saved cereal packages? They went out with the daily trash but the value of a cereal package did not always lie in the graphics on its front. Puffa Puffa Rice was just another cereal in a box until you checked the back where there was the complete information on an entire series of premium rings - a serious collectible in its own right.

As this is being published, colorful advertising art created by Stetson (hats), Winchester, and Colt, and scores of lesser known companies concerned with our 'Wild West', are serious collectibles. Be aware of sex discrimination in this field. Items featuring cowgirls will sell for as much as twice the price of those featuring cowhands.

Much advertising art is passed over because we may never turn over a trade card or postcard to read the message on the back. Of those who do, fewer still will look at the back of an old photograph. What you may find on it will be decorative borders or design, along with the name and sometimes the address and the specialty of the photographer and his studio.

A name alone without an address will be the 19th century photographer's admission that he considered himself an artist. So much so that he signed his work.

A favorite for the photographer's back were cherubs, who 2,000 years ago were the bearers of genius from the gods to artists, linking photographers with artists.

Photographers and advertising were also linked in the publishing of catalogs or booklets from any conceivable type of company including food producers. Here a merger of advertising and cookbooks found its obvious target - the housewife. Some catalogs were no larger than brochures or pamphlets. Other were miniature books featuring recipes applicable to the advertisers products and the fads and foibles of the era.

As paper collectors became social historians, so advertisers perforce were aware of contemporary mores and standards of taste. Even their harshests critics today admit advertisers are close observers of society and how it moves. It shows in their advertisements, their approach.

Magazines as a vehicle for advertising developed slowly. Before 1890, most magazines were regional or local. Be 1890, with the introduction of inexpensive half tone, advertising, not news stand price, became the key factor in a magazine's profitability. By 1900 several magazines, supported by advertising, could boast of one million circulation.

By 1910, color had been introduced and advertising became a billion dollar industry.

It seems strange that so many millions, so many billions of dollars have been spent to attract the buying power of American women. Yet women are a minority at a paper collectors show. Dealers excepted - most buyers are men. Someone explained it this way, "women don't collect paper, they spend most of their lives throwing it out."

BANNERS

To the military a banner is a flag to honor or follow. The botanist knows it as the upper petal of certain flowers. The newspaper person knows it as a large type headline running across an entire page.

Only the last might interest some paper collectors. Others would tend to view banners as unfolding strips of honeycombed or die-cut paper that celebrate a holiday or an event.

With an image better known than most movie stars, Aunt Jemima touts her pancakes on a banner, with an attached price of $425.

135

When the world's of entertainment and advertising meet, striking advertisements result.

ADVERTISING

It is left to the advertising collector to define the best of all banners which are those that aimed a message to use or buy - aimed at a receptive public.

Some were of paper printed for one time use and are rare. Others were of paper backed with linen or muslin that had a longer life span. Some few others were painted on canvas.

Banners sometimes bore name recognition. A pancake give-a-way banner, 54" by 32", featured the recognizable symbol of Aunt Jemima and her pancakes. It sold at a 1991 auction for $425.

In another area of this country, in May of 1992, according to a report in *Mid Atlantic Antiques* Magazine, a rare cardboard, die-cut overhead banner, promoting 'new' Post Toasties cereal, sold at a Franklin Auction Gallery sale in Franklin, PA, for $18,000 (plus ten percent). It came from the collection of B. and J. Santaniello. It said a lot for their foresight.

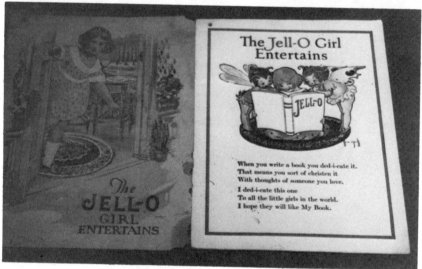

Everyone judges how best to get their message across: World's Fairs, corporations, the government, or the corner grocery store.

TRADE SIGNS

Trade sign is probably a misleading term. It brings visions of a gigantic fish, Paul Bunyan sized boots, or immense hand saws usually carved from wood which meant to distinguish the store front it enhanced from all others.

Trade symbol might be a better term for the paper collector's use. The cherubs - called putti - photographers occasionally used to distinguish themselves as artists being an eloquent example.

Trade symbols would be the elegant logos for which corporations pay king's ransoms - Cross and Blackwell or Gucci's, perhaps.

Trade symbols show best as package design. They also become more collectible.

The history of package design is a record of change in popular taste, of the variations of what the public wanted at various times.

Early package design is close to being true Folk Art. Medicine bottle labels of the late 19th and early 20th centuries were apt to show a bewhiskered gentleman, a bustle skirted lady, or a golden haired toddler, followed by a lengthy, over zealous description of the virtues of the bottle's contents. Paper mills, bakeries, or retail stores were want to show uninspired likenesses on package labels of the buildings they occupied. Collected today, they are enthusiastically described as quaint, primitive, or as true Folk Art.

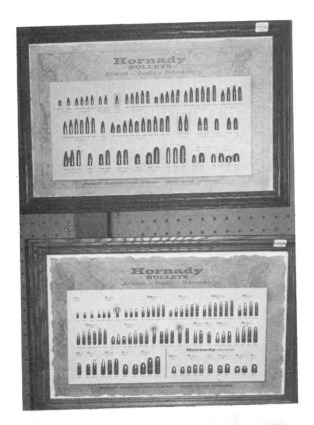

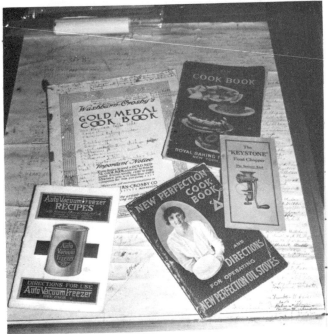

Advertisers seek to project an image, to entertain, or promote a cause. They also offer choice, a dream, or directions for preparing a meal - with their products. It isn't only Uncle Sam who points a finger to say, "I Want You".

ADVERTISING

Coffee can labels represent a serious line of paper collectibles. Trade names could be listed by the hundreds. Some of those names exist today on supermarket shelves such as Maxwell House, S.S. Pierce, Hills Brothers, Folgers and Ehler. Others disappeared leaving behind names invented with flights of fancy or just plain stodginess such as Millars Mountain Brand, Java and Mocha Swanell, Rosebud, Romeo-Walruth and Manz, Mo-Sam, Welcome Dainty, Araban, Council Cup, Glendora, and Golden Wedding. There were more - many more.

They were the early ones, used when packagers were happy to see their trade name used by the public whatever the occasion.

Times and people change, including manufacturers priorities. Packagers still like to see their names in print, but beware. Manufacturers have discovered sensitivity. If you use their names in print be sure to use a copyright symbol with it, otherwise, you collect another piece of paper - a lawyers letter.

WANTED POSTERS

The wanted poster still hangs on our post office walls. For many they are required reading, folk heroes to some few, open mouthed wonderment for others who may speculate, "wasn't that the man who asked me for directions yesterday?"

On those walls have hung the wanted posters of John Dillinger, Clyde Barrow, Bonnie Parker, and Alvin Karpis. As well known as these names are to current historians, they have never attained the mythology attached to the men who adorned the wanted posters of our Western Territories and states before and after the Civil War.

Texans may want to forget John Wesley Hardin, brave but bigoted, a quarrelsome killer. But Sam Bass? He's different.

As renowned as a train robber as was Jesse James, Sam Bass is spoken of as a hero. Most persons pictured on wanted posters were not. Not all killers and highwaymen received the accolade of a wanted poster - vigilante committees saw to that.

Among the longest surviving and most unlikely appearing desperados to make it to the wanted poster fame was Black Bart. Between 1875 and 1883 he held up twenty eight California stage coaches. After robbing the stage coach express box of its contents, he was apt to leave behind a few lines of verse.
Best known was:

I've labored long and hard for bread,
For honor and for riches,
But on my corns too long you've tred
You fine haired sons of bitches.
    Black Bart
    the Po 8

Using legwork as tirelessly as any precinct detective today, Wells Fargo Company detective, J.B. Hume, tracked down one C.E. Belton in San Francisco.

Belton, elegantly dressed, derby hatted, with a diamond stickpin and gold watch with chain, was finally identified as Black Bart, the Po 8.

Before then, in July of 1878, after robbing a Wells Fargo stage coach, Black Bart had left behind the completion of the first four lines of doggerel he had written earlier.

Here I lay me down to sleep
To nail the coming morrow.
Perhaps success, perhaps defeat
And everlasting sorrow.
I've labored long and hard for bread,
For honor and for riches,
But on my corns too long you've tred
You fine haired sons of bitches.
Let come what will, I'll try it on,
My condition can't be worse,
And if there's money in that box
It's money in my purse.
    Black Bart
    the Po 8

Human nature was no different in 1912, only the faces of those wanted for various offenses, and the amount offered as a reward. Photo by Howard Caine, Eastside Books.

OTHERS

Other categories? There is doubt that any one book could catalog all the paper advertising categories that exist. Right there is one - catalogs. Newspapers and magazine advertisements two others. The junk mail you receive that clutters up your mail box - that's a paper collectible. There's a private museum in California that specializes in just that - junk mail. At the moment, some Nabisco Foods Group advertisements, touting two hundred years of excellence have been appearing in collectible magazines. Subliminal implications? It may be implied but why not? The color and the graphics are excellent. The timetable is good: 1792-1992. Another gold mine of advertising label collectibles.

For collectors, the world is their oyster if it comes in a can with a paper label.

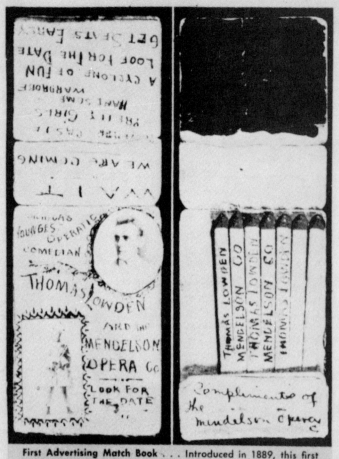

First Advertising Match Book . . . Introduced in 1889, this first book was created by the Mendelson Opera Company to sell seats to its New York opening. Manager of the troupe bought the books from Diamond; had troupe members handletter and paste pictures of the leading lady and comedian on them.

In 1889, the Mendelson Opera Company, in an attempt to sell more seats at its New York opening, bought book matches from the Diamond Match Company. The troup members hand lettered the matches and pasted photographs of the male and female leads on the covers. The result was the world's first advertising book match.

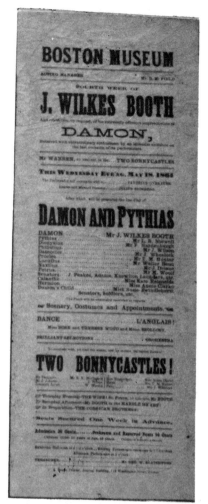

Plays in the 1860s featured actors famous in their time. Some became infamous for decades to come but were unknowingly advertised on posters aimed at those who could afford the price.

Everyone loves a circus and the circus advance men blanketed a town with posters advertising the delights to come.

Not only The Shadow knew. Advertisers such as the 'Blue Coal Company' knew the value of an entertainers name even if it was only a stage - or radio - name.

A Ballantines Beer die-cut from 1952 had been designed by Carl Paulson, a commercial artist, one of those people who drew the art work for those immense billboards that once cluttered the roadsides. This die-cut had a $100 price tag.

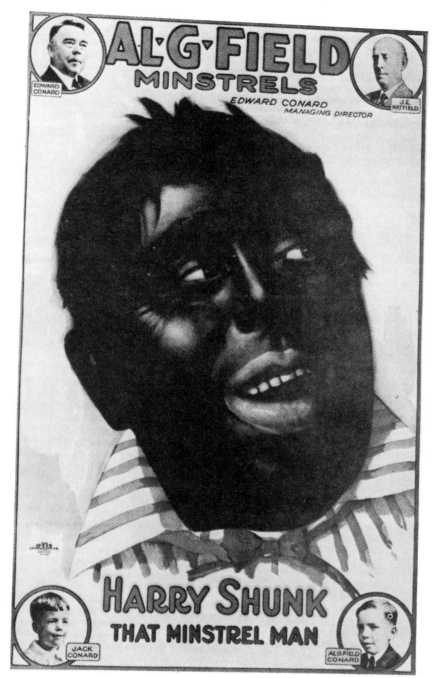

Minstrel men had their heyday during the 1800s/1900s. Posters were the accepted manner of advertising their coming appearance.

Advertising kept magazines alive, publishers solvent. It still does. But old advertising serves another purpose - it keeps collectors happy.

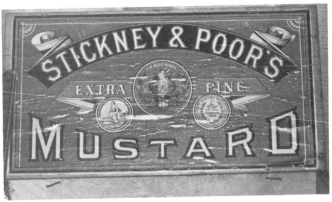

Nothing was so ordinary that it couldn't be used for advertising. The inside cover of a box could flash its message each time the box lid was opened. The latest message in 1992 said, ''I'm worth $45.''

Nothing small about this poster advertisement except its $45 price. Seven foot high and five foot wide, it boasted its 1910-1920s message to everyone nearby. Mid Atlantic Antiques Magazine.

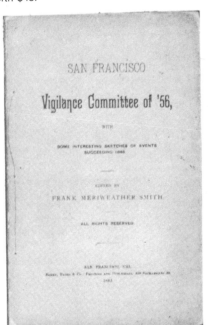

Scarce S.F. Vigilance report, Lot 343.

Some outlaws never lived long enough to warrant a wanted poster: vigilantes saw to that. Did a vigilante report make a lynching legal? This 1858 doesn't say.

The most wanted of men in the early 1900s, his name has become legendary with the passing of time. Being only a copy, not original, means this poster could be bought for a low four dollars.

Prices:

Big Band poster, 1900s, La Portes Blue Flame Ramblers Orchestra - $40

Calendar Girl, 1940s, unfolds four times for four views of bikini clad girls - $30

Gone with the Wind, c.1970, one sheet, near mint - $65

Ice Cream, orange, blue, white, for Icy Pi - $19

James Bond Moonraker, one sheet, c.1979, near mint - $49

Knoxville Tennessee World's Fair, 1982 - $25

Pancho Villa, $5000 reward, with two photographs of Villa, March 16, 1916, by Chief of Police of Columbus, NM - $1500

Wanted by the FBI, three pieces, 8"x8" side and front shots, fingerprints, description, relatives, alias, record and signature - $1200

U.S. Department of Justice, March 12, 1934, John Dillinger, with fingerprints, mug shots, criminal record, 8"x8" - $350

U.S. Department of Justice, May 21, 1934, Bonnie Parker, and Clyde Barrow, mug shots, descriptions, relatives, issued by John Edgar Hoover - $350

Howdy Doody Colgate cardboard standup - $30

Kendall Soap sign, 1875 - $100

Black and white, Harley-Davidson Motorcycle Co. Advertisements, 1910-1912 - $28

Borden's Elsie the Cow, color advertisements, 14 pieces - $48

White Rock Manufacturing, 8"x10" label, Superfine cotton, Lithograph, c.1850 - $20

Larkin Soap Box, cardboard, 7"x3" glycerine soap, orange flowers - $12

Columbian Exposition, small booklet, lithographed Pabst Brewing Co. - $15

Advertising fan, wood handle, Lititz, Manheim, Lancaster, PA - $5

Hershey's Ice Cream, heavy board, 23"x14", cones, with easel in back - $40

Nabisco, 3-D, Wild Animal Premium - $20

New Orleans World's Fair, 1984 - $40
New York World's Fair, Dr. Pepper, 1963 - $25
New York World's Fair, Spanish Pavillion, 1964 - $50
Red Cross (7) 1940s/1960s, full color - $54 all
Ringling Brothers, Barnum and Bailey's Shows, Feniell Jacobs, the Lion King, 1923 - $46
Stock Circus Poster with clowns, Mint - $225
Victor Phonograph, His Master's Voice, nine by thirteen inches - $15
WWII (6) by Abbot Laboratories, North Chicago, Illinois, 'Buy War Bonds' - $90 all
WWII, General Electric (6) 1942, 'It Can Happen Here' - $7.50
WWII, Marines (3) War Bond Drive, including flag raising on Iwo Jima - $22 all
Wrigley, two sided poster, black and white - $65

Associations:

National Association of Paper and Advertising Collectors, P.O. Box 500, Mount Joy, PA 17552, Phone: 717-653-9797, Doris Ann Johnson, Editor

Antique Advertising Association, P.O. Box 1121, Morton Grove, IL 60053, Phone: 708-446-0904

Books:

Package and Print, Alec Davis, Clarkson N. Potter, Inc., NY 1967

Magazines:

The Insider Collector, 225 Main Street, Suite 300, Northport, NY 11768, Phone: 516-261-8337

Auctions:

Olivers, Route One, Plaza One, Kennebunk, ME 04043

Anthony J. Nard and Company, U.S. Route 220, Milan, PA 18831, Phone: 717-888-9404, Tony Nard

Connestoga Auction Company, P.O. Box 1, Manheim, PA 17545, Phone: 717-898-7284

Richard Opfer Auctioneering Inc., 1919 Greenspring Drive, Timonium, MD 21093, Phone: 301-252-5035

Pettigrew Auction Gallery, 1645 South Tejon Street, Colorado Springs, CO 80906, Phone: 719-633-7963

CHAPTER XV

DIME NOVELS, ALMANACS

It was 1860. Longfellow, Nathaniel Hawthorne, and Walt Whitman were all being published in *The Atlantic* Magazine. Thackery was writing for *Harpers Monthly* along with a lady named Evans who preferred being called George Elliot. *Harpers Weekly* was running "An Uncommercial Traveler" by Charles Dickens, and Edward Zane Carroll Judson was counting off towards the 400 plus dime novels he eventually saw published underneath his byline of Ned Buntline.

Judson? Buntline? Who's he - they - to be listed with the literary giants of an age?

You never heard of the man whose life story was built on more blood and thunder than any Dime Novel that saw print? The man who survived his own lynching?

Think of Ned Buntline at a time when writers were paid a penny a line, Ned's income from writing Dime Novels was $20,000 a year. Today, with inflated dollars, the average magazine writer doesn't make that amount.

A spread of Dime Novels that a dealer displayed
at a Hartford, Connecticut paper show. They
were priced at eight dollars each.

Street and Smith published this in 1915. Price
then: 5¢. Price now at a recent show: $15

William Cody as he looked in 1870.

Another Buffalo Bill Weekly by Street and Smith published in 1915.

Frank Tousey published *Wild West Weekly*, This one was offered recently for $10.

The Dime Novel has usually been credited to the firm of Beadle and Adams in 1860. Yet it is hardly possible to write of Dime Novels without including Ned Butline's name, for he had been developing the concept for at least twelve years previously.

Even the *Readers Encyclopedia* by Rose Benet, credits him with at least three early novels of the genera: two in 1847, and Stella DeLorma or *The Comanche's Dream*, in 1860.

When in that year, Beadle and Adams discovered, with the publication of *Malaeska: The Indian Wife of the White Hunter*, that they had a 300,000 print winner, they started a trend that didn't end until shortly after the first World War. They published two novels a month for 32 years. They were thin little books, 6" high and 4" wide, that later enlarged and thickened. "Yellow-backed Beadle's," was the derogatory term from the competition. "Orange. They're orange, not yellow," was Beadle's reply.

Regardless of Buntline's, or Beadle's prolific output, neither was alone in their fields. Beadle and Adams had a print record of five million in the first four years. Others salivated and took off for a piece of this money.

A 1907 *Rough Rider Weekly*. The story illustrates the liberties writers took inventing Indian tribal names.

Tip Top Weekly introduced All-American boy, Frank Merriwell. Action remained the key word.

149

Elliot, Thomas, and Talbot, from Boston, jumped in about 1863 with The Brave's Secret or The Spy of the Ten. They didn't use yellow covers. Robert M. DeWitt of New York followed with *DeWitt's Ten Cent Romances.* The deluge became heavier with *Munro's Ten Cent Novels* joining. Eventually the list of publisher included such giants as Frank Tousey and Street and Smith.

Under their aegis the term Dime Novel became misleading. The price of a copy could be 6¢, 7¢, 8¢ or even 20¢. Half dime novels appeared, priced at a nickel. Regardless, the term Dime Novel persisted, became generic.

Buntline was always a front runner, whomever the publisher for whom he wrote. His competition would amount to at least 250 other writers. The difficulty here, for the collector, is that many wrote not only under their own names, but used pen names that could change with every novel they wrote. One excellent reason for this was the syndication of characters and authors - a practice that continued through the era of the pulps, to continue today with many paper back publishers.

Perhaps Buntline's most serious competition as a writer was one 'Colonel' Prentiss Ingraham, another whose life story was reputed to rival his Dime Novel output. As Beadle's most prolific author, he is said to have written more than 600 novels. There was also Edward L. Wheeler, creator of *Deadwood Dick,* and Anne S. Stephens. Actually she only wrote 200 Dime Novels, a mere nothing compared to Buntline's or Ingraham's output.

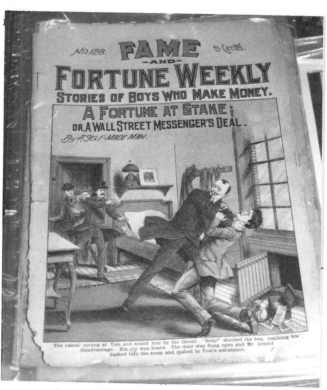

Fame and Fortunes formula for early retirement was save the boss or marry his daughter.

A 1914 *Wild West Weekly*, Frank Tousey, sold recently at a paper show for $10.

While *The Captain's Pig,* of which no copy is known, is thought to have been Buntline's first novel, about 1838, true Dime Novels came later. *The Mysteries and Miseries of New York,* 1848; *War Eagle* or *Ossiniwa, the Indian Brave,* 1848; or *The Comanche's Dream,* 1860, were all in print before Beadle and Adams discovered the gold in Yellow-backed Beadle's.

The basic story rarely varied. The good guys always won. Read any of the stories, under whatever cover title, available to the collector today, *Work and Win; Fame and Fortune; Frank Merriwell; Nick Carter, Secret Service;* Or *Buffalo Bill Weekly.* It was 'white hat' against 'black hat', good against evil. The villain never won. Who could conceive of Buffalo Bill losing a battle?

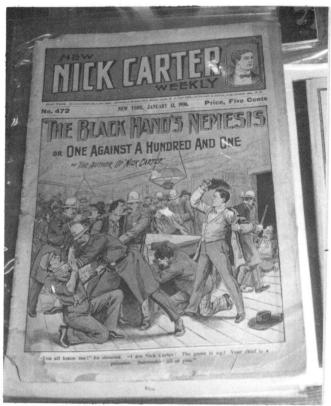

Nick Carter survived all the villians; goes on
fighting crime in today's paper backs.

It was Ned Buntline, who on meeting William Frederick Cody, in Fort McPherson, Nebraska, in 1869, re-christened that goateed showman, Buffalo Bill. Buffalo Bill he remained, while Ned began a series under that title. Later, after a disagreement between Cody and Buntline, Buffalo Bill stories were written by that other prolific writer, Prentiss Ingraham as his authorized biographer.

Who read these Dime Novels? Anyone with the price. With rising literacy, juvenile and adult imaginations were given what they craved most - a chance to experience the 'wild west' before it was all fenced in and tamed by barbed wire. To the Eastern sophisticate, the West was the natural home of desperados and rustlers, gamblers and gunmen, scalp hunting Indians and white hatted, clean shave, bath-a-week, upright lawmen and cow hands.

Any entrepreneur with access to cheap paper and a rotary printing press, could set out to supply this apparently inexhaustable urge. They churned out thousands of words for those who wanted to read stories of fearless detectives, women pirates, rags to riches work-a-holics, and cowboys with rifles that never missed.

The writers of these fantasies wrote fast. Buntline is said to have finished a 60,000 word novel in 62 hours, Ingraham, a 35,000 word novel in 24 hours. At a penny a line they had to work fast.

There were tricks. A typical passage might read:

"Knave."

"Sir?"

"Cur."

Slap!

"Duel?"

"Seconds?"

Happily such passages have faded into history though some of the protagonists still linger. Nick Carter still titillates, is still in print. By 1915, only a few of the best, Nick Carter, Frank Merriwell, survived. The pulps took over, giving way to comic books and serialized paper back heroes.

One hundred and thirty years after their alleged beginnings, Deadwood Dick, Buffalo Bill, Old Sleuth, Fred Fearnot, Wild Bill, and Fancy Frank are on the collector's want lists as are hundreds of others. The West has been tamed but readers and collectors remain for those great, old Dime Novels.

Almanacs are usually reasonably priced, mostly $10-$15. This one went for $185 with the claim
the cowboy on the cover made it more valuable.

ALMANACS

The forerunner of the modern magazine though ancient in concept, the word itself is of medieval Arabic origin. The first Almanac appeared in this country in 1639, published by William Pierce Mariner.

Followed by The Boston Almanac in 1692 and The New England Almanac in 1695, it was finally the work of two brothers who made the Almanac a true collectible. One James Franklin published Franklin's Rhode Island Almanac in 1728. The other brother - you may have heard of the name - published Poor Richard's Almanac in 1733 under the pen name of Richard Saunders. Most folk of that time knew him as Ben Franklin.

Put any of those older Almanacs on a book rack with today's versions and it might be difficult to say which was published when. They tend to have a generic appearance. Much of the content remains standard consisting of a notated calendar, phases of the moon, weather data and forecasts, recipes, and health and household hints.

Nor will price vary greatly except for those printed before 1850. These may be bought in the low hundreds with rare exceptions. After the 1850s, prices are comparable to the costs of today's versions of $5-$25.

There is a story, probably apocryphl, that Abraham Lincoln, as a lawyer, used an Almanac to defend a man accused of murder. Lincoln showed a page in an Almanac to a jury where it read, "the moon was riding low." How then could the defendent have used the light of the moon on the date in question, to strike? The jury is said to have believed Lincoln and the Almanac.

The wording in any Almanac may have been wild, the medical claims outlandish in the light of what we know today. Just remember that then - and until the first third of this century - cocaine, heroin, and opium were sold over the counter without a prescription. Most nostrums and patent medicines were laced heavily with alcohol and laudunum.

Medical knowledge may have improved but Almanacs change slowly, if at all.

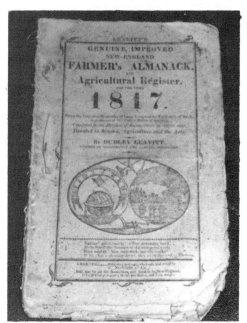

By 1817 when this Farmers Almanac and Agricultural Register was published, the ornate engravings to come were beginning to be used. Because of its poor condition, this one had only a $15 price tag.

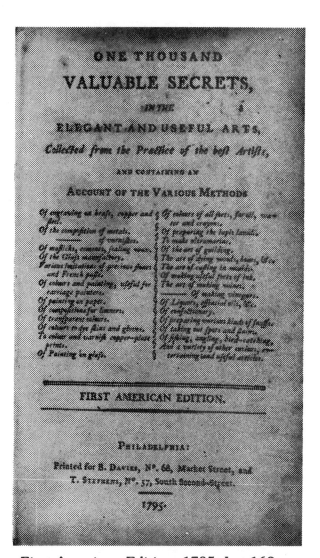

First American Edition, 1795, Lot 163.

Almanacs in 1795, when this First American Edition was printed in Philadephia for one B. Davis, had only a little of the appearance of later editions. Sotheby.

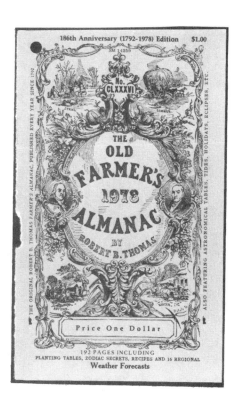

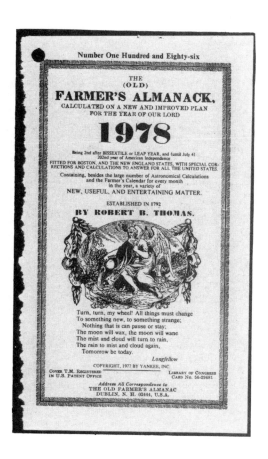

These two covers from 1978 Almanacs have a
recognizable appearance to any newstand
browser.

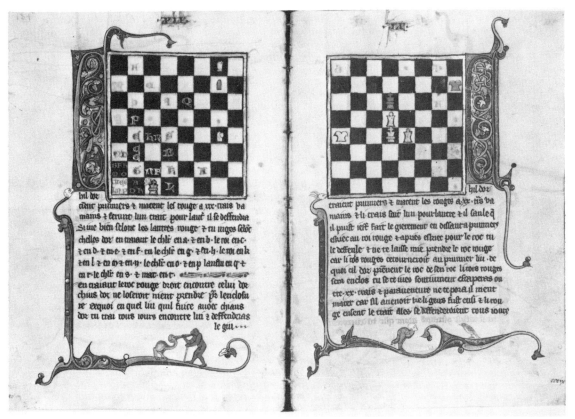

An illuminated manuscript of the 13th century once owned by J. Pierpont Morgan. Pierpont Morgan Library, M 108 f134 v 135

ILLUMINATED MANUSCRIPTS

Held by the Morgan Library in New York City, is a page from a 13th century, Franco-Flemish, illuminated manuscript of chess problems: Bonus Socius (The Good Companion or The Good Ally). It had once been owned by J. Pierpont Morga. As far back as then, the 13th century, chess problems were a mystery to the uninitiated,

The page illustrates what was then a source of joy to its practitioners. The detailed color, painstakingly applied by hand to a sheet of parchment. Joy was the practitioners only payment as the illustrators were monks. They toiled away for the greater glory of their beliefs and the recording of what was then, the world's knowledge. All was contained in lushly illuminated, wildly colored, and gilded prayer books, bibles, histories and devotionals, some containing portraits. The art of parchment illuminated books ended as printing began.

Few collectors of paper collectibles may ever have the privilege of owning an illuminated manuscript. Don't hope to find an unrecorded Book of Kells at a flea market, or Pierpont Morgan's sequel to Bonus Socius at a yard sale. Call them dream books or wish-I-hads. Enjoy them at museums and libraries, where major collections are stored under rigidly controlled climatic conditions.

Paper then, had a value of which we have no conception today. The parchment for these illuminated manuscripts was hand-made, irregular in shape. Trimmed to size to fit a proposed book, the trimmings were prizes to be saved and re-used. The generated a spin-off called quill work.

These bits and pieces of paper were further trimmed to size and rolled into curled and funneled shapes like the hollow quills of a birds feathered quill, hence quill work. Glued onto an object - a box, a vase, whatever - they were sized to prevent uncurling, then painted. As with the manuscripts from which they first came, the best of this quill work is to be found mainly in museums. Time and careless handling destroyed those pieces not protected by an official hand.

Occasional samples of quill work appear at yard sales and fleamarkets, mostly the work of patient home crafts persons.

A few collections of manuscripts follow. Enjoy them for what they are; icons of a collectors deep conviction that someday he'll own one.

Children's book authors used to prefer humanized animals as their protagonists. Currently, publishers seem to shy away from that concept. Robert Louis Stevenson's *Daisies*, remains one of the great children's book classics.

CHILDREN'S BOOKS

Children's books may not have the cachet of a Dime Novel or an Almanac, but they have one thing the other two don't - they cost more to the collector.

Why? Quite possibly because of the illustrations. They play a far more important role in evaluating a children's book than age, story, or author.

Strangely, Children's books are more collectible when printed after 1850 and before 1910. That period was when most of the great classics were written. Children's books may be collected by category or by story as well as by illustrator. The categories are numerous consisting of fairy tales, fantasy, and poetry; books of animals, sea creatures, and birds; books of travel and adventure, on and beyond this earth; books that pop up and become toys or teach about everyday things.

To each there is a reader, to each a collector. The best (translate highest) prices are from the great name auction houses.

CHILDREN'S SCHOOL BOOKS

There was the *New England Primer*, c.1830, which was somber and stern in outlook. *Webster's Elementary Speller* which was moral in tone with words too complicated to be clearly understood by a child's mind. There was also an 1860, *Warren's School Geography, Colburn's Arithmatic, Karper's School Geography,* and *Gin and Company's Reader.* Schoolbooks, textbooks, the names unknown to all but collectors of those small beginnings of a child's climb to an education.

Then there was William Holmes McGuffey. Even non-collectors know the name, *McGuffey's Eclectic Readers.* It's a small wonder that between 1836 and 1920, 120 million copies of McGuffey's six readers and one primer had been sold.

They shaped the mind of America's youth. In one room plank or log cabin schools across the country, a pen, a slate, berry juice ink and a McGuffey's Reader were all the necessities needed for an education. McGuffey wrote the First and Second Readers in 1836. Also the Primer. The Third and Fourth Readers appeared in 1837.

Revised in 1844, they were joined by a Fifth Reader in 1844 and a Sixth and final Reader in 1853. The last two were both written by his brother, Alexander. In retrospect, they presented an idealized rather than a real world to their young readers.

McGuffey's Eclectic Readers became the basic school texts in 37 states, and were translated for use in Puerto Rico and the Philipines. By 1911 they had gone through four more revisions.

Although there are seven books, there are five revisions for the five original books and four revisions for the two written by his brother. This means a complete set would number 40 books.

The publishers, Van Nostrand Reinhold, have put out a reprint of a seven volume, boxed set of *McGuffey's Eclectic Readers* at $47.95.

Since *McGuffey's Eclectic Spelling* in the original, has been sold for $5, the New Sixth Reader of 1866 at $10, and a set of nine, all original, at $32, buying reprints does not make sense. Unless you just want some nice, clean, new books on your bookshelves.

Prices:
Beadles Dime Library, Vol.3, #32, 1878 - $20
Beadles Half Dime Library, April 17, 1883 - $25
The New York Five Cent Library, June 30, 1894 - $11
Five assorted Dime Novels, show price - $40
Wild West Weekly, July 12, 1913, show price - $15
Nick Carter Weekly, Street and Smith, January 13, 1904 - $5
Wild West Weekly, July 24, 1914, Show price - $10
Secret Service, Frank Tousey, April 21, 1915 - $10
Work and Win, Frank Tousey, August 16, 1912 - $10
Lot - including Older Disney, Benji, Star Wars, E.T. dealer - $55

DIME NOVELS

Books:

Dime Novels: or Following an Old Trail in Popular Literature, Edmund Pearson, Kennikat Press, Port Washington, NY, 1929.

The Beadle Collection of Dime Novels, Dr. Frank O'Brien, 1922, published by the New York Public Library and may be found there.

The Life and Adventures of Ned Buntline, Frederick E. Pond, 1919.

The Dime Novel Western, Daryl Jones, Bowling Green, Ohio Popular Press, Bowling Green State University, 1978.

Almanacs:

Dime Novel Roundup, Michael L. Cook. An annotated index 1931-1981. Published 1983, Bowling Green, Ohio Popular Press, Bowling Green State University.

Children's Books, Book Collecting: A Comprehensive Guide, Allen Ahearn, NY: Putnam, c.1989.

Collections:

C.W. Post Campus, Long Island University, Northern Boulevard, Brookville, NY

Toronto Public Library, The Osborne Collection of Early Children's Books, Toronto 5, Canada

University of Minnesota, The Kerlan Collection, Minneapolis, Minnesota 55455

Pierpont Morgan Library, 29 East 36th Street, New York, NY 10016

Mail Auction:

Vintage Cover Story, P.O. Box 975, Burlington, North Carolina 27215. Bob Raynor, 919-584-6990. Occasionally Dime Novels appear midst the newspapers he specializes in.

Mail Order:

Same people, without auction:
Beadle's Pocket Library, February 11, 1885. $19.
Frank Reade Library, July 29, 1883, $17.
Diamond Dick, Jr., The Boy's Best Weekly, October 8, 1898. $17.
The Boy's Star Library, 1893, $17.
Wide Awake Library, June 7, 1890. $18.
The Boys of New York Pocket Library, July 22, 1882. $21

CHAPTER XVI

AUTOGRAPHS

Someone once said, "a man's signature reveals much about himself, sometimes even his name."

Well, yes. Maybe no. Signatures by themselves have minimal impact or value. To know the person who signed the letter, document, manuscript, or quotation, read the contents of that note, handwritten or typed. Even without a signature, the wording on the paper will reveal much about the author, his circumstances, or the times. Signatures - except for rarities - are of secondary importance.

More so if you stood in line at sports memorabilia show and then paid to have a current sports figure sign his name for you. They may never be worth the price you paid. Worse, as one pre-teen ager explained, "I asked him how his team would do this year. He didn't even look up. He sort of grunted or snarled, 'I get paid to sign my name. Not to talk.' "

Aside from such mass produced autographs of sports figures lack of value, the athlete's attitude may be another reason their signatures, so obtained, should be separated from the entire field of autographs. A separate genus should be authorized for those who like to pay to stand in line.

Such activity or lack of it, may eventually make some of them realize that there is more meaningful material available in the autograph field than such 'hurry up and pay' signatures. Names that will soon be only a statistic in a book of that sport.

It wasn't always so. Once sports figures were approachable. A collector of any age could talk to them before or after a game, even in a hotel lobby, and be assured of a smile and an autograph - for free. It was a personal approach with a personal response. It was autograph collecting in its most elementary form, satisfying an urge to have something valued from people felt to be important.

From such beginnings comes the true collector, those not satisfied with just a signature. These budding authograph collectors realize there must be more to their heroes than a sometimes illegible scrawl on a scrap of paper.

These nascent collectors go on to signed photographs, or use the mail to ask a question in hopes of a personal response. Eventually they realize the autograph field is so overwhelmingly large that they must specialize on a person, an event, an era in history. They can now start calling themselves autograph collectors.

A flashback at this moment will take us back to the time when athletes always had a moment to sign a scrap of paper or a program - back to the days of George Herman Ruth. 'Babe' to the world of baseball.

Babe was a willing and prolific signer. Nothing was more cherished, even in 1923, than a Babe Ruth autograph. Seventy years later this still holds true. But...

Authentication is paramount but often difficult. It was not uncommon for his second wife, Claire Hodgson Ruth, to sign checks in his name with her remarkably similar signature. He also used others, ghost signers, authorized to sign his name. They almost look like his signature - with several important distinctions.

The 'B' of a genuine Babe Ruth autograph will have a preliminary cursive stroke before the down stroke. The 'e' at the end of Babe will have this same cursive stroke and will look like a reversed number three rather than the looped effect of the normally written letter.

Many personalities have used secretaries to sign their correspondence. Charles DeGaul for one.

Other dignitaries use facsimile processes which vary with the type used. A rubber stamp imprints a facsimile. So does modern machinery designed to provide a reproduction of a person's signature automatically.

Here again are reasons to relegate signatures to secondary consideration. It is the contents of the document that reveals the value. The value to the collector, the dealer and the auctioneer. The value to the world as a historic document unveiling one more bit of our past as a people.

Not only well known names are valued, but also unknowns if the circumstances are apparent. A letter signed by ten Indian Chiefs appeared at a paper show. It's collector value was so significant that if it had not been part of business inventory the dealer would have enjoyed keeping it for herself.

A letter to Lord Byron, the Lord-in-Waiting to Queen Victoria, undated but researched to 1839, was signed, 'The Queen'. It specified who was to take her mother into dinner.

"Lord Cunyngham will take in the Queen and sit on her right. Lord Alberdeen will take in the Duchess of Kent and sit on her right, and Lord Melboume will take in Lady Durham and sit on the Queen's left."

George Anson, the seventh Lord Byron, succeeded his cousin, the poet Byron, in 1834.

A socially knowledgeable British subject was asked to comment on this letter.

"I don't question the authenticity of the letter, although it is doubtful it was ever written or signed by Queen Victoria personally. That's what secretaries or someone in charge of protocol did.

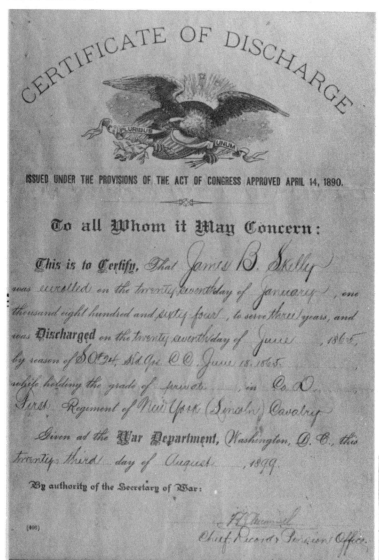

Discharge papers are valued for their historical content. Here, a Civil War private's discharge issued thirty four years after his last tour of duty. Similar papers at auction have sold in 1992 for $65-140. Courtesy Richard Steinhauer

A lobby card signed with the names of the actors and actresses who starred in the movie. Offered as facsimile autographs.

Babe Ruth's signature on his hat, as presented to Charles Mead, former Mayor of Riverdale, New Jersey, in 1928. Its visible 1992 price tag is $4,995.

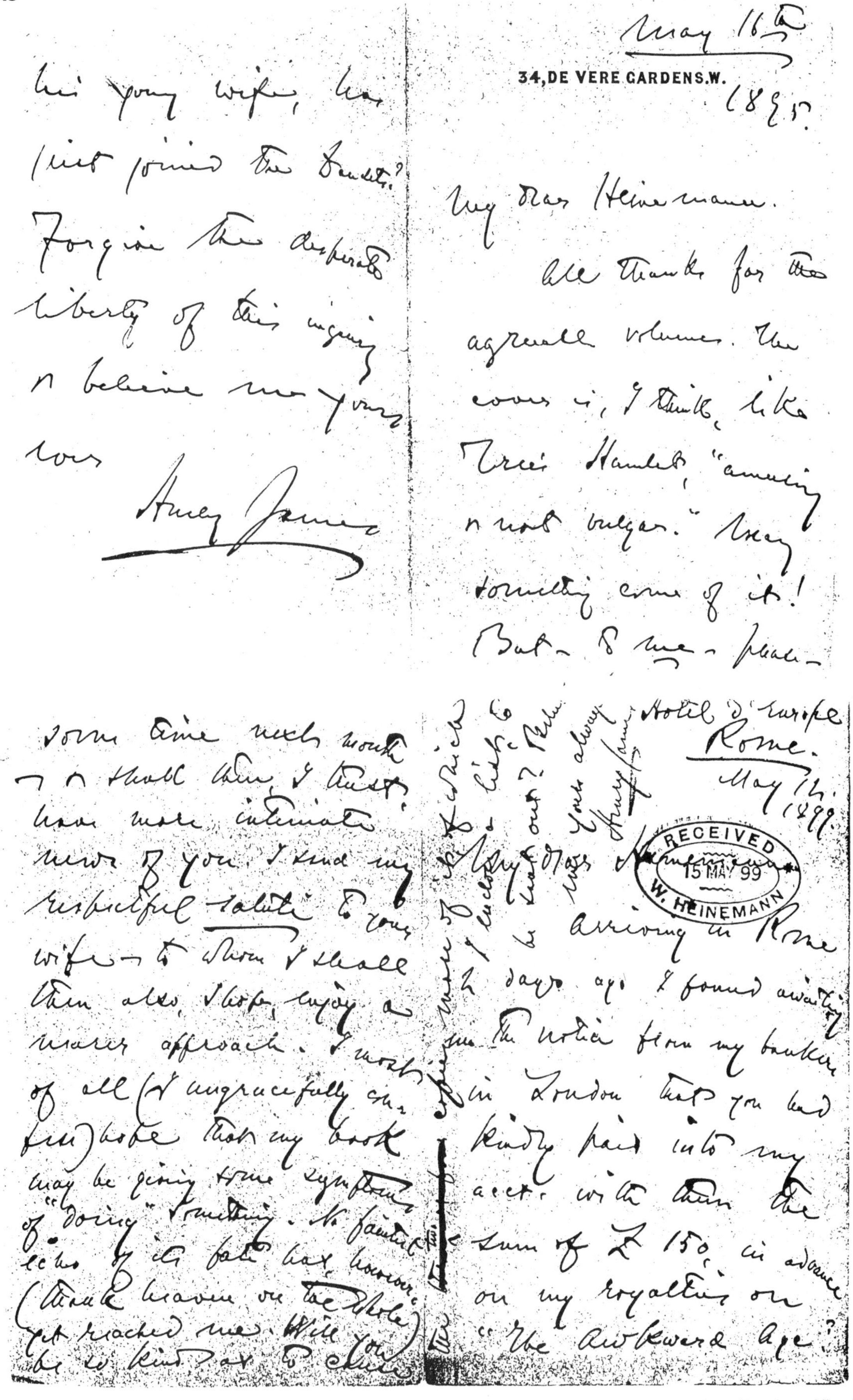
34, DE VERE GARDENS. W.
May 16th
1895.

My dear Heinemann.

All thanks for the agreeable volumes. The cover is, I think, like Tree's Hamlet, "amusing & not vulgar." May something come of it! But - to me - pleas-

his young wife, has just joined the bandit? Forgive the desperate liberty of this inquiry & believe me yours ever

Henry James

Hotel d'Europe
Rome.
May 17th
1899.

My dear Heinemann

Arriving in Rome 2 days ago I found awaiting me the notice from my banker in London that you had kindly paid into my acct. with them the sum of £150, in advance on my royalties on "The Awkward Age."

some time next month - & I shall then, I trust, have more intimate news of you. I send my respectful salute to your wife - to whom I shall then also, I hope, enjoy a nearer approach. I most of all (& ungracefully ...) hope that my book may be giving some symptoms of "doing" something. No faintest echo of its fate has, however, (thank heaven on the whole) yet reached me. Will you be so kind as to ...

... which I enclose to be sent out? ... Yours always Henry James

RECEIVED
15 MAY 99
W. HEINEMANN

Henry James (1843-1916), an American novelist, remains one of the more influential figures in American literature. His characters changed morally as well as psychologically as his story proceeded, usually with a sense of conflict between new and old world cultures. By 1897 James was living in England while retaining his love relationship with Paris and Rome. The pictured letter, with a Rome imprint, relates an incident concerned with his 1899 novel *The Awkward Age.*

Newport in 1860 made an important impression on Henry James life. While studying there he met and befriended John La Farge, the painter. Through, or because of, La Farge, James retained a life long interest in art.

Five hand written letters, three of which bear Henry James signature, written during the years of 1895, 1899, and 1904, discussing books, visits, and business. His business of course being the writing of books now considered classics. Courtesy Conrad Schoeffling, C.W. Post Campus, Long Island University.

A page of verse from a letter by George Meredith with this signature. Courtesy Conrad Schoeffling, C.W. Post Campus, Long Island University.

AUTOGRAPHS

"If the letter was to a personal friend, it would have been signed, 'Victoria'. If of a formal nature, it would be signed, 'Victoria Rex', followed by the list of her various titles and honors from the territories under British dominion.

"Judgement? Authentic, but written by her Chief of Protocol. Well worth a good price just for its content."

And more interesting than being told by a player he doesn't get paid to talk.

Any time period may produce autographs of interest, for by the simple stroke of a pen innumerable folk have assured themselves of a form of immortality.

A note to a public relations clerk at March Field in California, dated August 5, 1936, signed by Amelia Earhart, thanking the base for its hospitality, was accompanied by a request that her maiden name be used to identify her in photographic captions. It sold at an auction for $210.

Events from the past often overlap those of the present. A Revolutionary War journal written by Benedict Arnold included handwritten copies of letters Arnold wrote to George Washington in 1775. Arnold, then a Colonel in the Revolutionary Army, led 1,000 men through the Maine wilderness in an unsuccessful attack on Quebec. In 1992, the journal was stolen from a museum in Maine. The FBI recovered it in Chicago.

Such incidents add to the historic value of many autographs.

A check signed by George Herman Ruth in 1947 was priced at $750, while one signed by amid 19th century Vice President of the United States was offered for $2. It says something about the value of a politician as compared to a 1930s baseball player.

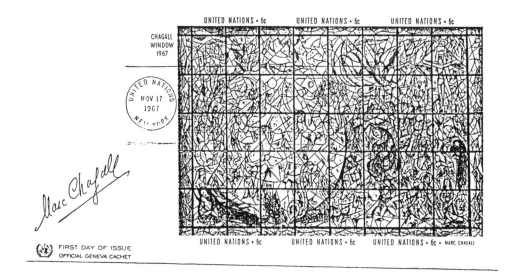

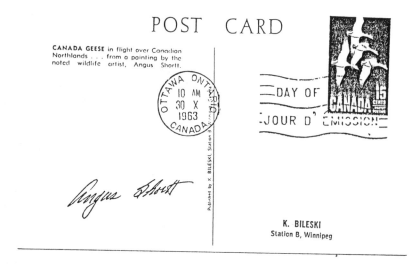

To collectors of first day covers and postcards, the signatures of the artists whose paintings were reproduced as postage stamps are valued, even though undoubtedly facsimile. Sutliffe Collection

BALTIMORE, February 15.

His Britannic Majesty's Speech to both Houses of Parliament.

NEW-YORK, February 9.
By the Brigantine Peggy, Capt. M'Neil, in 19 days from Tortola, we have received the following copy of His Majesty's most gracious Speech to both Houses of Parliament, on Thursday, December 5, 1782, which was brought to Tortola, from the Windward, by Captain Rodney, Son of Lord Rodney.

My Lords and Gentlemen,

SINCE the close of the last sessions, I have employed my whole time in the care and attention which the important and critical conjuncture of public affairs required of me.

I lost no time in giving the necessary orders to prohibit the farther prosecution of offensive war upon the continent of North-America. Adopting, as my inclination will always lead me to do, with decision and effect, whatever I collect to be the sense of my Parliament and my people; I have pointed all my views and measures, as well in Europe as in North-America, to an entire and cordial reconciliation with those colonies.

Finding it indispensable to the attainment of this object, I did not hesitate to go the full length of the powers vested in me, and offered to declare them FREE and INDEPENDENT STATES, by an article to be inserted in the Treaty of Peace. Provisional articles are agreed upon, to take effect whenever terms of Peace shall be finally settled with the Court of France.

In thus admitting their separation from the Crown of these kingdoms, I have sacrificed every consideration of my own, to the wishes and opinion of my people. I make it my humble and earnest prayer to Almighty God, that Great-Britain may not feel the evils which might result from so great a dismemberment of the Empire; and, that America may be free from those calamities, which have formerly proved in the Mother Country, how destructive Monarchy is to the enjoyment of constitutional liberty. Religion, language, interest, affections may, and I hope will, yet prove a bond of permanent union between the two countries. To this end, neither attention nor disposition shall be wanting on my part.

While I have carefully abstained from all offensive operations against America, I have directed my whole force, by land and sea, against the other powers at war, with as much vigour as the situation of that force, at the commencement of the campaign, would permit. I trust that you feel the advantages resulting from the safety of the great branches of our trade. You must have seen with pleasure and satisfaction the gallant defence of the Governor and garrison of Gibraltar; and my fleet, after having effected the object of their destination, offering battle to the combined force of France and Spain on their own coasts; those of my kingdoms have remained at the same time perfectly secure, and your domestic tranquility uninterrupted. This respectable state, under the blessing of God, I attribute to the entire confidence which subsists between me and my people, and to the readiness which has been shewn by my subjects, in any city of London, and in other parts of my kingdoms, to stand forth in the general defence. Some proofs have lately been given of public spirit in private men, which would do honour to any age and any country.

Having manifested to the whole world, by the most striking examples, the equal spirit and bravery of my people, I conceived it a moment not unbecoming my dignity, and thought it a regard due to the lives and fortunes of such brave and gallant subjects, to shew myself ready on my part, to embrace fair and honourable terms of accommodation with all the powers at war.

I have the satisfaction to acquaint you, that negotiations to this effect are considerably advanced, the result of which, as soon as they are brought to a conclusion, shall be immediately communicated to you.

I have every reason to hope and believe, that I shall have it in my power, in a very short time, to acquaint you, that they have ended in terms of pacification, which, I trust, you will see just cause to approve. I rely, however, with perfect confidence, on the wisdom of my Parliament, and the spirit of my people, that if any unforeseen change in the disposition of the belligerent powers should frustrate my confident expectations, they will approve of the preparations I have thought it advisable to make, and be ready to second the most vigorous efforts in the farther protection of the war.

Gentlemen of the House of Commons,

I have endeavoured by every measure in my power to diminish the burthens of my people. I lost no time in taking the most decided measures for introducing a better economy in the expenditure of the army.

I have carried into effect executions the several reductions in the civil list expences, directed by an act of the last sessions. I have introduced a farther reform into other departments, and suppressed several useless places in them. I have by this means to re-

gulated my establishments that my expence shall not in future exceed my income.

I have ordered the estimate of the civil list debt, laid before you last sessions, to be completed. The debt proving somewhat greater than could be then correctly stated, and the proposed reduction not immediately taking place, I trust you will provide for the deficiency, securing, as before, the repayment out of my annual income.

I have ordered inquiry to be made into the application of the sum voted in support of the American sufferers; and I trust you will agree with me, that a due and generous attention ought to be shewn to those who have relinquished their properties or professions from motives of loyalty to me, or attachment to the Mother Country.

As it may be necessary to give stability to some regulation by Act of Parliament, I have ordered accounts of the several establishments, incidental expences, fees and other emoluments of office, to be laid before you. Regulations have already taken place in some, which it is my intention to extend to all, and which, besides expediting all public business, must produce a very considerable saving, without taking from that ample encouragement, which ought to be held forth to talents, diligence and integrity, wherever they are to be found.

I have directed an inquiry to be made into what-ever regards the landed revenue of my crown, as well as the management of my woods and forest, that both may be made as beneficial as possible, and that the latter may furnish a certain resource for supplying the navy, our great national bulwark, with it's best material.

I have directed an investigation into the department of the mint, that the purity of the coin, of so much importance to commerce, may be always adhered to; that by rendering the difficulty of counterfeiting greater, the lives of numbers may be saved, and every needless expence in it suppressed.

I must recommend to you an immediate attention to the great objects of the public receipts and expenditure; and above all, to the state of the public debt. Notwithstanding the great increase of it during the war, it is to be hoped that such regulations may still be established, such savings made—and future loans be conducted, as to promote the means of it's gradual redemption by a fixed course of payment. I must, with particular earnestness, distinguish for your serious consideration, that part of the debt which consists of navy, ordnance and victualling bills; the enormous discount upon some of their bills shews this mode of payment to be a most ruinous expedient.

I have ordered several estimates, made up as correctly as the present practice admits, to be laid before you. I hope that such farther correction as may be necessary, will be made before the next year. It is my desire, that you should be apprized of every expence before it is incurred, as far as the nature of each service can possibly admit. Matters of account can never be made too public.

My Lords and Gentlemen,

The scarcity and consequent high price of corn, requires your instant interposition.

The great excess to which the crimes of theft and robbery, in many instances accompanied with personal violence, particularly in the neighbourhood of this Metropolis, has called of late for a strict and severe execution of the laws. It were much to be wished, that these crimes could be prevented in their infancy, by correcting the vices become prevalent in the most alarming degree.

The liberal principles adopted by you, concerning the rights and the commerce of Ireland, have done you the highest honour, and will, I trust, ensure that harmony, which ought always to subsist between the two kingdoms. I am persuaded that a general increase of commerce throughout the empire, will prove the surest sum of your measures with regard to that subject. I would recommend to you a revision of your whole trading system, upon the same comprehensive principles, with a view to its utmost possible extension.

The regulation of a vast territory in Asia opens a large field for your wisdom, prudence, and foresight. I trust that you will be able to frame some fundamental laws which may make their connexion with Great-Britain a blessing to India; and that you will take the proper measures to give all foreign nations, in matters of foreign commerce, an entire and perfect confidence in the probity, punctuality, and good order of government. You may be assured, that whatever defence upon me, shall be executed with a steadiness, which can alone preserve that part of my dominions, or the commerce which arises from it.

It is the fixed object of my heart to make the general good, and the spirit of the constitution, the invariable rule of my conduct, and on all occasions to advance and reward merit in every profession.

To enforce the full advantage of a government, conducted on such principles, depends on your temper, your wisdom, your disinterestedness, collectively and individually.

My people expect these qualifications, and therefore I call for them.

Baltimore: Printed and sold by M. K. Goddard, at the Post-Office, Market-Street.

From Baltimore, Maryland in 1782, comes this broadside with quotations from His Brittanic Majesty's speech to both houses of Parliament, wherein he offered to declare the American Colonies to be free and independent. Sotheby.

William F. Cody, known more widely as Buffalo Bill, proved his showmanship once again by signing postcards with both his birth name and his nickname. A postcard dealer had one identical to this at a show in 1992 for $145.

A photograph of a movie actress moves from a low ranking to a higher value when it includes a personal message and signature. Courtesy Ruth King.

Oliver Cromwell signature: an apparently un-happy man whose reign was noted for its rigidness and lack of ornateness - unlike his scroll-like penmanship. Rendell.

NAPOLEON I

CHARLES X AND LOUIS XVIII

LOUIS XVIII

NAPOLEON III

FRANCIS I

HENRY II

LOUIS PHILIPPE AND MARIE AMÉLIE

What would the analysts say of the block lettered signatures of these three Royals as compared to the mostly illegible scrawls of these French aristocrats? Rendell.

FRANCIS II

AUTOGRAPHS
Autograph prices from trade papers, dealers, auctions and shows.

Abbreviations:

ADS - Autographed document signed
AL - Autographed letter
AlS - Autographed letter signed
DS - Document signed
MDS - Manuscript document signed
SL - signed letter
SP - signed photograph
TLS - Typewritten letter signed

Prices:

Adolph Hitler DS, in German, two pages, commissions three Lt. Generals and ten Major Generals - $2750

Aid to volunteer, April 18, 1864, two eight by ten pages affidavit for wife from soldier in Wisconsin regiment, signed by Captain - $15

Alger Hiss, ALS, New York City, December 27, 1972 to Pulitzer prize winner, Mark Van Doren - $95

Audie Murphy, Medal of Honor winner WWII, signature and inscription on album page - $150

Benedict Arnold, MDS, signed B. Arnold, October 22, 1787, Supreme Court, St. John, Newfoundland - $2500

Buffalo Bill postcard with rodeo name and William F. Cody signatures, four dealers with four prices - $100-$700

Bryant Washburn, Movie star SP, eight by ten, photo by Hartsook, San Francisco - $35

Caroline B. Kennedy, ALS, both sides personal stationary, thank you for contribution to the Kennedy library - $150

Charles Dickens, ALS, 1839, London, to Edward Dowling, contains part of a seal - $1200

Civil War diary of Indiana soldier, 132 pages, detailed factual - $1800

Crossed Rifles on a check from Bridgeport, Connecticut, 1877, revenue imprint, RN-M2, from Sharp's Rifle Company, VF - $90

Dame Agatha Christie, ALS, November 23, 1966, holograph envelope, thank you for poem - $550

Damon Runyon, TLS, one page, 1935, payment letter for book received - $175

Diary of Rich boy, four months of non-stop activity, including comments on Douglas Fairbanks and Charlie Chaplin, college life in 1918 - $75

Don Whitehead, Pulitzer winning journalist, typewritten note, signed - $25

Eugene Sandowearly 20th century strongman, signature on card - $125

Father Flanagan, TLS, one page, 1941 - $225

Francis Scott Key, ADS, 1803, acknowledgement on receipt of letter - $525

George Gershwin, ADS, bank check on National City Bank of New York for $25 cash, June 7, 1935 - $2500

Grandma Moses, AL, autographed letter in pencil, handwritten - $1250

Harry S. Truman, TLS, as President on White House stationary, original envelope, thank you for neckties - $1250

Harry S. Truman, TLS, one page, 1971, get well letter, original envelope - $175

Heinrich Himmler, DS, in German as Minister of Interior - $895

Henry Clay, ALS, to B.O. Taylor, Esquire, accepting invitation - $295

Horace Greeley, ALS, on New York Tribune stationary, January 22, 1872, regarding newspaper matters - $85

James Michael Curley, Boston politician, typed, signed letter - $125

John Adams, SL, old signature and closing from a letter in another hand, with a vintage portrait - $1100

John Glenn, signature on illustrated United Nations cover, 1962, EX - $18

John La Farge, artist, ALS, New York, 1867, to Miss Beach, Rockville, New York - $125

Joseph Goebbels, ALS, on verso of German postcard, dated 1921 - $1750

Josephine Baker, TLS, in French, 1971, three paragraphs - $295

Juan Peron, as President, two pages, on personal, embossed stationary - $850

Kalakua, last King of Hawaii, signed card - $275

Louis Armstrong, signed program, Cave Theatre Restaurant, c.1962 - $165

Lenore Ulrich, early movie star, SP, eight by ten photo by Miskin, New York. On back, David Belasco presents 'Tiger Rose' at the Lyceum Theatre, 1918 - $25

Mamie Eisenhower, TLS, White House stationary, thank you for Christmas tree - $95

Mark David Chapman, John Lennon's Killer, ALS, 1989, requests where correspondent got address, polite but annoyed, original envelope - $275

AUTOGRAPHS

Martha Raye, TLS, 1942, answer to collector, self typed - $20

Mel Blanc, 1978, of Blanc with his cartoon friends, signed above printed name - $50

Milton Caniff, cartoonist, signed and inscribed magazine portrait - $45

Norman Rockwell, ALS, dated August 14, 1956 - $675

Oliver Wendell Holmes, Jr., ALS, while on Court complies with collector's request - $495

O.M. Hatch, Secretary of State of Illinois during Lincoln's trusted advisor. 1872 signed check from Tidgeley National Bank, revenue imprint - $15

Robert F. Kennedy, TLS, Office of Attorney General, June 17, 1964, to United States Customs Court Judge - $450

Rose Kennedy, ALS, from Antibes, August 13, 1961, declines invitation - $195

Sitting Bull, signature of a drawn scroll upon payment of one dollar fee, with authentification - $4200

Susan B. Anthony, ink signature, Rochester, New York, June 22, 1887, in her hand - $175

U.S. Grant, partly printed, signed check, made out to cash for $100. Two cent revenue stamp on corner - $1200

Victor Herbert, DS, Willow Grove Park music, account payable, 1908 - $350

Wilbur and Orville Wright, slip signed by both - $2350

William Jennings Bryant, ALS, Hotel Astor stationary, not date - $195

William Jennings Bryant, signature on card - $80

William Marcy 'Boss' Tweed, DS, as Deputy Street Commissioner, 1867 - $195

As of November, 1992, prices of original historical documents from the Kenneth W. Rendell Gallery follow.

ABRAHAM LINCOLN. Military appointment, 1861, as President. - $9500

DAVID BEN-GURION. Signed photograph of Ben-Gurion working at desk. $950.

FREDERIC CHOPIN. Copy of Histoire de Catherine II, signed in Paris 1845. - $25,000

CHARLES DICKENS. Third person letter, 1850 - $1500

RICHARD WAGNER. Thank you letter, 1863. - $6500

TY COBB. signed check, 1948 - $975

JEROME KERN. Thank you for thinking of me and project - $1500

SARAH BERNHARDT. "I am in the bustle of dressing. Come at once." - $750

ELVIS PRESLEY "I won't believe anyone any more." - $7500

ERNEST HEMINGWAY. French franc note signed in 1940. - $2750

GEORGE GERSHWIN. Signed musical quotation. - $12,500

LOUIS ARMSTRONG. photo. - $1750

PAUL GAUGUIN. "Hoping to meet you." - $22,500

SIGMUND FREUD. 1931 on the New Free Press. - $9500

P.T. BARNUM. signed autobiography 1888 - $2500

AMELIA EARHART. Signed airmail envelope. 1929. - $2500

SAMUEL L. CLEMONS. Autograph quotation. - $9500

GRETA GARBO. Signed closing quote. - $4500

MARK CHAGALL. Signed color reproduction. - $950

RAYMOND CHANDLER. Fine contract. - $3750

U.S. GRANT. A criminal's pardon as President. - $1500

WALT DISNEY. "On the value of an education." - $3500

AGATHA CHRISTIE. Confusion on death of her mother. - $1500

MAE WEST. signed photograph. - $750

CHARLES A. LINDBERGH. Photograph with mother signed before historic flight. - $6750

ROBERT E. LEE. signed letter - $12,500

ERWIN ROMMEL. "You have not a minute for me anymore?" - $5750

DWIGHT D. EISENHOWER. Signed printed D-Day message. - $3500

ENRICO CARUSO. signed photograph. - $3500

FRANK LLOYD WRIGHT. Signed 1942, "the boys are on the way here from the desert." - $3000

ALBERT EINSTEIN "The support of cultural life-" - $12,500

KNUTE ROCKNE. Signed Notre Dame rule book 1916-1917. - $3750

JOHN F. KENNEDY. Letter on coming session of Congress. - $2000

MARTIN LUTHER KING. Signed book of Montgomery bus boycott. - $2750

LETTERS

Women may be a minority amongst paper memorabilia collectors but in one field they have always outshone men. Women save letters. Not all of them romantic in tone or content. Personal accounts of events, large or small, fill the well read pages.

During our Civil War, an enlisted man advertised for a correspondent. A young lady answered the advertisement. Beginning in August 1863 and ending in August of 1868 when they were married, he wrote more than 100 letters to her. Some were written from the field between skirmishes, some offering glimpses of a long distance romance. As a collection, they were a personal side light to a war's drama and intrigue.

Would a man have saved those letters? Unlikely. Would a woman? Any woman would.

This lot of letters sold at an auction for $1,800. See how much smarter women are than men?

Not everyone can turn down an offer of help gracefully. P.T. Barnum did so nicely as this letter notes. Photo from Robert Pelton, Barnum Museum Collection.

169

A caricature drawn by Picasso was included in a letter to his friend Appolinaire. Courtesy Conrad Schoeffling, C.W. Post, Campus/L.I.U.

Letter from a Queen. Meant for Lord Byron, it may have been written by the Chief of Protocol. Regardless, its significance lies in its social history.

Maria Jane Taylor
March 1829

LIEUT. JAMES MOODY'S

NARRATIVE

OF HIS

EXERTIONS AND SUFFERINGS

IN THE

CAUSE OF GOVERNMENT,

Since the YEAR 1776;

AUTHENTICATED BY PROPER CERTIFICATES.

THE SECOND EDITION.

LONDON:

Printed; and sold by RICHARDSON and URQUHART, at
the Royal Exchange; WILKIE, St. Paul's Church-Yard;
FAULDER, Bond-Street; and S. HAYES, Oxford-Street.

MDCCLXXXIII.

For a different view of the Revolutionary War, this account of Lt. James Moody's trials as a loyalist spy who intercepted Washington's dispatches, blew up munitions, enlisted loyalists to fight the colonists, was captured and escaped is the stuff of late night movies and a Sotheby auction.

RED-JACKET
A SENECA WAR CHIEF.

PUBLISHED BY E. C. BIDDLE, PHILADELPHIA.

A history of the Indian Tribes of North America, from the early 1800s, with portraits of American Indians, were painted mostly by government artist 'King'. Sotheby.

Le voyage et na-

uigation/faict par les Espaignolz es
Isles de Mollucques.des isles quilz
ont trouue audict voyage/ des Roys
dicelles/de leur gouuernement & ma-
niere de biure/auec plusieurs aultres
choses.

Cum priuilegio.

❡ On les bend a Paris en la maison de
Simon de Colines/ libraire iure de lu
niuersite de Paris/demonrât en la rue
sainct Jehan de Beauluais/ a lensei-
gne du Soleil Dor.

A first edition of the most authentic account of the first circumnavigation of the world, written by Antonio Pigafetta in Paris, c.1525, described Magallan's feat.

JOURNAL

OF THE FIRST SESSION OF THE

SENATE

OF THE

UNITEDSTATESofAMERICA,

BEGUN AND HELD

AT THE

CITYofNEW-YORK,

MARCH 4th, 1789,

AND

IN THE THIRTEENTH YEAR OF THE

INDEPENDENCE OF THE SAID STATES.

NEW-YORK, Printed by THOMAS GREENLEAF,
——M, D C C, L X X X, I X.——

This journal of the first session of the United States Senate in New York on March 7, 1789, deals on April 6th with the announcement of Washington's and John Adam's selection to be President and Vice-President of the United States. More important are proposed amendments to the Constitution, being the core of the Bill of Rights. Sotheby.

NARRATIVE

OF A

JOURNEY ACROSS THE ROCKY MOUNTAINS,

TO

THE COLUMBIA RIVER,

AND

A VISIT TO THE SANDWICH ISLANDS, CHILI, &c.

WITH

A SCIENTIFIC APPENDIX.

BY JOHN K. TOWNSEND,
Member of the Academy of Natural Sciences of Philadelphia.

PHILADELPHIA:
HENRY PERKINS, 134 CHESTNUT STREET.
BOSTON: PERKINS & MARVIN.

1839.

In 1834, John Townsend, under Captain Wyeth, in company with Thomas Nuttall, made a journey across the Rocky Mountains to the Columbia River. This is the narrative. Sotheby.

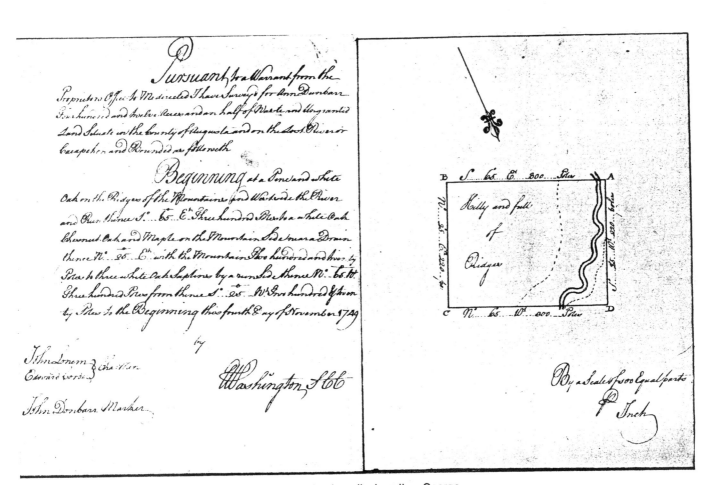

The school books all describe George Washington as a surveyor. Here an autographed manuscript survey of 4 November, signed G. Washington, SCC. One of the earliest Washington surveys known as he was 17 at the time. Sotheby.

May

3 Mr. Daingerfields Negro Bricklayer
   Guy came here to Work. —
4 Finished Planting Corn at all Places
10 Counted the Tobo. Ho. at _____
   as follows viz. — of —
   Cooper _____
   Dung'd Ho. in Peach Orchard — 3500
   Ditto in Apple Orchard — 3500   12,500
   New ground — 12500
   Old Ground _____ — 10700
   Large Cut in Corn field Fence 22000
   Middle Cut _____ adjoin'd — 9200.
   Small Cut near Woods Do. — 1500.
   Round New Tobo. House — 8500
   Branch between _____
   Do. Ho. old Gd. S. side Run — 13000
11 Tol'd my Sheep as follows — viz. & Cut & Mark'd
   Ewes in all — 104   Ewe Lambs — 38
   Weathers Do. 29   Left for Rams — 4
   Rams — 6   Weathers — 8
   _____   139   Left for Killing — 18
   _____ 66
   Note. ye above includes falling Sheep
   Ewes & Lambs —
11 Put 31 Hides in Soak for Tanning —
   Guy began ye Garden Wall, after having built
   a drain in ye Kitchen, laid the hearth, & repair'd
   the back.
   Do. brought 5 Cows & Calves from _____
13 Got a Cask of Lisbon Ale from Mr. Marshal Price _____
   Do. Agreed for Do. Mr. Bell Work for £51 _____
15 6 Cows & Calves from _____ 3 _____ & from Ck.
22 Young Countifs & Black Mare cover'd by Al. Hanson _____ Hon.
28 Planted ab't 50 or 60,000 — being the first — Top put on _____
   Roan's bay & Sorrel cover'd by Mr. Hoyes _____ ravell'd
   English bay & Black cover'd by Ariel
30 Chesnut Mare — cover'd by Col'o. H. County & Col'o. return'd
   Do. Roan Mare & old Black cover'd by Mr. _____
   Do. White Mare & Franklin cover'd by Do.

July. —

27 Bank _____ cover'd by _____
28 Corn planted in _____
29 Replanted Too. — _____ went to Work at Bells
30 good Season — _____ best part of Tob.

July. —

3 Got 194 bush. _____ in Bells
4 My Mares came home from Mr. Hoyes
   _____ _____
   Finished Plant'g & replant'g at all Do.
23 Put my Wheat at A, B, & C, & Do.
   Do. finished first cutt'g of Hay
   finished plow'g behind Garden.
   Carpenters went to Reap'g at Posey.
   Mares brot. from Mr. Digges's
   Tol'd my Sheep as follows —
      6 Rams at Johnsons
      12 Ewes at Do.
      64 Do. _____ large
      1 Do. put into _____
      13 Weathers put into Do.
      16 Cut g. in pasture
      112 old Sheep besides one at Col'o. Fox
      12 Rams _____ put into _____
      8 Weathers Do. in grass g.
      38 Ewe Ditto   in Ditto
      200 in all & besides put'd Ewes & _____
   _____ cattle for fall g. upon Do.
      2 old Steers from D. King formerly
      1 old Cow from Do.
      2 old Steers from there to Day.
      1 old Cow from Muddy hole
      2 old Oxen — Home _____
      1 old Cow Do. Do. — which came from _____
      9 — in all —
   Nancy _____ left this

From a more mature Washington in 1762, of eight
diary pages discussing planting, cattle raising,
slaves and finance. Sotheby.

174

PROCEEDINGS

OF A

BOARD

OF

GENERAL OFFICERS,

HELD BY ORDER OF

His Excellency Gen. WASHINGTON,

Commander in Chief of the Army of the United States
of AMERICA.

RESPECTING

Major JOHN ANDRÉ,

Adjutant General of the British Army.

SEPTEMBER 29, 1780.

PHILADELPHIA:
Printed by FRANCIS BAILEY, in Market-Street
M.DCC.LXXX.

Intrigue comes alive on these pages when Major John Andre is found guilty and letters by Benedict Arnold threaten Washington if Andre's life is forfeit. Sotheby.

JOURNAL of the PROCEEDINGS

against the Conspirators at NEW-YORK, 1741.

At a Supreme Court of Judicature held for the Province of NEW-YORK, at the City Hall of the City of New-York, on

TUESDAY, 21st APRIL, 1741.

PRESENT,

FREDERICK PHILIPSE, Esq; Second Justice.
DANIEL HORSMANDEN, Esq; Third Justice.

The Grand-Jury called.

The following Persons appeared, and were sworn, Viz.

Mr. ROBERT WATTS, Merchant, Foreman.

Messrs. Jeremiah Latouche,
Joseph Read,
Anthony Rutgers,
John Mc Evers,
John Cruger, jun.
John Merritt,
Adoniah Schuyler,
Isaac De Peyster, } Merchants.
Abraham Ketteltass,
David Provoost,
Rene Hett,
Henry Beekman, jun.
David Van Horne,
George Spencer,
Thomas Duncan,
Winant Van Zant.

Mr. Justice PHILLIPSE gave the Charge to the Grand Jury as followeth.

"Gentlemen of the Grand Jury,

"IT is not without some Concern, that I am obliged at this Time to be more particular in your Charge than for many preceeding Terms there hath been Occasion. The many Frights and Terrors which the good People of this City have of late been put into, by repeated and unusual Fires, and burning of Houses, give us too much Room to suspect, that some of them at least did not proceed from meer Chance or common Accidents; but on the Contrary, from the premeditated Malice and wicked Purposes of evil and designing Persons; and therefore it greatly behoves us to use our utmost Diligence by all lawful Ways and Means to discover the Contrivers and Perpetrators of such daring and flagitious Undertakings: That, upon Conviction, they may receive condign Punishment: For although we have the Happiness of living under a Government which exceeds all others in the Excellency of it's Constitution and Laws, yet if those to whom the Execution of them (which My Lord COKE calls the Life and Soul of the Law) is committed, do not exert themselves in a conscientious Discharge of their respective Duties; such Laws which were intended for a Terror to the Evil-Doer, and a Protection to the Good, will become a dead Letter, and our most excellent Constitution turned into Anarchy and Confusion; every one practising what he listeth, and doing what shall seem good in his own Eyes: To prevent which, it is the Duty of all Grand Juries to enquire into the Conduct and Behaviour of the People in their respective Counties; and if, upon Examination, they find any to have transgressed the Laws of the Land, to present them, that so they may by the Court be put upon their Tryal, and then either to be discharged or punished according to their Demerits.

C 2

In 1741, the so called Negro plot (which included some whites) had a great idea: burn the city of New York. It's been tried since on several occasions without success, but this first edition, printed by James Parker, describes a little known vignette of the city's early history. Sotheby.

Paul Cezanne, a Post-Impressionist from France at the turn of the century comes this auto--graphed letter signed, dates Fountain blue, July 6, 1905, notifying an art supply house of receipt of one order of paints and canvas, and increasing a follow up order not yet received. Sotheby in 1976 offered this letter for $5000.

A Bible containing the old and new testaments translated into an Indian language in the late 17th century. Sotheby.

Quakers, in *America*, that are zealous against this and all other Iniquity, to whom my Soul is nearly united in Spirit, bleſſed be the Lord my God, for ſo great a favour for evermore. And I believe ſome of other Profeſſions alſo, whom I dearly love ; and I have ſome Hope the Number of all Sorts, that truly fear God and Love his Truth at Heart, will increaſe, which I ſhould rejoice to hear and ſee, although Things ſeem to look dark at preſent. *B. L.*

Abington, the 3d of the 3d Mo. 1736, *between 3 and 4 this Morning.*

IT was again revived in my Mind, the Practice of Slave-keeping, and thus to query.

Whether it is not as wicked and ſinful a Practice to keep and trade in Slaves, as to commit the following Evils and filthy Abominations, which are now in Cuſtom I ſuppoſe by Jew and Gentile, to whom our brave Slavekeepers allude, *Abraham* and the Law. That is to ſay, Keeping many Wives and Harlots or Concubines, going to and making uſe of Harlots when they pleaſe, and Mankind too ; and many other Things mentioned in the Old Teſtament, and other Hiſtories, and by *Peter Charron* in his Book of Wiſdom, page 324. *The*

The 15th of the 1ſt month, 1736,7.

JOHN MILTON wrote a Treatiſe concerning *the likelieſt Means to remove Hirelings out of the Church*, which I gave to King *George* the I. and to the preſent King and Queen, that they might ſee what a Company of deſtructive Vermin they had about them. And I think there is as much need now to keep ſuch as are of the ſame Spirit out of the Church, or it is in great Danger in the Opinion of ſome ſeeing worthy Friends, who can ſee beyond Profeſſion, Formality or worldly Intereſt.

That Spirit has ſomething in view ; the good of the Belly, a rich Wife or Husband, carrying on a good Trade, or to be exalted, and to get or keep up a ſtrong Party for ſome Deſign, baſe enough; and under this Cloak of Deceit, accuſe others of ſeeking a Party. Now when this Spirit goes forth with Authority from the outward Church, then our Meetings are or may be ſure to be grievouſly peſtered, with noiſe if not nonſenſe. It ſeems as if ſome of our Miniſters (I was going to ſay many) have forgot the great Benefit of Silent Meetings, if ever they rightly knew it, that they are ſo reſtleſs in them, and muſt

R be

From the Franklin Press, came one of the earliest books on the abolition of slavery printed in America. RARE: deemed most important, dated 1737. Sotheby. 176

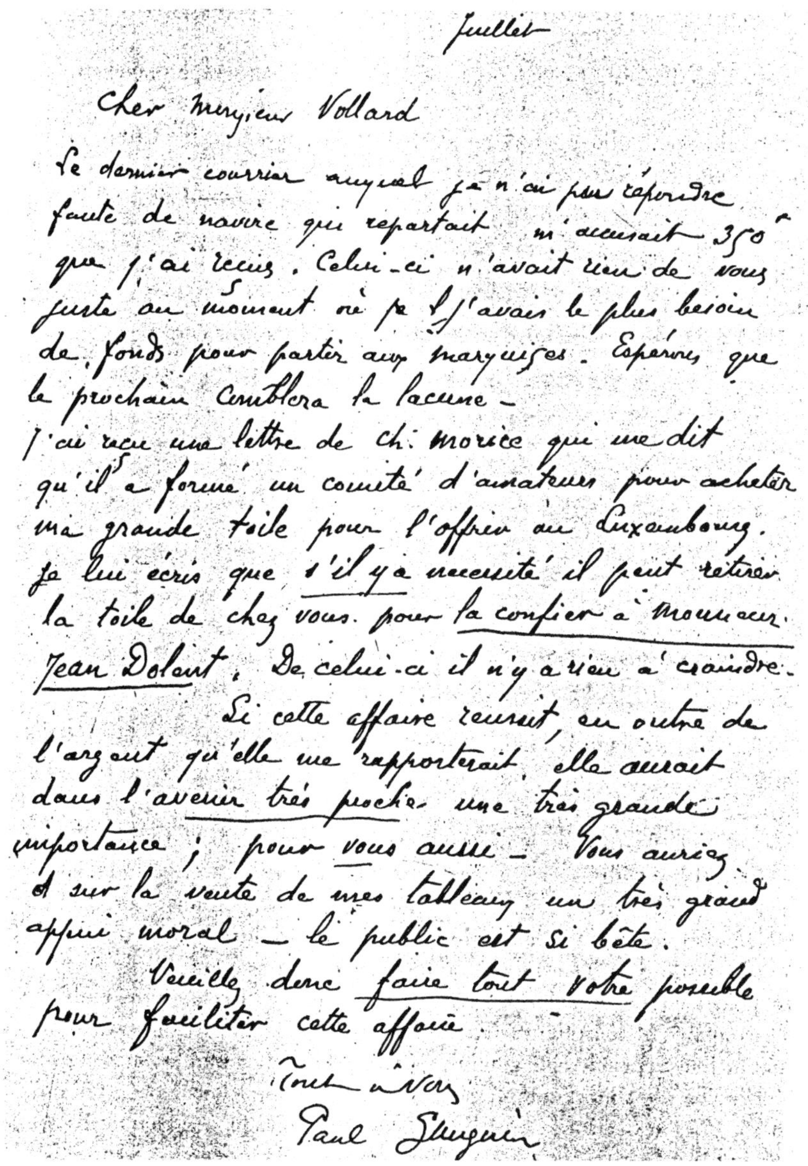

Juillet

Cher monsieur Vollard

Le dernier courrier auquel je n'ai pas répondre faute de navire qui repartait m'accusait 350f que j'ai reçus. Celui-ci n'avait rien de vous juste au moment où j'avais le plus besoin de fonds pour partir aux marquises. Espérons que le prochain comblera la lacune –

J'ai reçu une lettre de Ch. Morice qui me dit qu'il a formé un comité d'amateurs pour acheter ma grande toile pour l'offrir au Luxembourg. Je lui écris que s'il y a nécessité il peut retirer la toile de chez vous pour la confier à Monsieur Jean Dolent. De celui-ci il n'y a rien à craindre.

Si cette affaire réussit, en outre de l'argent qu'elle me rapporterait, elle aurait dans l'avenir très proche une très grande importance; pour vous aussi – Vous auriez sur la vente de mes tableaux un très grand appui moral – le public est si bête.

Veuillez donc faire tout votre possible pour faciliter cette affaire.

Tout à vous
Paul Gauguin

Paul Gauguin: the universal cry of humanity was evident in Gauguin's letter to his agent: send money. Paul did something we would all like to do. He sold everything (his paintings) and sailed to a South Sea island, in his case Tahiti.

Due to historical accidents, postal stamps sometimes became secondary to an event. Stamps on flight covers of Zeppelins were one of the occasions when the Graf Zeppelin burned and crashed in Lakehurst, New Jersey. Because of this event flight covers may be offered for up to $100 at some shows.

Philip V, King of France, 1316-1322, was evidently a man concerned with details, minute or gross. He tried, during his reign, to reform and unify coinage, weights, and measures. His careful script, could have been a page taken from an illustrated manuscript. Rendell.

PAPER CURRENCY

Paper money owes its existence to emergency situations such as revolution, invasion, inflation all being within that classification. It is not a new idea. China produced the world's first paper money about A.D. 200.

It was the Mongols under Kublai Khan who were first to pay their soldiers by issuing paper military money. Predictably, it was at that time that China experienced its first paper money inflation.

Six hundred and twenty years later, in 1880, on another continent, one William Michael Harnett offered another form of paper money - a trompe l'oeil painting (one that tricks the eye) of American paper currency. He found himself between the expressions of his art and the dictates of the law in the form of the Treasury Department. He spawned an entire school of imitators.

Harnett's paintings of paper currency pose no difficulty in dating. Yet dating real paper money less than fifty years old may often be difficult even for the experienced collector.

One of the reasons is simple. Like all paper collectibles, there is just such vast quantities and varieties to be had. Governments are tempted to overissue paper money in times of stress. Look no further back than the German mark of the French franc in the early 1920s for proof. Or to our own Civil War.

The United States printed notes commonly called 'greenbacks'. Although they later obtained parity (only because the North won), in 1864, the one dollar greenback note brought only 35¢ in its gold backing. Again, for the same simple reasoning, there was just so much of it.

CHECKS

Checks are an exercise in faith. Positive belief there is money in the offeres bank account to cover. It has been said that 90% of all money transactions in the United States are made by check or credit card. It is also possible that a percentage of these same checks will bounce.

Paper collectibles have only one worry when buying a signed check and that is to make sure the signature is genuine and not a facsimile. The same skills are used to determine the authenticity of a check's signature as are used for any other form of autograph. In other words, don't accept a check on faith alone, even those a hundred years old that a bank once cashed.

Checks are low valued collectibles, evident by the price tag on these checks from a Louisville, Kentucky bank.

SPORTS EQUIPMENT

Sports equipment has only peripheral interest to a paper collector, mostly because of autographs. Here again don't line up and pay to have a bat or ball or glove autographed. The value you hope for will never be there. Too many signatures by the player and no historic interest in the item you offer to be signed are the major flaws against any significant rise in value.

As in any collectible field, go for the best you can afford. You may hesitate before paying $12,000 for a baseball bat signed by Babe Ruth and used by him in a game. Or even $500 for a baseball signed by both Dizzy and Daffy Dean. But an Official American League game used baseball signed by Hubble and Heimben for $140 or a Lou Gehrig Christmas card from Lou's tour of Japan, and sold for $50, may fit your finances.

They will offer as much collector joy as the more expensive items with less money to lay out for security and insurance. If you think about it, a Lou Gehrig postcard is a real find, a real paper collectible.

Magazines:

The Autograph Collector's Magazine, P.O. Box 55328, Stockton, CA 95205, Phone: 209-473-0570, Joe Kraus Editor/Publisher

Manuscripts Magazine of the Manuscript Society, 350 North Niagra St., Burbank, CA 91505, David R. Smith Executive Director

Associations:

Manuscript Society (See **Magazines**)

Universal Autograph Collectors Club, P.O. Box 6181, Washington, D.C. 20044-7388, Phone: 202-332-7388, Robert A. Erickson

Professional Currency Dealers Association, P.O. Box 573, Milwaukee, WI 53201, Phone: 414-282-2388, Kevin Foley Secretary/Treasurer

World Paper Currency Collectors, American Numesmatic Association, 818 North Cascade Ave., Colorado Springs, CO 80903-3279, Phone: 719-632-2646

American Society of Check Collectors 2115 Roman Court, Warren, MI 48092, Phone: 313-573-0796

Museums:

The American Numismatic Society, Broadway and 155th Street, New York, NY 10032, Phone: 212-234-3130

Farmers Bank, 19 Bollingbrook Street, Petersburg, VA 23803, Phone: 804-733-2400

Johnson County, Jim Gatchel Memorial Museum, 10 Fort Street, Buffalo, WY 82834, Phone: 307-608-9331

U.S. Army Finance Corps Museums, M.G. Emmett, J. Bean Center, INdianapolis, Indiana 46249, Phone: 317-542-2169

Wells Fargo Historical Museum, 420 Montgomery Street, San Francisco, CA 94163, Phone: 415-396-2619

AUTOGRAPHS

Prices:

Movie star autographed photograph, 8"x10", Bryant Washburn by Hartsook, San Francisco - $35

Movie star autographed photography, 8"x10", Lenore Ulrich by Miskin, NY. On back, David Belasco presents 'Tiger-Rose' at the lyceum Theatre 1918 - $25

Check, National Exchange Bank, signed Theodore Francis Green, governor of Rhode Island 1933-37, U.S. Senator 1937-81 - $9

A 1665 deed signed by Charles Calvert, property of Kingsley Greene, seal tag and remains of original wax seal - $140

John Adams, older age signature and closing from a letter in another hand with vintage engraved portrait - $1100

Susan B. Anthony, ink signature with Rochester, NY, June 27/87 in her hand, matted with oval frame - $175

Charles Dickins, ALS, 1839, London, to Edward Dowland, part of wax seal gone, bold signature $1200

Rich boy's diary, four months of non-stop activity, including Douglas Fairbanks and Charlie Chaplin, college life in 1918 - $75

Pair of crossed on check from Bridgeport, CT, 1877, revenue imprint, RN-M2, from Sharp's Rifle Co., VF - $90

Aide to volunteer, April 18, 1864, a two, 8"x10" page affidavit for wife from soldier in Wisconsin regiment, signed by Captain - $15

O.M. Hatch, Secretary of State of Illinois during Lincoln term. His trusted advisor, 1872 signed check from Ridgeley National Bank, revenue imprint - $15

William Jennings Bryant, ALS, Hotel Astor 1 letterhead, two pages, no date - $195

Oliver Wendell Holmes Jr., ALS, while on The Court. Complies with collectors request plus photograph - $495

Adolph Hitler, DS, in German, two pages, commissions three Lieutenant Generals and ten Major Generals - $2750

U.S. Grant, partly printed signed check made out to cash for $100. 2¢ revenue stamp on corner - $1200

CHAPTER XVII

MONEY: PROMISES, PROMISES

Checks are a promise of money. So is paper currency. It is a promise that a government will honor these engraved or printed bits of paper, or exchange them for coinage or metal. The variations in form, color, value, or historic significance make of checks, and particularly currency, prime collectibles.

They are only the appetizers of a long menu of paper hoardings. Stocks and bonds are another form of money, more volatile in worth, and not readily exchanged for currency.

Since checks, currency, stocks, and bonds are promises by governments or corporations, so are other forms of paper issued by these same entities.

Stamps by their very use are a promise that the mail will be delivered. For other uses there are flaws. Issued as commemorative stamps (sheets of 25, 50, or 100 are usual) may be bought for about five percent less than their face value. The postal authorities will accept them as postage at par.

Somewhere between their issue date and their below face value sale by a dealer, stamp collectors did not take seriously to these highly promoted commemorative issues and rejected them as collectibles. They had been printed by the millions and were now a glut on the market. Discounting to large users of stamps for commercial mailing purposes helps to unload these unwanted sheets.

This is not a deep, dark secret. It has been going on as business as usual for many decades.

Stamps take other forms. They serve as an official notice that a tax has been paid and that a mortgage is legal.

A ticket to board a train, a plane, or a steamship is another promise - a promise that transportation between two or more destinations will be provided by the transportations owners or employees in order to honor that ticket.

When the old map makers filled in unexplored areas with the words, "here be demons", they were only foretelling what occasionally happens to the purchaser of a ticket, "here be problems." More so among airline companies than with trains or ships. Weather may make railroad tracks impassable, or hold up the sailing schedule of a ship, however, they do not 'bump' passengers as will an airline which quite often will oversell the seating capacity of a plane.

Such events are part of the turbulence of the 20th century. It makes the colonialism of the past centuries seem peaceful and placid. A time when promises appeared to be kept by governments and corporations. The key word is 'appeared'. Paper promises were just that - paper promises. It's always been safer to believe in a postage stamp on a piece of mail.

More Confederate money is collected in this country than foreign currency, so say the dealers. The ease with which it is found, the attached history, and its social significance are all part of its collectibility.

Stamps are not only used for postage. Like The Federal Migratory Waterfowl Stamps they are a form of license. Others from this country or abroad are never used as postage but collected, filed, and hoarded away as collectibles. Sutliffe Collection. High in interest, how in price. Prices average from less than $1 to just under $5.

STAMPS

Postage stamps have been collected since the first penny black was issued by the British government in 1840. Stamps are a form of money that may be exchanged for the delivery elsewhere of a letter or a package. Stamps also enter into a form of collecting called 'topicals'. This is a special category whereby collectors pursue only stamps with a special type of picture regardless of country. Paper collectors become doubly fortunate. Stamps are paper with a whole range of stamps issued that pertain to a specific collectible field.

Many countries have issued stamps depicting Disneyana characters. Our own nation has issued stamps showing major collectibles from Fine Art to painted tin ware.

There is another stamp form that has become increasingly popular as a collectible and that is the so called 'Duck Stamp'. This is also a promissory note. It promises you won't be arrested and charged with violation of the game laws if you are caught hunting with one.

Prominent names in the world of art become involved in the production of these stamps. A different stamp is issued each year with a different species shown.

First issued in 1934, Federal Migratory Waterfowl stamps are the easiest to find. Check what is being offered at sporting auctions. There are also National Wild Turkey stamps and Federal Bird Hunting stamps. Still reasonably priced are the Golden Federal Migratory Waterfowl stamps issued in 1983/1984 to commemorate the 50th Anniversary edition of Federal bird stamps

Names well known in the art world have contributed their skills with water colors or oils for these stamps aiding in their increasing popularity. William C. Morris, Phil Schaler, David Maas, John S. Wilson, Al Gilbert, Martin Murk, James Harlman, James P. Fischer, Robert Bateman, and Maynard Reece are among those whose art is increasingly collected in the form of Federal hunting stamps.

Stamps such as these have been issued for years without committing themselves to the current trend of 'gimmicks'. Odd sizes, stamps with only half the picture unless you buy two, are some of the ploys being used by emerging nations (and some that emerged hundreds of years ago) to sell stamps meant only to be placed in albums rather than be used on mail. Since there is no delivery expense to the issuing government, the gimmick stamp, other than printing cost, is almost pure profit.

RAILROAD AND STEAMSHIP TICKETS

Rail and ship tickets are minor segments of collectibles, yet they have their adherents. While they may never achieve the popularity - or price - of a 1926 World Series Yankee Stadium ticket stub, that may be all to the good. It means the collector will never have to pay $200 for one, as someone did for that World Series ticket stub.

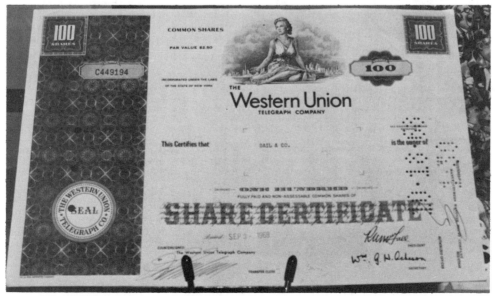

Former evidence of power or wealth, now worthless, except as collectibles, these share certificates are master pieces of the engraver's art.

STOCKS AND BONDS

Stocks and bonds represent ownership of an incorporated business or participation in a debt owed by a municipality. Anyone interested only in this aspect should read *Money Magazine*, *Moody's*, *Baron's*, or *Fortune*. Fortunately for paper collectors there are other delights to owning capitol shares and bonds, particularly if the companies involved are no longer in existence with their historic importance, graphics, or their abilities to shed light on a moment in the past.

When viewed as collectibles, the characteristics that were an integral part of their issue still remains. The terms that describe these now collectible papers.

The engraved certificate was once evidence of equity. 'Authorized stock' would be the maximum number of shares the company was allowed to issue without amending its charter.

If the company, at some time in its future, bought back some of its outstanding stock, these shares became 'treasury stock' or were canceled. What is left in the hands of investors is 'outstanding stock'.

There may be more than one class of a stock issue, evident on a certificate. Original offerings are usually 'common stock'. There may also be issues of 'preferred' or 'Class A' stock.

Some preferred stock is 'convertible'. It may be exchanged for a specified number of shares of common, sometimes at a previously set price.

Attached to or with the certificate may be coupons, which are exchanged for 'declared dividends' usually of cash, sometimes for more stock. If the coupon is exchanged for a 'stock dividend', the erstwhile coupon clipper did not get richer. All he did was to acquire a new certificate he didn't own previously.

Stock certificate prices, old certificates, from companies no longer in existence, do not follow the ups and downs of the stock market. Instead they follow the vagaries of collector's whims.

Actually certificates with defunct companies have changed little in prices over the past several decades. Mostly are still low prices, apparently following the cost of living curve.

The low prices of these 'wall paper' certificates are a boon to collectors.

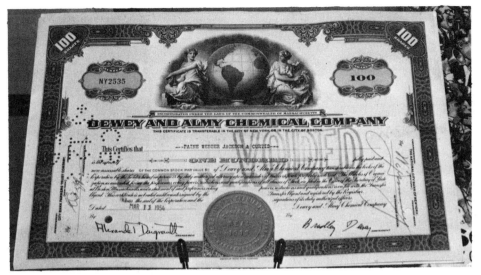

It is not necessarily the price of these bits of
colorful paper that lures collectors. Mostly it's
the engravings and the historical background.

Many are printed by companies that make bank
notes for foreign countries.

Although in a sense they look like legal tender,
their values fell faster than the value of the
American dollar. At least that's still worth
something.

On the other hand, share certificates of the long defunct United Cigar Store Company of America, was shown at a paper show in 1992 priced at $35. Now if they would only accept one at a supermarket.

But even supermarkets may join the ranks of companies that once were, as this Grand Union Company 100 share certificate suggests, along with its two companion certificates.

Once there is no longer a basis for copyright infringement, share certificates become fair game for graphic designers who buy the engraved papers for unusual ideas. They will pay $5 to $35 or more, gladly, for designs that appeal to their sense of value.

MONEY

Prices:

Alabama Gold and Copper Mining Company, New Mexico, 1899, signed by Pat Garrett - $1,950

American Express Company, 1863, signed by Henry Wells and William Fargo, company founders - $525

American Telegraphone Company, 1907, District of Columbia - $25

B and O Railroad Company, 1893, New York, 50 shares incorporated 1827 - $30

Bird Aircraft Corporation, New York - $12

Baltimore and Ohio Railroad Company, 1893, old steam engine and cars - $28

Banco Central Mexico, 34 coupons - $10

Bank of America, 1853, Top, large eagle, bottom, small eagle - $15

Bank of Orange County, 1862, Goshen, New York, woman, garden tools, stock color blue - $20

Bay State, Gas Company, 1908, Indian vignette - $6

Bonanza Division Company, Leadville, Colorado, 1883 - $40

Boston and Albany Railroad Company, cancelled, 1919 - $25

Boston, Clinton, Fitchburg, New Bedford Railroad Company, 1878, Indian maiden - $21

Boston, Clinton, New Bedford Railroad Company, 1876, seal on left - $14

Boston, Hartford, Erie Railroad, $1000, 50 coupons - $65

Boston, Hartford, Erie Railroad Company, 1863, $1000, 50 coupons, three RN stamps - $50

Boston, Erie Railroad Company, Inc., Connecticut 1863, dates also 1865 as issued, two trains and eagles - $35

Boston - Providence Railroad Company, 1867, brown 25 stamp - $22

Boston - Providence Railroad Company, 1874, train on bridge - $15

Camden and Philadelphia Steamboat Ferry Company, 1873, New Jersey, steamboat and trains - $80

Capitol School, State of Missouri, County of Tarry - $6

Carbon Building and Loan Association, 1919, Red Lodge Montana, marked cancelled - $6

Certificate #1, First National Bank of Bisbee, Arizona Territory, 1904 - $90

Chambersburg and Bedford Turnpike Road Company, 1818, Pennsylvania, $5, used as money Chicago, Burlington, Quincy Railroad Company, 1899, stamp on back - $20

Cincinnati and St. Louis Railroad Company, November 25, 1882, EX - $12

City of Carey, State of Kansas, 1905, Water Extension Enlargement Bond - $6

Clark Automatic Telephone Switchboard Company, 1903, Providence, Rhode Island, eagle on bottom - $15

Confederate, $1000, 1864, 5th series, 50 coupons - $35

Confederate, $1000, vignette Jefferson Davis, overview of Richmond, seven coupons - $38

Columbus Piqua Indiana Railroad Company of Ohio, letter with stock sold at tax sale - $35

County of Lawrence, Territory of Dakota, 1887, $500, trains and mountains - $30

Eastern Airlines, New York - $12

Eureka Mining Company, State of Rhode Island, two document stamps - $10

Everglades Club Company, USA, State of Florida, 1936, with coupons - $10

Everglades County, Florida, $1000, 1928, 10 coupons - $9

Federal Migratory Waterfowl Stamp and print, by Edward J. Bierly, of Ross's Geese, 1970-1971, signed - $300

Federal Migratory Waterfowl Stamp and print, by David Maas, 1974-1975, wood ducks, signed - $300

First Exchange, 1857, New York, ships and trains - $30

First Exchange, Memphis, Tennessee, 1878, for $1065 - $15

General Oil Company, Harris County, Texas - $12

General Oil Company, State of Texas, fancy red bond - $8

Government, $100, 1841, ten coupons on, with 50 Broken Bank treasury note N-21, Houston, Texas, signed by Sam Houston, 1837, in frame - $175

Guanajuato Development Company, New Jersey, 1906 - $6

Idaho Consolidated Mines, Arizona, eight vignettes - $15

Illinois Central Railroad, 1963, engines - $9

Indian Spring Oil Company, 1865, 25¢ brown stamp - $25

Iron and Steel Plant Company Ltd., 1980, ten shares at 10 pounds sterling - $6

Kay Hardy Mining Company, San Jose, California, Forest Sierra County, California, 1920 - $12

Lehigh Valley Railroad Company 1890. Pennsylvania, brown stamp top right - $30

Mexican Telephone Company, 1880, New York City - $6

Mining Stock, Diamondfields, 1911, signed by gunman Diamondfield Jack Davis - $425

Missouri, Kansas, Texas, 1908, steam engine - $13

Nevada Greenback Wonder Mining Company, 1907, Reno, Nevada, mountains in center - $35

MONEY

New Bedford Railroad Company, $1000, 1876, with 20 coupons, State of Massachusetts - $65
Nevada Mining Company, made out to Harriet A. Green, letter on back from G.E. Stone, 1913 - $25
New London Ship Company, Connecticut, now Electric Boat - $10
Northern Railroad, Boston, 1864, 25¢ brown stamp, red seal - $30
Old Colony Railroad Company, $1000, 1896, trains, horse and wagon - $30
Owyhee Land Irrigation Company, 1894, horses, cows, large stream - $10
Pan American World Airways, for $10,000, world globe with two men, seal at bottom - $15
Parrot Silver and Copper Company, 1899, Montana, parrot, arm and hammer - $35
Pepper Well Petroleum Company, Boston and Canada, 1865, oil wells, paddle ship, railroad - $25
Pennsylvania, Lehigh Valley Railroad Company, Philadelphia, Pennsylvania, 1899, train - $20
Portland Soldier, Sailors Monument Association, 1883, eagle on flag - $35
Rockdale Gold Mining Company, Colorado, unused, VF - $24.50
St. Lurie Rod and Gun Club, West Palm Beach, Florida, trees, paddleboat - $6
Santa Fe Gold and Copper Mining Company, 1913, New Jersey - $15
Second Exchange, New York, 1934, for seven pounds, seven shillings, eleven pence, sterling - $30
Second Exchange, New York, 1855, for 53 pounds, three shillings, six pence, signed, two women, two warriors - $30
Set of Federal Migratory Waterfowl Stamps, 1934-1978, uncanceled, EX - $750
Set of six National Wild Turkey Stamps, 1976-1980 - $25
Stamp for Special Tax, United States Internal Revenue Service, manufacture of cigars, 1880 - $22
State of Georgia, 1885, 25 shares South Western Railroad Company, two trains and an eagle - $20
Stissing National Bank, Pine Plains, New York, 1881, girl, dog and safe - $18
Tashmoo Land Company, now Martha's Vineyard, 1891, Massachusetts, two settlers - $30
Third Exchange, Kidder, Peabody and Company, Boston, 1865, left side, paid in 600 pounds sterling - $35
The Horseman of Rhode Island, vignette of horse, seal, 1915 - $15
Toledo, Delphos, and Burlington Railroad Company, June 3, 1862, locomotive and tender - $12
Uncas National Bank, 1895, sail ship on bottom - $10
Union Mutual Insurance Company, New York, made out to Margaret Walton, 1875 - $40
Union Mutual Insurance Company, 1871, sailship and sailor - $45
U.S. Nut and Bolt Company, 1897, New Jersey, horse, and wagon - $8
Union Consolidated Oil Company, 1902, banknote printed - $75
Verde Mines Milling Company, 1929 - $12
Vermont Central Railroad Company, train, ships, man steel engraved - $80
White Horse Mining Company, 1901, Yukon and Alaska Territories - $60
Wire Gold Mining Company, Ramsey and Fairview, Nevada, 1909, two donkeys with packs - $15

Museums:

The Calvin Coolidge Memorial Foundation, Inc., Plymouth, VT, 05056

Cardinal Spellman Philatelic Museum, Inc., Weston, Massachusetts 02193

Age of Steam Railroad Museum, Dallas, TX 75226

Forney Transportation Museum, Denver, CO 80202

Portholes Into The Past, Medina, OH 44256

San Diego Maritime Museum, San Diego, CA 92101

To determine if old stocks have any value, send a photocopy of the old stock or bond certificate to:
Stock Market Information Service, Inc.
235 Dorchester Boulevard East
Montreal, Canada

A fee of $20 is the usual cost.

MONEY

Books:

Money of the World by Richard G. Doty, Grosset and Dunlap, NY 1978.

The Story of Paper Money by Yasha Beresiner and Colin Narbeth, Arco publishing, Inc. 1973

Confederate and Southern States Currency by Grover C. Criswell, Criswell and Criswell Publications, 1976.

Magazines:

Linn's Stamp News, Amos Press, Inc., P.O. Box 29, Sidney, OH 45365, Phone: 513-498-0801

Stamp Collector Van Dahl Publications, P.O. Box 10, Albany, Oregon 97321-0006, Phone: 503-928-3569

Paper Money - Society of Paper Money Collectors, P.O. Box 1085, Florissant, MO 63031, Gene Hessler, Editor

Associations:

Bond Club of New York care of E. Necarsulmer, III, C.J. Lawrence Morgan Center, 12th Floor, 1290 Avenue of the Americas, New York, NY 10104, Phone: 212-468-5622

Bond and Share Society care of R.M. Smythe and Company, 26 Broadway, New York, NY 10004, Phone: 212-943-1880

International Society of Worldwide Stamp Collectors, 825 East Torry Street, New Braunfels, TX 78130, Phone: 512-629-0370, Herb Holland, Secretary/Treasurer

Ships on Stamps Unit, 3613 Kanawha Ave., SE, Charleston, WV 25304, Phone: 304-925-7211, William A. Coffey, President

CHAPTER XVIII

EXOTICA

Within reason, paper collectibles could mean anything from cocktail napkins to junk mail. It takes in a selection that may seem inane until one discovers books are available on most subjects, the Brittanica's have paragraphs or pages on their history, magazine articles appear regularly, and collector club news is read eagerly as are collector newspapers and magazines.

Match covers have been collected almost since their invention. Coffee table books have been written describing the graphics involved in cigar bands. Firecrackers, diaries, Worlds Fairs, ink blotters, and railroad time tables are frequently seen in collector magazine want advertisements.

Paper collectibles are fantastically varied. It's the thousands of flyers stuck under your windshield wipers, hung on your doorknobs, or shoved into your mailbox. It's the single summons given by Police Constable Gateensky in Suffolk County, NY, in 1935, to a teenaged driver from Hyannisport, Massachusetts, for crossing a double yellow line. The boy lived it down to become United States President John F. Kennedy.

The summons (paper of course) became a museum exhibit. Most paper collectibles don't. They become the prizes of collectors who sense something of value, to history or to themselves.

Paper collectibles can be:
- cigarettes in their cardboard boxes from the 1950s, selling for $65.
- old premium playing cards customized as advertising give-a-ways, with a current value mostly between $20 - $35.
- the labels once placed on the top face of a keg of soda fountain syrup, on which one sentence proclaims, "all cocaine removed"
- Old diaries that show the miasma of a teenagers mind, or the lucid description of a traumatic experience years later. Or as Letts of London is doing. It is the United States subsidiary of Charles Letts and Company. In 1988 they sponsored a search for antique American diaries. They were particularly interested in those of social or historical interest, especially those with colorful anecdotes of American life in previous centuries.

The company has a distinguished collection of old diaries in London, which is occasionally sent here for exhibition. Among their collections is the original Letts diary, published in 1812, an 1857 diary by the Bishop of Norwich, and Victorian thumb size diaries.

The company believes that diaries provide the most accurate and personal accounts of a century's history.

And paper is:

- old letters that dignify a corner of a room at the Barnum Institute of Science and History, in Bridgeport, Connecticut, where books accompany the letters of one Phineas Taylor Barnum, better known to friend and sucker alike as P.T. The books and letters celebrate his life and times. They include one written on early circus stationary
- Dolly Dingle cutouts for $2
- catalogs from manufacturers, supply house, and nurseries, mostly at a cost of $20 - $100
- vintage sewing patterns, easy to find, attractive alongside collections of clothing and fashion related items.

In the early 1850s, diagrams with brief sewing instructions made their appearance in Godey's Lady's Book. Miniaturized, it was up to the reader to enlarge them to a scale that would fit.

By the 1870s, *Harpers Bazaar* began publishing a most confusing set of up to thirty dress patterns on a single page. Each pattern used a different style of line drawing to differentiate it from the others.

In 1863, the name most pattern collectors recognize appeared. The name of Ebenezer Butterick. He introduced the first paper patterns in a range of sizes. Made first from stiff paper, he later switched to thin tissue paper. In 1868 he put out his own magazine *Metropolitan Monthly*.

A number of pattern followed his lead, including the use of their own magazines. These eventually became fashion magazines. These style periodicals and paper patterns continued their relationships - the best known around the turn of the century being Butterick, McCalls, and Vogue.

Vintage sewing patterns and fashion magazines are easily found and are reasonably priced with $5 being average.

Dating is not onerous. Sometimes a pattern date is on the envelope, otherwise comparing the dress style with fashion magazines of the period will give a reasonably accurate dating.

EXOTICA

And paper is:

- house programs from 1892-1898, 1929-1931, 1944-1945, early administration records, or posters relating to events pertaining to the Carnegie Hall Corporation (the Carnegie Hall) in New York City. The corporation wants these with enough desperation that they advertise their wants in paper collector's trade papers
- old milk carton, somehow never thrown out with the trash, which help in the study and documentation of the history of the fluid milk industry. There is a National Bottle Museum in Ballston Spa, New York, that features these housewives throw-a-ways.
- old railroad timetables. The first of which was published in the Baltimore American newspaper in 1861. There is a collectors club in Pennsylvania whose members not only collect these eye straining railroad schedules. They also read them. Futhermore, paper is:
- fruit crate labels, sadly missing now that shipping companies have converted from wooden crates to cardboard cartons. Mail order advertisers in the collector magazines, and dealers at shows are most likely to be the best sources. Unless of course, you know of a warehouse about to be demolished.

Air Force pilot's wives used an excellent play on words as a title during WWII for their privately printed cook book. Limited in edition and distribution, its only price basis is what a cook book collector is willing to pay. Ordinarily, one such as this, in fine condition, would sell for $25.

Who saves cereal boxes? Someone must as they appear at collectible shows regularly with prices that can go to $75. Some have games, premium listings, or a child's construction project imprinted on the back panel which adds to its desirability - and price.

196

The rarest labels are from the 1880s, when fruit growers in California tried using colorful labels as a promotion in the fight against an influx of foreign fruit.

San Francisco lithographers, their appetites and skills honed by their production of 19th century's florid stock certificates, were the logical lithographic legatees of these new fruit crate labels. The 1906 California earthquake that almost destroyed San Francisco, did destroy one of the areas best known lithographers - the Mutual Lithographic Company - almost automatically making of their fruit crate labels, prize rarities.

Don't plan on retiring if you should find one of these rarities. $100 would be an excellent price. Plan on spending less, perhaps $5, for an average label.

And paper means:

- cookbooks whose collectors are history buffs, more interested in the history of foods and the preparation of these comestibles than in the orderly pages of recipes.
- cigar bands. You like to collect cigar bands? Try a different approach. Find the February, 1933 issue of *Fortune*, where you will find twenty cigar bands specially printed on one side only of cigar band paper.
- old wine labels, laboriously removed from the bottles.
- schematics, meticulously scaled diagrams of mechanical or other contrivances, carburetors, old diving bells, or machine guns.
- origami, that fascinating art from the Japanese where paper is folded into one inch long cranes painted in ten colors of the humpbacked, monotone likeness of a water buffalo.
- match covers, whose enthusiasts will never run out of new covers to collect.
- book jackets, which are easier to carry than the whole book, are prettier to look at, and are a lot cheaper, $8 being an average show price.
- and papier mache. When the Chinese invented paper it was a crude process requiring hand trimming of the edges. Too valuable to discard, these inventive folk reworked the scraps into the form we known as papier mache.

By the 10th century, the art of papier maché had reached Europe. By the 17th century it had become a Folk Art craft in America. In the 19th century women had taken up the art, making the party favors that were found on Victorian dining tables. Each piece of whimsy matched the season.

On one of its cyclic lows momentarily, its prices are better than reasonable. As a recently popular television advertisement used to say, "the prices are insa-a-a-ane."

As are most paper collectibles. That's part of the fun. Enjoy.

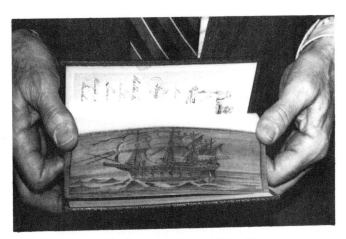

Exotica is a fore-edge water color of c.1830 that only shows when the pages are riffled so. This one sold for $500. A price of $2000 to $10,000 is not unknown for an early fore-edge. Later ones bring them $200-1000.

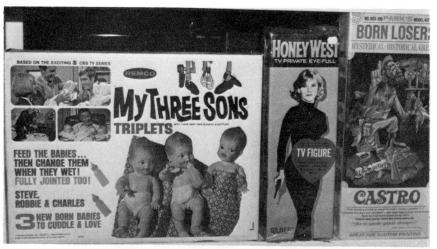

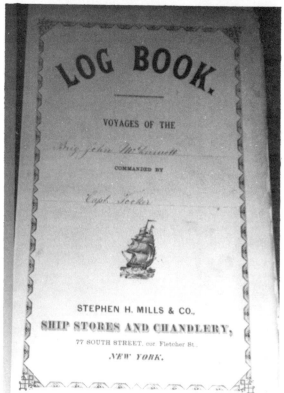

It is also a cookbook written and published by United States Air Force pilot's wives whose pilot husbands might not make it home. It is the cereal boxes thrown out daily, the graphics of a television series toy spin-off, and the log book kept by a ships master when sail and wind and muscle alone moved a ship.

The wide range of paper collectible may be seen on this page. Top: flies, lures, a postcard (not shown), a sporting club news booklet, and two record books of game and fish kills; sold for $900 at a Spring 1992 Sporting Collectible auction. Center: a lithograph from the book *The Education of Mr. Pipp* by C.D. Gibson, 1906, published by R.H. Russell, show priced at $55. Bottom: at the Hartford Papermania Show in Connecticut, a New York City dealer found that schematics of Browning machine guns, even with French descriptions, sold readily at $45.

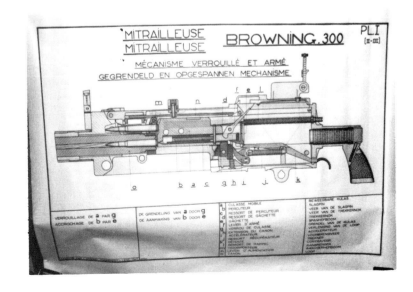

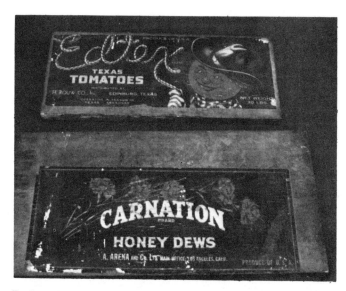

Far from the last, exotica is the graphic colors of fruit crate labels on the end pieces of wooden crates, both long gone.

Book covers - dust jackets to a librarian - decorate the wall of a University entrance hall, invitations to read.

Fans were once an important give-a-way for advertisers. No longer fashionable, since the appearance of electric fans and air conditioning, their value to collectors is higher than their prices, some as low as two dollars. The popsicle-like stick fans from 1910-1920 had, right to left, prices of $10, $14 and $28.

Fans could be and were made of paper, cotton, or silk. The ribbing was often of ivory, bone, wood, mother-of-pearl, gold leaf applique, or bleached bone. The fans themselves could have come from Spain, France, Britain, China, or anywhere. Some of the best were made 1780-1820, and bring prices of $345 to $750.

Fruit crate art ran the gamut of a lithographers imagination; the more colorful the better it was accepted. $100 would be a top price. $5 is more common.

Fruit crate labels were and are the most commonly found but lithographers - and corporations - didn't stop with fruit, as this Salmon label proves.

The most colorful of all labels were to be found on cigar box covers and cigar bands. A Vermont mail auction house offered the graphics of Old Queen cigars on a cedar box from 1895-1900 for $45.

die Karte - la carte - the Menu

The first menu has been recorded but was undoubtedly oral: Esau's red lentil pottage.

Even Apicius, for all his flaunting of Roman culinary wealth could not top that simple, Bible recorded, menu. Menus, oral or written, have shown us much of what we know of ancient life, as well as recent. If read carefully, menus tell us of more than food or table manners. They are recordings of life styles, political, military, personal, or historical.

The menu listed great recipes of the past that still find their way to our table. Apple Charlotte is recognizable though two centuries from its beginning. The French meat en daub, was recorded in a cook book in the 14th century. We not only stand upon the shoulders of our ancestors, we select their achievements from a menu and are fed upon their culinary advances.

While the first written restaurant menu probably appeared in 19th century Europe, the best of all menus may be those of fictitional heroes and heroines.

By the 1830s, Delmonico's in New York City, offered a ten page menu in English and French. But the menu from a *Christmas Carol* (1843) by Charles Dickens, was more widely known for its roast goose, sage and onion stuffing, gravy, applesauce, and Christmas pudding.

A recent phenomena, the collecting of menus may have been influenced by the souvenir menus offered aboard cruise ships and sometimes, though rarely, proffered by railroads and airlines. The most valuable are those with covers engraved by notable artists for dinners honoring more notable personalities, who may add their autographs. For example, the menu for Major General Leonard Wood in 1917 by the Lotus Club as an example.

No matter how fine the engraving, how honored the guest, its memory will never live as long as the menu of Oly Koek, crullers, and sweet cake, from Washington Irving's 1820 Legend of Sleepy Hollow. Or the menu inspired by Nero Wolf's hour long speech on the glories of American Cuisine at the fictional Kanawha Spa in West Virginia.

Rex Stout's fictitional detective never autographed that equally fictitional menu of baked oysters, terrapin, turkey, and rice croquetts. But other, real life personalities have, adding not only a cachet to the collector's prize, but additional value as well.

Many collectible menus are mind boggling in their ornateness and the lavish use of foods and liquors. When overcome by 16, 20 or more course menus from the self satisfied flaunting of an era's superabundance, it's nice occasionally, to remember John Steinbeck's Breakfast menu in 1938 - Biscuits (Southern Style).

Menu collecting is not a fad. The Johnson and Wales Culinary Institute in Providence, Rhode Island, with thousands of restaurants, ship, plane, hotel, and diner menus on file, sent the White House menus of our President's on a successful, country wide tour. On a smaller, but eclectic scale, is Massachusetts. Lou Greenstein's progress as a food consultant to national TV culinary shows to the complimentary role of a menu collector. They go well with his thousand cook books and equally numerous kitchen collectibles.

The first Southern cookery book, 1824, Lot 120.

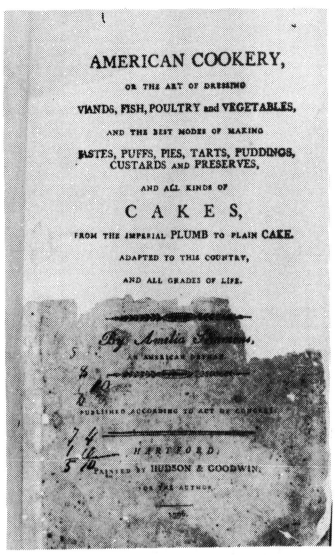

The first cookbook by an American, First issue, 1796, Lot 150.

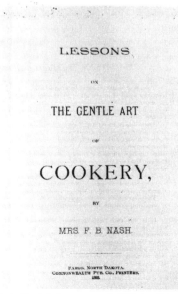

Early North Dakota regional, 1892, Lot 500.

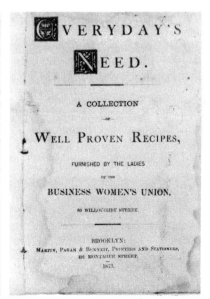

1873 Brooklyn charitable imprint, Lot 486.

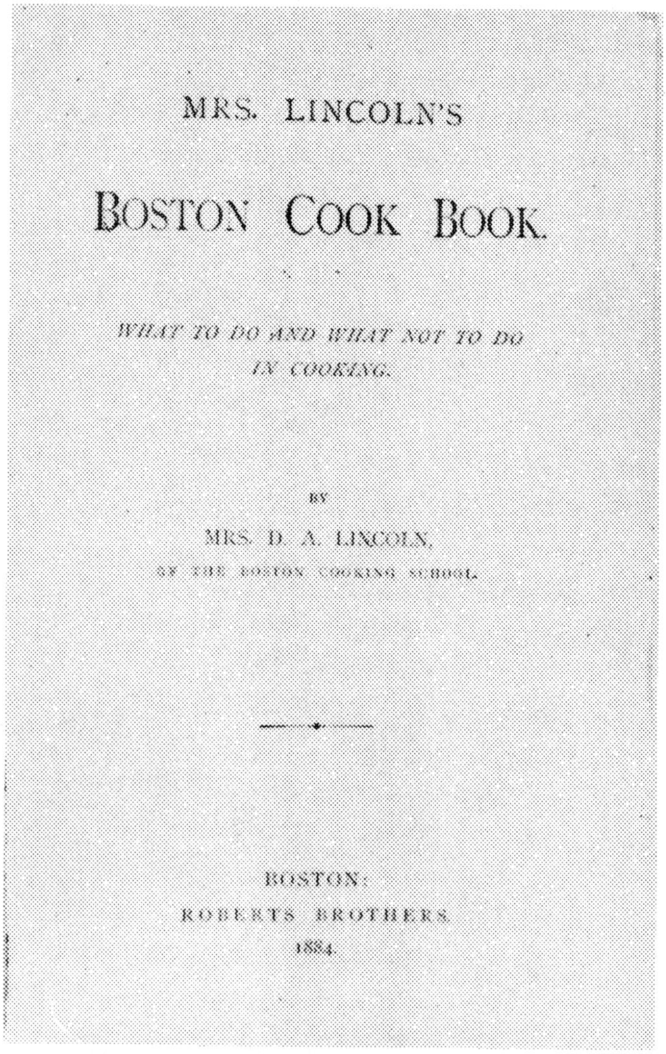

MRS. LINCOLN'S

BOSTON COOK BOOK.

*WHAT TO DO AND WHAT NOT TO DO
IN COOKING.*

BY

MRS. D. A. LINCOLN,
OF THE BOSTON COOKING SCHOOL.

BOSTON:
ROBERTS BROTHERS.
1884.

THE

BOSTON COOKING-SCHOOL

COOK BOOK.

BY

FANNIE MERRITT FARMER,
PRINCIPAL OF THE BOSTON COOKING SCHOOL.

BOSTON:
LITTLE, BROWN, AND COMPANY.
1896.

Mrs. Lincoln's Boston Cookbook, First Edition, 1884, Lot 280.

Fannie Farmer's Boston Cooking-School Cookbook, First Edition, Lot 217.

Cookbooks should not be under an 'exotic' heading, they deserve value guides of their own. However, the first Southern Cookery Book of 1824, and the first cookbook by an American, issued in 1796, deserve to be called exotic, in addition to Mrs. Lincoln's Boston Cookbook of 1884, and Fannie Farmer's Cooking School Book, of 1896. Peripherally then, all cookbooks are exotic.

Cookbooks, or booklets, from the 1940s and
1950s mostly come with low prices of $1-$10.

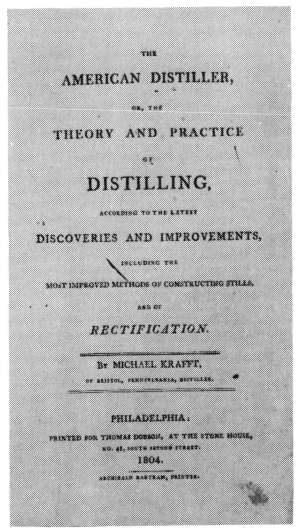

Krafft's important work on distilling, 1804, Lot 80.

Distilling was a technical achievement in 1804,
despite it's thousands of years old history. In the
Prohibition era it was still a technical
achievement but had been simplified to where
any home owner could brew his own.

Menus arranged for dinners with military over-
tones are not rare. A menu for Major-General
Leonard Wood in New York, organized by the
Lotus Club on February 10, 1917 is rare. More
so when the front page is especially designed
by Thomas A. Sinclair. The menu opened with
appetizers, went on the Striped Bass Mandarin,
then to roast plover, and ended with cheese,
coffee and cigars, plus brandy. Lou Greenstein.

A collage of 1950s and 1960s menus for Les Ami's d'Escoffier. It worked out to one menu for one meal each year. The first, in 1939, was exclusively for sixty members and guests. Lou Greenstein.

In 1913 Railroad menus were worth reading - and food worthy. The Lehigh Valley Railroad featured sirloin steak for $1 and little neck clams for 25¢. Lou Greenstein

A July 4th, 1913 menu from the New Ocean
House, Swampscott, Massachusetts went all out
with this die-cut beauty. Lou Greenstein

From the same New Ocean House came this
collection of different menus from the early
1900s. Lou Greenstein

As famed today, at a higher price, as it was in 1926, this United States Senate menu featured a then favorite, old fashioned bean soup - at 20¢ per bowl.

From Boston's Quincy House of 1890, we may consider a menu whose mulligatawny, salt cod with pork scraps, green goose, and corned mutton were menu standards.

The Henry Siegal Restaurant seated one thousand diners at any one sitting. With a chicken dinner at 60¢, prime ribs at 35¢, and lobster for 75¢ it's no wonder. It is of interest that chicken was the high price meat at that time, higher in cost than prime rib of beef. Chickens were for laying eggs, not for men who claimed you had to be tough to raise a tender chicken. Lou Greenstein.

In 1924, when John F. Hylan was Mayor of New York City, the Democratic National Convention was held in that city. Among the honored guests Guggenheim and Hayes. They ate well off salmon, beef, and hearts of romaine. Rubber chicken? Not for those politicians.

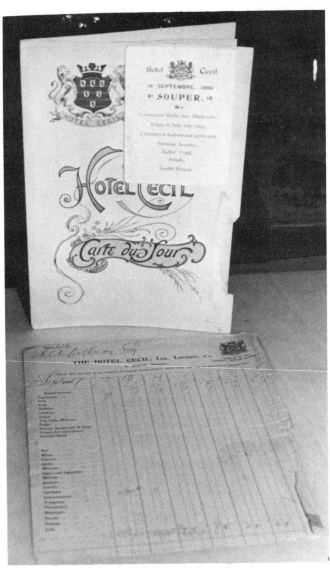

An actual bill rendered by the Hotel Cecil, London, in 1890. Despite centuries of oral, politician, and actual fights and denigration of all things from the other side of the Channel, the menu was in French.

A fixed price, American plan menu from the Fifth Ave. Hotel of New York City, in 1860. Widgeon, venison, and black duck were offered daily in season. Lou Greenstein.

211

Nov., 1894.

Welcome to
Rear Admiral Henry Erben
United States Navy
City Club
New York, Saturday Evening, November 10th
1894

"He laid his hand upon the Ocean's mane
And played familiar with his hoary locks."

A menu created for a welcome dinner for Rear Admiral Henry Erben, USN, at the City Club, New York City, Saturday evening, November 10, 1894. He had fought in the Civil War, participated in the laying of the Atlantic cable and fought pirates in China. He had led a full life and deserved a full menu.

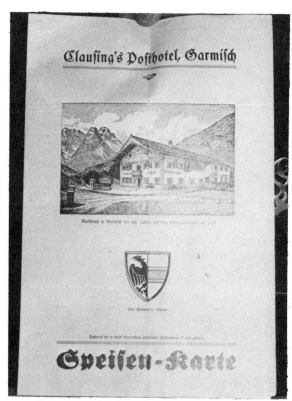

Claufing's Pofthotel, Garmifch

Speifen-Karte

Menus and good food may be had in any language, any country. A Speisen-Karte (menu) from Glaufing's Post Hotel, Garmisch in pre-war, 1936 Germany. Lou Greenstein.

WIENER
RATHAUSKELLER

FÜR GESCHLOSSENE GESELLSCHAFTEN
ODER EINZELVERANSTALTUNGEN STEHEN DEN P.T.-GÄSTEN LOGEN
SOWIE GRÖSSERE GESELLSCHAFTSRÄUME ZUR VERFÜGUNG

OTTO KASERER

A German Rathskeller menu of 1936. A half chicken was 90¢, and roast beef eight cents, in old German marks. Lou Greenstein.

A 1929 souvenir menu from the S.S. Republic of the United States Line. In addition to the expected foods it also noted a musical program. Lou Greenstein.

A menu may be blank as this one. Fountain offerings during the 1920s to the 1950s were usually handwritten on cards like this one, almost always with a fresh faced, wholesome girl practicing eye contact with a susceptible teenager.

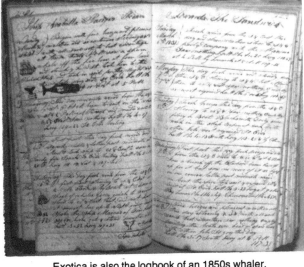

Exotica is also the logbook of an 1850s whaler, handwritten daily by the ship's master. The whale profiles indicate captured whales and the barrels of oil obtained. Sounding whale flukes show the one that got away. Suffolk County Historical Society.

THE

DYER'S COMPANION;

IN TWO PARTS.

PART 1st CONTAINING

Upwards of one hundred receipts for colouring woollen, cotton or silk cloths, yarn or thread, all kinds of colours and shades, so as to make them lasting and permanent, upon the newest and most improved plan in dying ; with directions for dressing cloth, and some observations and directions as to the use of colours and dye-stuff, and the properties and effects thereof—calculated for the use of artists, private families, and the encouragement of manufactories, &c.

THE 2d PART CONTAINING

Directions for jacking and varnishing leather ; to make Oil-Cloth, Lacker Brass, and Tin-Ware : To colour feathers, fur, and hair ; to prepare paints, varnishes, &c. to stain wood different colours ; to colour hats, either in whole or any particular part ; together with a number of medical receipts, which have been found beneficial, and highly approved by the faculty.

CONTAINING ALSO—

Many discoveries and improvements, not before made public.

BY ELIJAH BEMISS.

NEW-LONDON :
PRINTED BY CADY & EELLS,
FOR THE AUTHOR.

The Dyer's Companion (1804), Lot 18

A

USEFUL GUIDE,

FOR

GROCERS, DISTILLERS,

HOTEL & TAVERN-KEEPERS,

AND

WINE AND SPIRIT DEALERS.

OF EVERY DENOMINATION ;

Being a Complete Directory

FOR

MAKING AND MANAGING ALL KINDS OF WINES AND SPIRITUOUS LIQUORS ;

CONTAINING THE MOST APPROVED AND VALUABLE RECEIPTS.

1st. For making Artificial and Imitation Wines, Brandies, Rum, and Gins.
2nd. For lowering Brandy, Rum, and Geneva down to Proof.
3d. For Brewing and Managing Ale, Beer, Porter, Cider, and Vinegar.
4th. For making and distilling all kinds of French and English Cordials.
5th. For Salting, Curing, Pickling, and Preserving Beef, Pork, and Fish.
6th. For making the best Pickles and Preserves, and putting them up for sale, according to the London plan.
7th. For Preserving Fruits and Vegetables, fresh and good, throughout the year.

Many of these receipts are from Manuscripts, and have never before been published. The whole forming the most complete body of useful and valuable information on this subject, ever promised to its readers.

BY WILLIAM BEASTALL, Chemist.

New-York :
PUBLISHED BY THE AUTHOR,
No. 49 DELANCY-STREET.
C. Bartlett, Printer.
1829.

The Complete Grocer, 1832, Lot 40.

Where else would you put 'The Dyer's Companion', printed in 1804, or an 1829 edition of 'Making and Managing all kinds of Wines and Spiritous Liquors'? Where else? Under exotica.

American Fruit Product Company labels (6) Duffy and Motts brands - $5
Blotter - Dionne quintuplets, girls as infants, Phospho-Soda advertisement - $15
Blotters (44) 1929 Dodge Truck, Lone Ranger for Bond Bread, Hick's Capudine, etc. - $29
Blotters (10) unused, Association of American Railroads, 1939-1942 - $15
Cigar Box label, Abraham Lincoln end label, profile - $18
Cigar Box label, Cuban Sport, man, yacht, horse - $5
Cigar Box label, inner lid, Cupid's Best, cupid offering cigar to woman - $25
Cigar Box label, First Cabinet, embossed label, five members of Cabinet, Van Dam Cigar Company - $6
Cigar window sign, 1910, paper, Smoke the Eventual Five cent Cigar - $14
Cook Booklet, 1927, Griswold Manufacturing Company, Aunt Ellen's Delicious Dutch Oven Disher, Good - $18
Cook Booklet, Prudential Insurance, 1910, Teddy Bears - $25
Drug bottle labels (20) Charleston, South Carolina - $10
Drug bottle labels, (20) Camden, South Carolina - $10
George Washington fan, 1932 - $15
Golf Advertising fan, c.1900, paper and bamboo, Golf Queen Perfume advertisement - $20
Matchbooks and matchboxes (60) - $7
Matchbook collection, c.1940s, album - $10
Matchbook, Lincoln Mercury 100 club - $5
Matchbook, 1956, Lincoln Premier Capri - $5
Matchbox cover, Draft George Wallace for President, Save our Land, Join the Klan - $23
Menu, 70th Birthday dinner for Harry S. Truman, May 1954 - $15
Menu(s) (12) 1939, Italian steamship, Saturnia, color covers, classic stories - $60 (all)
Menu, Monarch of Bermuda, Lincoln's Birthday menu, February 2, 1939 - $7
Menu(s) (50) 1920s-1940s Railroad and Steamship assortment - $90
Menu, RMS Rotterdam, 1937, Art Deco cover, VG - $10
Menu, Short Line Railroad Association, October 1939 - $7
Menu(s), (4) steamship Queen Elizabeth, June and July 1950 - $10 (all)
Menu, S.S. Normandie, 1939, Daragnes cover - $20
Menu, unused, blank, ice cream parlor type - $5
Murad Cigarette Box c.1900, Egyptian scenes, VG - $15
New York Keuka Lake Grape labels (3) and one from Fancher, New York, Tomato - $5
Pillsbury Cook Book, 1913 - $12
Punchboard, Poker Pots, 12"x19" - $35
Riverside Cook Book, Rock Island Stove Company, Illinois, 64 pages, VG - $15
Rimford Cook Book (2) 1911-1913, girls on covers, Mint - $25 ea.

Sources:

Antique and collectible magazines are a must for any serious collector. The painless sources of information of the mundane and the esoteric. Nothing is too lustrous nor too minute in collectible favor not to be mentioned, if not featured, in one or another of the hundreds of generalized or specialized magazines or newspapers dedicated to the collector. One or the other of the following will be of interest to the beginner or the advanced collector.

The list is not all inclusive. There are many more, including newsletters from clubs or associations, and specialized and local collectors newspapers, that are not on this list. They will be worth the effort to locate.

Antique Monthly - 2100 Powers Ferry Road, Suite 125, Atlanta, GA 30339, Phone: 404-955-5656

Antique Review - Ohio Antique Review, Inc., 12 E. Stafford Street - P.O. Box 538, Worthington, OH 43085, Phone: 614-885-9758

Antiques Showcase - Amis Gibbs Publishers, Ltd. Highway 169, P.O. Box 260, Bala, Ontario, POC IAO, Canada

Antique Trader Weekly, Babka Publishing Co., P.O. Box 1050, 100 Bryant St., Dubuque, IA 52001, Phone: 319-588-2023

Antiques and Auction News, Engle Publishing Co., Route 230W, P.O. Box 500, Mount Joy, PA 17552, Phone: 717-653-9797

EXOTICA

Antiques and Collectibles Hobbies, Lightner Publishing Co. 1006 South Michigan Ave., Chicago, IL 60605, Phone: 312-939-4767

Antiques and Fine Arts, Fine Arts Publishing Co. 255 N. Market Street, Suite 120, San Jose, CA 95110, Fax: 408-298-3057

American Collectors Journal, P.O. Box 407, Kawanee, IL 61443, Phone: 309-853-8441

Antiquarian, P.O. Box 798, Huntington, NY 11743

Antique Collecting, Antique Collectors Club, 5 Church St., Woodbridge, Suffolk IP12 IDS England, Phone: 0394-385501

Antique Collector, National Magazine Co. Ltd., 72 Broadwood St., London, WIV 2BP, England.

Antique Dealer Collectors Guide, IPC Magazines, Ltd. King's Reach Tower, Stamford St., London SEI 9LS, England, Phone: 01-261-5000

Antique Market Report, Web Communications, P.O. Box 12830, Wichita, KS 67277

Antiques and the Arts Weekly (The Newtown Bee) Bee Publishing Co., 5 Church Hill Road, Newton, Connecticut 06470, Phone: 203-426-3141.

New England Antique Exchange - RFD3, P.O. Box 1290, Augusta Road, Winslow, ME 14901, Phone: 207-872-5849

Massachusetts Bay Antiques, North Shore Weeklies, Nine Page Street, P.O. Box 293, Danvers, Massachusetts 01923, Phone: 508-777-7070

Michigan Antiques Trading Post, 509 E. Michigan Ave., Lansing, MI 48912, Phone: 517-372-1216

Jersey Shore Art and Antiques, The Valente Publishing House, Inc., P.O. Box 176, Bay Head, NJ 08742

Renniger's Antique Guide, P.O. Box 495, LaFayette Hill, PA 19444, Phone: 215-828-4614

Journal of the Print World, Editor/Publisher Stuart Lane, 1000 Winona Rd, Meridith, New Hampshire 03253-9599

Antique Week, Mayhill Publications, Connie Swaim Editor, P.O. Box 90, Knightstown, IN 46148, Phone: 1-800-876-5133

Canadian Antiquer and Collector, P.O. Box 70, Station Q, Toronto, Ontario N4T 2PI, Canada, Phone: 416-867-9716

Collector's Showcase, 2909 Keats St. Number 1, San Diego, CA 92106, Phone: 619-222-0386

New York-Pennsylvania Collector Drawer C Fishers, NY 14453

Maine Antique Digest - Sam Pennington/Editor, 71 Main Street, Waldoboro, ME 04572, Phone: 207-832-7534

New England Antique Journal, Turley Publications, 4 Church Street, Ware, Massachusetts 01082, Phone: 413-967-3505

The Paper and Advertising Collector, The National Association of Paper and Advertising Collectors, P.O. Box 500, Mount Joy, PA 17552, Phone: 717-653-4300

Paper Collectors Marketplace - Watson Graphic Designs 470 Main Street, P.O. Box 127, Scandinavia, WI, 54977, Phone: 715-467-2379

West Coast Peddler, P.O. Box 5134, Whittier, CA 90607, Phone: 213-698-1718

EXOTICA

Yesteryear, Yesteryear Publishing Co., P.O. Box 2, Princeton, WI 54968, Phone: 414-787-4808

Collector's News and Antique Reporter, 506 Second Street P.O. Box 156, Grundy Center, IA 50638, Phone: 319-824-5456

MidAtlantic Antiques Magazine Henderson Dispatch, P.O. Box 908, Henderson, North Carolina 27536, Phone: 919-492-4001, Lydia A. Tucker, Editor.

Toybox, Long Publications, Julie L. Semrau Mgr/Editor, 8393 E. Holly Rd., Holly, MI 48442, Phone: 313-634-0301

The Paper Pile Quarterly, P.O. Box 337, San Anselmo, CA 94960, Phone: 415-454-5552

R.M.S. Bulletin, Rathkamp Matchcover Society, Ruth A. Richmond - 25 Front Street, Williamstown, MA 01267

Postcard Collector, Joe Jones Publishing Co., 121 N. Main St., P.O. Box 337, Iola, WI 54945, Phone: 715-445-5000

The Insider Collector Victoria Publishing, P.O. Box 98, Elmont, NY 11003, Phone: 516-326-9393

Mass-Bay Antiques 133 Main Street, North Andover, Massachusetts, Phone: 617-237-2576

CHAPTER XIX

PROTECTION

Finally! You've found it, that one piece of paper for which you've sought so long. You have bought it, taken it home, admired it there on the table.

Now what? That's not the be all and the end all. Now it's time to think about protecting your prize. First call your insurance agent, right? wrong. What are you going to tell him. That you've bought a winner?

The first task is to document your new acquisition. You do this for your own benefit and your family's, and for the insurance company and the government. That piece of paper listing the facts about your collection may be of immense value some day. Insurance companies love documentation. They pay out few insurance claims without it.

You document your collection for insurance companies and your family so both may know its value. The Internal Revenue Service may have an interest some day. Proper documentation might save your heirs both problems and money. The document goes into a safe or a bank's safe deposit box.

Now, if something happens, a fire or theft, you have a written record, something insurance people insist on seeing before they settle. Inadequate documentation means inadequate insurance settlements. You know the historical significance of your collection, its value. Does your family? Document thoroughly.

That's a beginning. Now, how do you physically protect your collection, that paper memorabilia you love so well.

Don't do anything to your collection that is not reversable. Don't use staples, sticky tape, or glue. All three have been used indiscriminately before. The few words that follow are not intended as a substitute for the services of a trained, professional conservator or restorer. They are merely basic first aid to help your collection endure, survive.

What do you collect? What is your passion? Postcards? Photographs? The worst place to store them may possibly be an album. According to Frank Cormier, a New York City based conservator, the albums themselves may cause damage, by the acids in the pages of the album if of paper, or by bonding themselves permanently to the pages.

Plastic pages that are sealed may look safe. They are not. They can sweat on the insides. Some plastics will exude an oily substance. Both will damage or otherwise stain the contents. Learn the uses of powdered erasers for paper cleaning

by consulting the people at an art supply shop. Dust photographs, don't wash them. Never spray your photographic prints with clear lacquer. It pulls the emulsion away from the paper. Keep your photographs framed in glass.

Photograph or copy everything.

Old paper collectibles, printed on wood pulp, highly acidic papers can crumble or fragment. Rather quickly if handled too much. The advantage of the photo or copy, if the collectible is not framed under glass, is that a rare or not so rare collectible can be made available for display or bragging without damage to the original.

For books with weak bindings, such as comic books, Disneyana, cookbooks, and catalogs, as well as hard cover books, use preservation enclosures or library binders. These are no more than carefully folded, non-acid papers or cardboards that exclude light while the collectible is stored in a cool, dry area. An identification label on the outside of the folder or envelope is acceptable.

The subject of light in relation to collectibles is a subject not often considered. Yet light, from the sun or artificial, is an enemy of all paper products. Light will even change the color of glass.

Light makes paper fade whatever form the paper takes.

Museum and library supply houses may be the best source for materials to protect a collection. Your yellow pages will list them, as will *Thomas's Directory*, which you will normally find in the reference section of your local library.

These sources can supply archival plastics and tapes, zipper bags, glass domes, postcard supplies, and acid free tissues and papers.

Archival plastics, for the beginning collector, are the only plastics used by museums because they are the safest, and will preserve your collectibles for decades. They maintain the same clarity without yellowing or bleeding oils or acids, as the more readily available consumer plastics will. They come in sizes to fit baseball cards, postcards, or magazines, in fractional sizes, standard or large for the paper currency collector, and in sizes for stereo cards and photographs. One such source (there are many) is:

Eezee Products Company
Division of Ship's Treasures
1749 Central Street
Stoughton, Massachusetts 02072
Phone: 617-341-3640

PROTECTION

Even the use of acid free paper is not the complete answer to a collection's protection. True, it will last longer. But the other side of acid free is alkaline. This in itself will act as a deterioration agent.

But reasonable care is better than no care at all. With some thought, and that some reasonable care, your paper collectibles should oulive your insurance agent. Even with this, and your eventual use of ultra violet filters on your lights, the pages of newspapers, pamphlets, books, or any folded papers, should be checked each month seeking evidence of deterioration or mold.

One of the many experts in the fields of restoration and preservation is author and lecturer:

Carolyn Price Horton
430 West 22nd Street
New York, NY 10011
Phone: 212-989-1472

Temperature and humidity control brings the collector to decision time. How much is the collector willing to pay to protect the collection. In terms of dollars is it worth the outlay as compared to the value of the collection. For many collectors the usual answer is no. Paper is normally low keyed, low valued. Then there are autographs, first editions of comic books heroes, postage stamps, and high priced rarities without end.

Humidity, the water vapor in the air, is always a hazard to collectibles. If the humidity is too low, moisture will be drawn from paper causing it to become brittle. Humidity that is too high will cause paper to absorb moisture. This releases the acids or alkalines causing a rapid deterioration of the paper.

A simple solution for the average collector is a low priced humidifier or dehumidifier. Depending on the climatic conditions where the collection is housed, either one may be your answer. Local hardware stores or appliance outlets are the usual sources.

Steady temperatures are best. Above 70 degrees Fahrenheit - 21 degrees Celsius your collection may be at risk from mold or insects. Low temperature will do little or no damage. The best storage for valuable photographs is in a frost free refrigerator. "I'm bringing home company, Martha. Thaw out my photographs, please."

It is fluctuating temperatures that are worrisome. It causes paper, among other substances, to expand or contract. It causes structural stress in the paper's fibrous structure. As well as causing humidity to rise in closed or sealed areas. Humidity and temperature control should be considered a single problem. Temperatures between 60 and 70 degree F. 16 and 24 degrees C, are relatively secure boundaries, as is a relative humidity of 40% to 60%.

There are instruments to measure humidity and temperatures in the room where your collection is housed. Some are relatively cheap, such as a paper hygrometer to measure humidity or as expensive as an aspirated psychrometer which measures the humidity and temperature of a room.

When you have gone that far you are treading in the rarified atmosphere usually observed in museums. As such they are beyond the parameters of this book. When the collector goes that far, much of the fun, the joy of paper collecting is lost to an everlasting search for security.

For those who wish to dig deeper into this subject read:

Manual For Museums by Ralph H. Lewis
National Park Services - U.S. Department of the Interior - 1976
Washington, D.C. 20405
For sale by the Superintendent of Documents
U.S. Government Printing Office
Washington, D.C. 20405
Stock Number 024-005-00643-5

Most collectors will leave such exotics to curators and conservators, remaining what they are, some of the world's lucky people addicted to paper collectibles.

REPRODUCTIONS

Reproductions are not a 20th century inspiration. The ancient Egyptians used to make copies of a Pharaoh's treasures to sell to visiting Greeks and Romans.

The turn of this century saw many repros of Colonial furniture which are collectibles today. Glassware reproduced in this century has becomee a major problem. Wallace Nutting, whose copies are noted proudly in show catalogs, advertised his reproductions in the 1930s.

Motherhood may be the world's second oldest profession, but it is running neck and neck with the forging of antiquities. So why would anyone believe paper collectibles are immune?

Because of normal low valuations? Check the auction records, then ask yourself, "What recession?" Prices are rising. Where there are high prices there are those who would take any advantage, including forgeries and the selling or reproductions as originals. The temptation is too great.

The problem is not necessarily one of recognition, of the ability to see or feel a difference between an original and a copy. It is both a problem of a collector's continuing education and, sadly, of too many dealers who have learned to 'tell the tale' and believe that is sufficient.

The collector should be aware of what is happening around him. Many paper collectibles are from the 20th century. Board games, jig saw puzzles, cereal boxes, books, postcards, and posters among them. Many are undated, yet have manufacturers, or printers, names and addresses.

If you can pinpoint a zip code, or lack of one, you may be able to place the piece before or after 1963, when zip codes came into being. Dates are important. Reproducers have been known to use the wrong date or zip code.

Do you have research sources? Research librarians from public or University libraries are beyond value in helping to prove authenticity. Cultivate them.

Actually reproductions have a place in today's market. They make excellent substitutions when the price of an original is beyond reason, providing they are marked as reproductions. There is the rub. Too many reproductions come with paper labels, easily removed. Too many collectors are careless when buying, they don't use common sense.

Examine the item. No matter how carefully it was protected, even if if had been stored in a shaded, climate controlled room, the item should still show age. Wood pulp papers are not acid free, eventually such paper will deteriorate. Because of these built-in acids, the paper will crumble, fragment

Is the aging too uniform? Do the age marks inside a piece have the obsolutely same aging as the exterior? Why? There should be a difference.

Ask questions. A legitimate dealer will answer fairly. He won't claim it came from a Vanderbilt mansion, as one vendor tried at a Southampton show, in an area you know was uninhabited 100 years ago and still is. If the dealer knows where an item came from, the legitimate delaer will say no. If he doesn't he'll tell you honestly.

Most reproduction specialists will cut corners in the production of their copies. If one of these takes an event program and scrawls a participants name across the cover, that will often elevate its price from single digit to triple, or better. Check the autograph against a known original. A simple procedure but how many do so?

You say you can't do that at an exhibit. You can cover yourself. Buy the item if you must, but ask the dealer for an agreement in writing whereby he will buy the item back if it doesn't check out as to the dealers description. If he won't give such a guarantee, back off. You don't need the frustration of buying a possible reproduction. It's your money, protect it.

It is not necessary to be paranoid about reproductions. They have their place. Certainly many collectors buy them knowingly. Even with inflated incomes, not many collectors can come up with $451,000 for a T206 Baseball card. Nor, even $12,000 for a Hitler signature on a letter. Reproductions fill these holes in your collection until the moment you can afford the original.

Reproductions, known on the street as knock-offs, are not necessarily only of four, five or six figure amounts. Cereal boxes have been reproduced. Why cereal boxes? For the backs of the box. Cheerios of the 1930s had three different towns printed on the backs. Their current values makes them worth reproducing.

Conrad Schoeffling, of the C.W. Post Campus, Long Island University in New York, said, "In its taste and delicacy, in its originality, and in its elaborations of color and design, the *Book of Kells* must by placed among the wonders of the world.

Consider: there is only one *Book of Kells*. It is listed as Ms58, Trinity College Library, Dublin.

Must the scholars and collectors of the world travel to Eire to see this treasure? Here is an example where reproductions are in the interest of all. Authorized reproductions of the book have been made. The cost is so extravagant, $14,000,

REPRODUCTIONS

only major libraries and universities can afford one. But you, can enjoy seeing a copy of this magnificent book without traveling to Dublin.

The *Book of Kells* has nothing to do with the American Antique's Association's concern that they consider the escalating sales of reproductions to be totally out of control. Their concern is with unmarked reproductions. Permanent marking of all reproductions is their goal.

Siding with the Association is the Quilters Guild of Indianapolis, in major conflict with the Smithsonian Institute in Washington, D.C.

The Smithsonian has decided to allow four historic quilts to be reproduced by a company that uses Chinese labor. American quilt makers have objected strenuously.

Like many foreign imports, these quilts have arrived in this country with easily removed labels of their country of origin and fabric content. Right now, the unethical dealer is selling them as antiques to a naive public.

The United States quilt makers, through The National Quilting Association of Ellcat City, Maryland, amongst others, want the Smithsonian to cancel its contract with the Columbus, Ohio importer. So far, the major concession by the Smithsonian, has been to order permanent 'Made in China' labels on the imported quilts, and to have printed in indelible ink 'Copyright 1992 Smithsonian Institute' on the back of each quilt. It's a bit late. Label stripped quilts are already here.

Have you ever looked over a major show and wonder 'where do they find all these antiques and collectibles'? Now you can stop wondering. Some of them come from China.

*****

INDEX